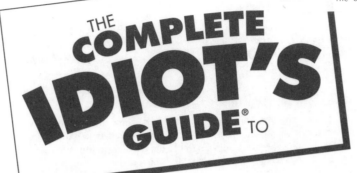

THE COMPLETE IDIOT'S GUIDE® TO

The Perfect Wedding

Fourth Edition

by Teddy Lenderman

ALPHA

A member of Penguin Group (USA) Inc.

In loving memory of Dorothy Penner, my mentor and dear friend, and for all the support and friendship the Association of Bridal Consultants has given me, I dedicate this book.

Publisher: *Marie Butler-Knight*
Product Manager: *Phil Kitchel*
Senior Managing Editor: *Jennifer Chisholm*
Senior Acquisitions Editor: *Randy Ladenheim-Gil*
Development Editor: *Lynn Northrup*
Senior Production Editor: *Christy Wagner*
Copy Editor: *Cari Luna*
Illustrator: *Chris Eliopoulos*
Cover/Book Designer: *Trina Wurst*
Indexer: *Heather McNeill*
Layout/Proofreading: *Rebecca Harmon, Mary Hunt*
Graphics: *Tammy Graham, Laura Robbins, Dennis Sheehan*

Contents at a Glance

Contents

Foreword

The good just continues to get better with this new version of *The Complete Idiot's Guide to the Perfect Wedding Illustrated, Fourth Edition.* Teddy Lenderman has done it again, taking the best from the previous editions and adding some new material to update this edition. But the biggest change is the book's new look—you'll find it packed with beautiful photographs taken by professional wedding photographers, including a color insert—sure to give you some great ideas when planning your own wedding.

Since Teddy's first edition of *The Complete Idiot's Guide to the Perfect Wedding* was published several years ago, the wedding industry has grown from a sleepy cottage industry worth about $32 billion a year to a $120 billion-a-year megabusiness, and it continues to grow at an incredible rate. When Teddy joined the Association of Bridal Consultants in 1986, there were about 120 members. Membership today exceeds 3,400 in almost 30 countries on 6 continents.

What does all of this mean to you, the bride or the wedding professional? Weddings have grown increasingly complex in the past two decades. Divorces, remarriages, and extended, nontraditional families complicate everything from whose name goes on the invitation to who sits where in the church. A mobile society (the U.S. Postal Service reports 17 percent of Americans move each year) means more guests are traveling considerable distances to share that special day with family and friends. This has led to the weekend wedding (you really can't expect people to travel across the country for a 20-minute ceremony and 1-hour reception, now, can you?). Weekend weddings mean more events—and more expenses. Teddy shows you how to get the wedding you want while sticking to a budget. Finally, the traditional family wedding planners—the bride herself and her mother, sisters, cousins, and aunts—most likely are working and don't have the 80 or more hours it takes a professional to plan today's wedding.

That is where Teddy and other wedding professionals and this book come in. If you choose to do it all yourself, you'll find this book an invaluable guide for all the decisions you'll have to make. Teddy's even included worksheets designed to help you choose wedding vendors and keep track of various details. If you do hire a wedding consultant (wise move!), read on, for you will find in these pages the wit and wisdom you need to ask intelligent questions, things that will help you and your coordinator do just that—coordinate.

I first met Teddy at an informal Association dinner in Indianapolis, Indiana, in July 1986. Her personality filled the room the same way it fills these pages. From her first forays into wedding consulting, she has developed her business, Bearable Weddings by Teddy, into a recognized industry leader. She served for many years as the Indiana state coordinator for the Association of Bridal Consultants, providing local information, networking, and mentoring, helping many get started in the business. An early leader in wedding education, she is a Master Bridal Consultant™—the highest educational designation the Association offers—one of only 33 in the world. And she was the first recipient of the "Miss Dorothy Heart Award," the only award the Association presents, for her passion for weddings.

If these aren't good enough reasons to read this book, there is one more … it's fun!

Gerard J. Monaghan
President
Association of Bridal Consultants
New Milford, Connecticut

Introduction

Today's weddings are as different as the couples being married. Gone are the "cookie-cutter" weddings of past decades. Unique, personalized weddings are the trend. The average age of the bride and groom today is 26 and 28 respectively. Today's wedding couples are more mature, have their careers well in place, and are eager to get the planning process started. Many times the couple pays for the wedding and reception themselves or split it with one or both sets of parents. There are all kinds of options out there for the engaged couple; from having a weekend wedding to flying off to an exotic destination wedding site, to the traditional wedding at home. Many couples plan their weddings from long distance. Whatever your plans or ideas, it sometimes seems that you have to be a genius to pull off a successful wedding.

Thousands of complex questions are just lurking out there, waiting to be answered. It's hard to know where to go or whom to turn to for help. You've never done this kind of "adventure" before. Even if you're a vice president of a huge corporation, you start thinking, "I must be an idiot. I don't have the faintest idea where to begin!"

Well, you're not an idiot—not even close. You are, however, about to become a wedding consumer. You will have lots of questions, and you will need many, many answers.

You deserve honest answers to your questions and some guidance from someone who knows this industry inside and out. You also deserve to be treated with respect by vendors. This book tries to answer your questions and provide you with the information you need to work with your vendors. It also attempts to guide you through the months of planning that await you.

Weddings, although one of life's most traditional events, have changed over the past several years. And this book has also changed, too. There is still some focus on traditional wedding ceremonies and receptions, but it keeps you current with the latest trends and new ideas. It emphasizes using your uniqueness to its fullest to make this wedding yours. *Personalize* is the buzzword in weddings now. There are many choices out there. Mom and Dad may not be in the picture to help. And they might not be paying for this wedding. There are changes, but with a little help from this book, you will be able to glide through this process without much friction.

This book is the result of the experience and satisfaction I have gained in helping more than 360 couples enjoy the wedding of their dreams. In 1985, I began my wedding consulting business, Bearable Weddings by Teddy. In the ensuing 18 years, I have shared ideas and learned from countless other wedding professionals through seminars and conferences. I have learned the hard way how to choose competent and professional vendors and how to avoid potential nightmares. I have also broadened my horizons through the give-and-take of teaching a noncredit course, "How to Plan and Enjoy Your Wedding," for Indiana State University in Terre Haute, Indiana.

I've always been a believer in continuing education, and in 1993 I obtained the highest level of recognition that the Association of Bridal Consultants awards: Master Bridal Consultant. It took me seven years to achieve that, but my learning never stops. I learn so much from the brides and grooms I've had the pleasure of working with—that alone could fill a book.

I've been where you are right now about 360 times. I know the frustration you are feeling, the intimidation, and the feelings of being overwhelmed at the same time that you're so happy you could just burst.

Well, slow down. Take a deep breath and get ready for some major work on understanding the wedding industry. That knowledge will help you gain an insight into a field you probably know nothing about. Once you have some understanding and knowledge of what is out there as far as the wedding industry goes, you will be better equipped to be an intelligent wedding consumer. That's the name of the game.

You wouldn't rush right out and buy a new car without first studying the car industry and trying to figure out what is best for your particular needs and value. No, you'd pick up brochures, talk to friends and family, go into the car dealership and look around, ask questions, and get a feel for what's out there. Right? So what's so different about shopping in the wedding industry?

That's what this book is all about. You—the bride and groom—will learn what can help make your life and the lives of your family and friends so much easier as you plan for the big day. It's really not difficult, but it will require some time and energy on your part. The sole purpose of this book is to take the overwhelmingly complicated task of planning a wedding and make it E-A-S-Y.

How to Use This Book

Before you spend a dime, I suggest that you read this book from cover to cover. Try not to get so carried away with the romance and the newness of being engaged that you lose your sense of perspective.

Use a highlighter to mark the points you need to understand more fully. Take notes on possible vendors you want to contact. Really use this book! Its unique design will give you all the help you need. The more you use it, the easier your planning will be. Do not rush right out and reserve a catering hall, for example, before you read this book. Let me help you determine what to look for in a facility that's going to be a big part of your wedding day and your wedding dollars.

Become an intelligent wedding consumer, and spend your dollars wisely. Understand your responsibilities, and figure out the best way to approach them. Most of all, enjoy! This should be one of the most pleasant, fun-filled, exciting times in a couple's life. This book can help with that. It won't make the process of planning perfect, but it can help take the bumps out of the road to a very bearable—and wonderful!—wedding.

Here's how this book is organized:

Part 1, "Don't Spend a Dime Yet!" gets you off on the right foot. I'll talk about understanding the ever-growing wedding industry and how to get started on this wonderful adventure of planning your wedding. I'll share some tips on finding a good bridal consultant. I'll tell you about the different formalities of weddings and how to determine which fits your ideas and needs so you can decide on a realistic budget for your big day.

Part 2, "First Things First," talks about how to find the right ceremony site and what choices are available. It also discusses the types of reception facilities available and those that will be part of your overall budget. I'll discuss your wedding party and the various "jobs" you can give to friends and family. A part of the planning that often gets left to last is planning the rehearsal dinner. I'll cover that, too. And finally, you'll learn all about planning the perfect honeymoon.

Part 3, "Putting It All Together," covers lots and lots of planning ideas. I'll go into detail about the reception menu and your liquor responsibilities, how to find the right florist for your taste, and choosing the music for both the ceremony and reception. I devote a chapter to finding that perfect gown and tux, and discuss the wide variety of transportation ideas that are available now. I'll also share tips on finding and working with a photographer and videographer. And I round out this part with chapters on invitations, favors, and budget-saving ideas.

Part 4, "Help! My Family Is Driving Me Nuts!" is pretty much self-explanatory. I'll talk about the wedding stress that accompanies most wedding planning processes and what you can do to help yourself stay sane. I'll talk about divorced parents, the "control" issue, and ways to get help if you need it.

Part 5, "Special Weddings," discusses just that—all kinds of special weddings. I'll cover theme weddings such as holiday weddings and garden weddings, and tell you about the latest trends in personalizing your wedding. You'll also find out about popular weekend weddings and destination weddings.

Part 6, "Surviving the Big Event: Tales from the Altar," talks about the preparation for the wedding day, starting with the rehearsal and moving right through the reception. A favorite part of these books has been the trends from bridal consultants all over the country. These fine ladies and gentlemen tell you "what is hot and what is not" in their part of the country and offer some words of wisdom along the way. And the final chapter, one of my favorite, features real-life couples who have had their weddings and lived to tell about them. These couples share with you, the potential bride and groom, ideas they loved about their own weddings and things they would do differently.

You'll also find three valuable appendixes. Appendix A gives you a list of books and magazines to help you in the planning process. In Appendix B, you'll find worksheets to make it easier to choose and work with major vendors. For example, the "Photography Worksheet" gives you plenty of space to fill in the information you need to keep on file for your records. I hope you'll use these worksheets. I didn't add them simply to fill pages. They are there to help you stay organized. Finally, Appendix C offers a planning check-off list to help you keep track of all the details in the months leading up to the wedding.

Extras

To help you get the most out of this book, you will see the following special information boxes scattered throughout:

Bouquet Toss

In these sidebars I share wedding trivia and stories of other couples just like you who are planning their weddings.

Wedding Woes

Check these sidebars for cautions about possible pitfalls and solutions to common problems you might encounter.

Teddy's Tips

In these sidebars I offer expert tips that can help you be more efficient or save you money.

Nuptial Notes

Check these sidebars for simple definitions of wedding terminology.

Acknowledgments

I cannot believe this is the fourth edition! And a totally new version at that. The hundreds of photographs featured in this new illustrated edition are wonderful additions! Whoever would have thought that a bridal consultant from the Midwest would be asked to write a book on weddings. Three editions later, I'm finishing up this fourth edition.

My thanks to Alpha for having the confidence and trust in me to write another edition. To my acquisitions editor, Randy Ladenheim-Gil, your support, humor, patience, and understanding have meant a great deal to me. It has been a pleasure to work with you. Thank you very much. To Lynn Northrup, my development editor—what a joy it has been to work with you. Your kindness, understanding, and encouragement will always be remembered. You are quite a lady. And to all the other "behind-the-scenes folks" at Alpha Books, thank you, too. You are the ones who make my job easy.

Because of the many photographs in this edition, I owe a HUGE thank you to all the wonderful photographers and bridal consultants who lent me their fantastic images. These are some of the most outstanding photographers in the country. They cover weddings from coast to coast. A big thanks to Michael Colter of Colter Photography in Indianapolis, Indiana. Michael was my mainstay, providing hundreds of photos and spending hours upon hours with me trying to find that "perfect" picture. No matter where our paths take us, I will always be indebted to him.

If you find one of these photographers or consultants in your area and decide to use them for your wedding, please tell them where you saw their work and read their name.

These fantastic photographers and consultants include:

Colter Photography—Michael Colter
Indianapolis, Indiana
317-946-2044
www.colterphotography.com

Wyant Photography, Inc.—Jim and Lois Wyant
Zionsville, Indiana
317-873-2282
www.wyantphoto.com

Broadway Photography, LLC—Kymberly Henson and Jay Bachemin
Cincinnati, Ohio
513-621-1595
www.broadwayphotoandvideo.com

Garbo Productions—Margaret Busk
Chicago, Illinois
773-477-4210
www.garboproductions.com

Diane Alexander White Photography
Chicago, Illinois
www.DAWhitephotography.com

Morris Fine Art Photography—Denise Morris
Columbus, Indiana
812-342-0736
www.morrisfineart.com

Front Room Photography—Neil Kiekhofer and Eron Laber
Bay View, Wisconsin
414-294-0080
www.frphoto.com

Frank Event Design—Frank Andonoplas
Chicago, Illinois
773-275-6804
www.frankeventdesign.com

Wolfe Photography—Jennifer Wolfe
Chicago, Illinois
www.WolfePhoto.com

The Wedding Casa—Norma Edelman
San Diego, California
619-298-9344
www.weddingcasa.com

Photography by Chana and Don—Chana Groh and Donald Groh
San Diego, California
619-255-6966
www.photobychanaanddon.com

Stephanie Cristalli Photography
Seattle, Washington
206-783-8985
www.stephaniecristalli.com

Curtis Rhodes Photography—Curtis Rhodes
Seattle, Washington
206-782-3681
www.crhodes.net

Hudson Designer Portraits—Bruce Hudson
Renton, Washington
253-271-9709
www.hudsonportraits.com

Kurt Smith Photography—Kurt E. Smith
Kingston, Washington
360-297-8938
www.kurtsmithphotography.com

Melanie Blair Photography—Melanie Blair
Seattle, Washington
206-285-7717
www.melanieblair.net

Craig Larsen Photography, Inc.—Craig P. Larsen
Redmond, Washington
425-885-5552
www.craiglarsen.com

Janet Klinger Photography—Janet Klinger
Seattle, Washington
206-622-7478
www.janetklinger.com

Aisle of View—Merry Beth Turpin
Kirkland, Washington
425-427-2277
www.aisleofview.com

C.B. Bell, III—Artist/Photographer
Seattle, Washington
206-551-3096
www.CBBELL.com

Chuckarelei Studio—Chuckarelei
Seattle, Washington
206-767-9833
www.chuckarelei.tripod.com

The Wedding Specialist—Mimi Doke
Lake Havasu City, Arizona
928-453-6000
www.weddingspecialist.net

Tony Campbell, Photojournalist
Indiana State University
812-237-3788
www.indstate.edu

Jeff Hawkins Photography—Jeff and Kathleen Hawkins
Altamonte Springs, Florida
407-834-8023
www.jeffhawkins.com

BBJ Linen—Lanie Hartman
Skokie, Illinois
847-329-8400
www.bbjlinen.com

Orange Enterprise, Inc.—Association of Wedding Gown Specialists
Orange, Connecticut
1-800-501-5005
www.WeddingGownSpecialists.com

Photography by Monique Feil—Monique Feil
San Diego, California
619-583-1150
www.moniquefeil.com

Michael Rosenberg Photography—Michael Rosenberg
Seattle, Washington
www.michaelrosenberg.com

Trademarks

All terms mentioned in this book that are known to be or are suspected of being trademarks or service marks have been appropriately capitalized. Alpha Books and Penguin Group (USA) Inc. cannot attest to the accuracy of this information. Use of a term in this book should not be regarded as affecting the validity of any trademark or service mark.

Accredited and *Master Bridal Consultant* are trademarks of the Association of Bridal Consultants.

In This Part

Don't Spend a Dime Yet!

You're engaged to a wonderful person. You've been floating on cloud nine since the proposal. You've announced the good news to your family and friends, and now you can't wait to get started on the wedding plans.

Planning a wedding is a big deal, and the wedding business is big business. The more you know about the industry and how to use it to your advantage, the better your planning will be and the more relaxed you'll be when you finally walk down that aisle. So catch your breath, let your feet touch down for a moment, and ready yourself to read Part 1. I'll introduce you to some of the things you should know before you write that first check. You'll find advice on how to start your planning, which questions to ask, and where to go for help. You'll learn how to determine the type of wedding you want to have and how that decision can affect your wedding budget.

In This Chapter

- ◆ Big business: understanding the wedding industry
- ◆ Getting organized
- ◆ Checking out bridal shows
- ◆ Should you work with a bridal consultant?
- ◆ A pro picks the best wedding websites

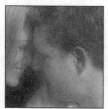

Chapter 1

Taking Your First Steps Toward the Altar

You wouldn't go out and buy the first car you saw without doing some research on its qualities or gas mileage; you might even consult *Consumer Reports* for expert tips. Likewise, you wouldn't have brain surgery without first consulting and interviewing several doctors. And you wouldn't go looking for the perfect home without the help of a reputable real-estate agent. The same is true for the wedding industry. You need to understand what's out there and what's available before you start spending those precious dollars.

So before you make that first purchase, you need to understand what the wedding industry is all about and how to get yourself organized. In this chapter you'll also find the best online resources to help you along your path to wedding bliss.

Understanding the Wedding Industry

The first thing you need to know about weddings in this country is that the wedding industry is big business. In 2002, the most recent figures available, the wedding industry grossed between $72 and $106 *billion*, second only to the holiday season in retail! That figure doesn't cover just the wedding itself. It also covers things like the rings, the honeymoon, and setting up your new home.

Understanding how big the industry is might give you some perspective on why you don't want to rush right out and reserve the first reception site you see. This wedding process will cost you some money—you don't have to break the bank to have the wedding of your dreams, but you do have to plan wisely. (I'll tell you how to set up a budget you can live with in Chapter 2.)

This couple has just set the date. *(Photo by Jeff Hawkins Photography)*

Finding a System to Keep Yourself Organized

The number-one suggestion I make to the brides I work with is to find and use some kind of organizational system. It doesn't matter what this is, whether it's a three-ring binder, a CD-ROM program, or a folder with pockets. (Obviously, this book will be a big part of your system, and it should be.) The type of system you choose to use really doesn't matter. What matters is that you use it. Keep everything that relates to your wedding in this planner: receipts, contracts, material swatches, a calendar with appointments marked, phone numbers of all your vendors, and reminder lists. Make sure you have this planner with you whenever you visit a vendor. Even if you're not an organized person, force yourself to become more so. Your planner should be so much a part of your being that when you are without it, you feel like you are missing something. I cannot stress this enough. If you are organized, you will be able to enjoy the whole planning process so much more.

Teddy's Tips

Be patient with yourself! Taking some time now to read and understand what you need to do will pay off later. Keep every receipt, and keep them together in one place! You never know when you might have to produce one quickly.

Bridal Shows

So you've figured out a system you're comfortable with and one that you will use. Now what? Depending on how much time you have, you may want to attend a bridal show in your area. Bridal shows are great ways to meet the vendors from your area whose services you will be using. These shows are usually promoted by area merchants to let the community know what wedding services are available in the area. The usual format for such events might include time to talk with individual vendors, a fashion show by area bridal shops, and sometimes drawings for door prizes the vendors provide.

What to Expect

The whole idea behind bridal shows is twofold: You get to see what's available in your area, and the vendor gets your name and address for possible contact. The bride and groom, or the parents of a bride or groom, can browse the different vendors (jewelers, caterers, florists, and photographers, to name a few) and get a feel for what they have to offer. Sometimes, you will be able to tell whether a vendor can provide what you need by just looking at the booth setup. If crepe-paper streamers and balloons decorate the booth and you're thinking more in terms of satin ribbon and crystal, then you should look at other displays.

How to Get the Most from a Bridal Show

Brides who get the most from these shows talk to the folks behind the booth tables and hear what they have to say. Is it a hard-sell? Does the product look like something you would want to have at your wedding? Are the vendors personable? Do they seem to know what customer service means? Pick up any handouts or brochures they offer, and make notes in your planner on items you particularly like. When you get home, you can spread out your notes and brochures and see what's available. This can give you a good starting point.

The real reason the vendors at a bridal show agree to give up an entire Sunday is that they receive a list of all attendees at the show. You probably will receive some flyers or direct-mail pieces from some of the vendors following the show. Many times, you will receive additional coupons or discounts from these vendors after the show.

This happy couple is walking on air. *(Photo by Jeff Hawkins Photography)*

The Role of the Bridal Consultant

Working one-on-one with the bride and her family from the engagement to the honeymoon, or any point in between, the *bridal consultant* can ensure that all aspects of your wonderful day happen as you had planned. Some couples hire consultants as soon as they announce their engagement. I've actually had mothers call me for advice and counsel before their daughters even have a ring, much less have a date chosen. Other couples choose to hire a consultant near the end of the process—six weeks or so from the actual wedding day—to pull together those loose ends and to oversee the rehearsal and wedding day activities. The bottom line here is that you should decide just how much you want to involve the bridal consultant. You're the boss; the final choice should always be yours.

> **Nuptial Notes**
>
> A **bridal consultant** works directly with the bride and groom, or the couple's parents, to help facilitate the wedding. Most bridal consultants have independently owned businesses. Their expertise is in finding the right vendors to meet your budgetary needs and keeping you on track with your check-off list as you count down the days until the wedding. The bridal consultant is there to help you have *your* dream wedding at the best possible price.

How to Find the Right Consultant for Your Wedding

You can look in the Yellow Pages as a first step in locating a competent bridal consultant, as long as you review the listings carefully. The best method, however, is to ask friends and family for names of consultants they have worked with. Many vendors will also recommend bridal consultants in their area they have worked with and whom they feel comfortable with. In addition, the church may have worked with bridal consultants they felt especially good about having at the wedding.

Look for a bridal consultant who is a member of an organization of wedding professionals. This generally indicates that the consultant is continually learning, attending conferences to further her knowledge, and keeping aware of changes and trends in the wedding industry. You should always ask the bridal consultant for references.

The Association of Bridal Consultants (ABC)

You can also get the names of consultants in your area by contacting certain trade associations, such as the Association of Bridal Consultants (ABC). This is the largest organization for bridal consultants in the world. In 1982, ABC had just two members worldwide; as of April 2003, it has a worldwide membership of more than 3,400 members, and that number climbs higher each year.

This association is located in Connecticut call them (860-355-0464; fax 860-354-1404) or e-mail (Office@bridalassn.com) and they will be happy to give you names of members in your area.

You might decide that you just want to bend a consultant's ear for a couple hours to help you get started. I've had several brides who were getting married away from my area make an appointment to get some advice about how to begin. That's fine. If that's all the help you think you'll need, then definitely take that route.

> **Bouquet Toss**
>
> There are no "wedding police" out there. If you truly want to do something at your wedding or during the planning stages that may not be proper etiquette, get some impartial advice. Try to determine whether the custom truly is not in good taste or whether it simply wasn't a custom practiced at the turn of the century. It may be one no one would bat an eye at in the year 2003 and beyond.

Using the Internet: Show Me Your Sites!

The Internet has grown so much since I last updated this book in 2000 that the changes are hard to keep up with. The websites you can choose from are endless, and the mass of information can boggle the mind.

Michael Connors of WdWEB.Company—Wedding Detail—Party Detail, in Traverse City, Michigan, has been in the wedding business for the past 17 years. He knows the websites you should know about like the back of his hand.

In the following sections, Michael shares which are the most popular sites to browse and offers "must-see sites" for each item of the planning process I discuss. Please understand that websites change very frequently. As of this writing, all of these sites were active and well established.

Bridal Shows

Three main websites that feature wedding shows are …

- www.bridal-shows.com
- www.bridalfashionshows.com
- www.bspishows.com

Bridal Consultants

The Association of Bridal Consultants (ABC) has made it easy to find a consultant in your area by allowing you to send in an e-mail request. They will locate a consultant near you and send you his or her information.

- www.afwpi.com
- www.bridalassn.com

Wedding Portals/Directories

Wedding portals/directories are the easiest way to find information on weddings. A portal is like a mall, but everyone in the mall or "portal" is in the same type of business—the one-stop shopping for weddings. Caterers, bridal shops, coordinators, clergy, and so on, from your area are all located in the same place. This allows you to stop searching the web and start concentrating on viewing products and contacting professionals. Michael's must-see sites are as follows:

- www.theknot.com
- www.weddingchannel.com
- www.weddingdetails.com
- www.weddingnetwork.com

Honeymoons on the Web

The Internet has opened the door to finding fun and exotic places for your honeymoon. Many locations you may have never heard of before. The Internet also puts pictures, videos, and detailed information right at your fingertips, making your choice much easier. Some sites to visit are …

- www.honeymoondetails.com
- www.honeymoons.com
- www.unforgettablehoneymoon.com

Wedding Stores Online

There are several sites that have thousands of products, from favors to centerpieces and everything in between. By checking out these sites, you will come up with a multitude of ideas, products, and options to fit your budget and taste. Once you decide on your wedding theme and colors, it will be very easy to visit these online stores and order without having to drive around the state. To make good use of these sites, make a list of products you want to order, their prices, and the website; then make another notation on this list that shows when you ordered an item and a phone number for that order. Sites to see include the following:

- www.modernbride.com
- www.theweddingshopper.com
- www.weddingdetails.com

Bouquet Toss

You think you have problems? How would you like to select a new wedding ring every year? That's what the primitive brides had to do. Their rings were circles of hemp or rushes woven together into the shape of a circle. Because the fibers disintegrated over a period of time, women had to replace their rings every year!

Personal Bridal Pages

Should you have a web page? The answer is YES! It will save you time and money and will help you communicate better with your family and friends. Imagine your page with a picture of the two of you and a little background information. Then add a brief synopsis of your jobs, hobbies, and heritage so that friends and family can get better acquainted with you. Post your wedding date, time location, and reception information and include a map (a must for out-of-town guests). Also, include where you are registered for gifts. Many national chain stores are online and linked with their stores all over the world. Two websites that allow you to set up your own personal web page for your wedding free of charge are the following:

- www.theknot.com
- www.weddingdetails.com

These two sites also offer wedding advice via e-mail.

He just popped the question, and she said "yes!"
(Photo by Jeff Hawkins Photography)

Online Bridal Registry

It has never been easier to register online. With thousands of items to choose from and all those extra ones you want to register for, you can't miss. Online registry offers you the convenience of registering where you like without having to worry about whether or not a certain store is in your area. Perhaps you would like to add a glass vase from Macy's in New York to your list, but most of your friends and family live in Idaho. Online registry is the answer, allowing friends to order conveniently and safely over the Internet. Check out these registry sites:

- www.a-weddingday.com
- www.alifetime.com
- www.giftpoint.com
- www.theweddingshopper.com
- www.weddingnetwork.com

Wedding Planning Sites

These websites offer links to all areas of planning, from consultants to florists to photographers.

- www.theknot.com
- www.weddingchannel.com
- www.weddingdetails.com

Destination Weddings

These sites offer help with planning a wedding in another location. As you'll learn in Chapter 18, a destination wedding is a wedding you plan from one area and all of your guests travel to the wedding. It is usually held in a vacation location such as Disney World or Hawaii, someplace special.

- www.unforgettablehoneymoon.com
- www.weddinglocation.com

Invitations

These websites can connect you with help in choosing your invitations, programs, place cards, and other wedding papers. You'll read all about it in Chapter 12.

- www.ed-it.com
- www.elite.com
- www.invitesgalor.copm
- www.mvsweddinginvitations.com
- www.regencythermo.com

Wedding Woes

I highly recommend ordering invitations from an expert vendor in the field with whom you can sit down and discuss the order in person. There are too many chances for mistakes if you order invitations online or over the phone. And then, it's your word against the vendor's as to who made the mistake.

Wedding Traditions

Weddings that call for unusual special effects or costumes to carry out the wedding theme can be found at the following websites. Yes, the second site is real and it *is* about costumes. Halloween weddings are fun, fun, fun, as you'll see in Chapter 17!

- www.medieval-weddings.net
- www.scarycostumes.com
- www.weddingdetails.com/lore

Tuxedos

Refer your groom-to-be and his groomsmen to the following sites for information on tuxedoes:

- www.afterhours.com
- www.fubu.com
- www.tuxedos.com

Gown Preservation

When the big day is over, check these sites for information on preserving your wedding gown:

- www.wedclean.com
- www.weddinggownspecialist.com

Pure romance. *(Photo by Jeff Hawkins Photography)*

The Least You Need to Know

- The wedding industry has become big business, grossing many billions of dollars every year.
- Use a system of organization—a CD-ROM program, a notebook, or a folder—to hold your receipts, brochures, fabric swatches, vendor phone numbers, appointment calendar, and so on.
- Attending a bridal show can be a good way of learning about wedding vendors and comparing prices and services.
- Working with a bridal consultant can help you make sure all aspects of your big day go as planned.
- Check out the Internet for information regarding anything and everything to do with your wedding.

In This Chapter

◆ How formal do you want your wedding to be?

◆ How the level of formality affects your budget

◆ Money matters: setting a realistic budget

◆ Determining whom to involve with the finances

◆ Be willing to compromise!

Chapter 2

Simple or Extravagant? Setting Your Budget

This chapter talks about the financial part of the wedding. Ugh! I know it's not a popular topic, but it's necessary. Without a realistic budget in mind, you'll be overspending long before you know it.

Before you set a budget, though, you need to understand several factors to make your wedding dollars count. The first question to ask yourself is how formal you and your partner would like your wedding to be. Have you always dreamed of a large formal church wedding, or is a relaxed outdoor wedding with just family and a few close friends more your style? And you'll want to discuss what the important elements of the wedding and reception are that you and your groom want included. Sit down with each other and go over "What's Important to Us" worksheet in Appendix B. Prioritize your ideas so you know how you want to divide your precious wedding dollars. If wonderful photography is high on your list, for example, make a note of that so that when it comes time to divide the overall budget, you'll know that's one area in which you want to allocate more money.

Blue Jeans or Black Tie?

Determining how formal you want your wedding to be will help you establish the basis for your overall wedding strategy. The level of formality you choose determines, to a great extent, the overall cost of your wedding. It's a good idea for all participants—the bride, the groom, the in-laws, and anyone else with a financial interest in this wedding—to sit down together and figure out just how detailed and formal you want this affair to be. Essentially, you can choose from the following four levels of formality:

◆ Ultraformal
◆ Formal
◆ Semiformal
◆ Informal

Let's take a closer look at what each level entails.

Ultraformal: Glamorous and Glitzy

The most formal type of wedding you can have is *ultraformal.* This is the kind of wedding a movie star, royalty, or the President's daughter might have. Of course, you can have this type, too, and it doesn't necessarily mean you have to have it in a large church. Ultraformal weddings usually include the following:

◆ Usually more than 500 guests
◆ A large wedding party—9 to 15+ bridesmaids and groomsmen
◆ Elaborate decorations and floral arrangements
◆ A variety of music selections both at the ceremony and reception
◆ A formal served dinner
◆ Place cards and menu cards at the table
◆ Formal programs for both ceremony and reception
◆ A detailed bride's gown, with beading and pearls (the bride might also have a separate gown for the reception); the bridal gown is always full length, with, most times, a cathedral-length train (the longest type)
◆ A veil (either short or full length)
◆ If the reception is after 6 P.M., the groom and his groomsmen should be in white tie and tails. If the reception is before 6 P.M., formal black tie is the attire.
◆ Full bar
◆ An evening reception (after 6 P.M.)
◆ Favors for the guests
◆ Formalwear for the guests, with men in tuxedos and ladies in long gowns

This handsome couple poses for a formal picture. Note the large bouquet, full-length veil, and groom in a black tux. *(Photo by Colter Photography)*

This little princess completes the wedding party for the ultraformal wedding. *(Photo by Melanie Blair Photo)*

Featured at an ultraformal wedding, this stunning floral arrangement was about five feet in height! *(Photo by Garbo Productions)*

A large factor in determining how formal your wedding will be is deciding how many guests you want to invite. Start with a number you can comfortably entertain at the reception, and divide that number by four. This process can vary depending on your personal family situation, but normally the bride's parents, the groom's parents, the bride, and the groom all submit guest lists. There may be duplicates on the lists, so check for that. If that number is too high, begin eliminating names by whatever means you can determine. Many families invite only those friends who know the bride or groom well, leaving out business associates. Many couples want those in attendance to be only people who are special to them.

Formal: Elegant and Graceful

The *formal* wedding currently is the most popular type of wedding in most parts of the United States. A formal wedding normally includes:

◆ 150 to 350 guests

◆ Three to eight bridesmaids and groomsmen

◆ Either seated dinner or heavy hors d'oeuvres or grazing stations

◆ Full or limited bar

◆ Several musical groups for ceremony and reception

◆ Brides' gowns can be elaborate or more simple, to suit the bride, but still full length with either a chapel- or cathedral-length train

◆ A veil (either short or full length)

◆ Men in the wedding party wear tuxedos

◆ Favors are still usually given to guests

◆ Guests wear suits and ties for the men and cocktail dresses or suits for the ladies

These pretty maids all in a row await the bride. They are carrying "tussie mussies," a Victorian silver flower holder. *(Photo by Colter Photography)*

Here's one bride who just decided to take a break. I think all this picture taking is getting to her. Wonder what she's thinking? Her veil is a cathedral length and she is wearing long above-the-elbow gloves. *(Photo by Colter Photography)*

This pretty bride in a formal gown looks a little nervous as she takes her walk. Notice the ties on the men's tuxes instead of bow ties. *(Photo by Colter Photography)*

Wedding Woes

Weddings tend to grow in size and complexity. Think carefully now about your options and what you want to include. As you start adding to your must-have list, the complexity and costs can easily begin snowballing!

Semiformal: Tasteful and Dignified

The *semiformal* wedding generally includes:

- ◆ 100 to 200 guests
- ◆ One to four bridesmaids and groomsmen
- ◆ Men in wedding party may not wear tuxedos
- ◆ Bride is dressed more simply; may wear flowers or comb in her hair instead of veil
- ◆ Decorations are more simple
- ◆ Reception might consists of hors d'oeuvres and limited bar
- ◆ A disc jockey or small combo may provide the music

This formal full gown of tulle and lace is accented with a satin ribbon around the bottom of the gown. The bride is wearing a tiara to hold her veil. The groom is wearing a classic tuxedo. *(Photo by Wyant Photography)*

Here's an example of how levels of formality can cross over into each other. While this couple had 200 guests and extensive food, they chose blazers and slacks for the men, street-length dresses for the bridesmaids, and the bride did not wear a veil. Also notice how the wedding party is circled around the couple for the ceremony. *(Photo by Colter Photography)*

This happy groom is wearing the newer tie look with his tux. *(Photo by Colter Photography)*

This handsome groom wears a button at the collar instead of a bow tie. *(Photo by Jeff Hawkins Photography)*

Here's a lovely bridal veil that can easily be removed for the reception. *(Photo by Jeff Hawkins Photography)*

Informal: Casual and Comfortable

An *informal* wedding is usually conducted either in a judge's chambers, in a home setting, or outdoors. Most times, an informal wedding includes the following:

◆ Fewer than 50 guests

◆ Just one honor attendant each

◆ Simple food, such as cake and punch or champagne for the toast

◆ Simple décor, such as one floral arrangement, with the bride carrying a simple bouquet

◆ Both bride and groom wear simple suits, or the bride may opt for a street-length wedding dress or day dress

◆ Couple may choose to have a larger party later to celebrate their marriage with family and friends

How the Level of Formality Affects Your Budget

The type of wedding you decide to have—ultraformal, formal, semiformal, or informal—plays a huge part in determining the overall cost of your wedding. The standards that determine the level of formality, however, are not carved in stone, and there are no hard-and-fast rules. Your wedding may cross over into a couple formality levels, but you do need a starting point. Choose the level of formality with which you are most comfortable and which seems to fit best within your budget.

This bride chose street-length dresses for her maids. Her gown is simple, and she is not wearing a veil.
(Photo by Wyant Photography)

Teddy's Tips

The average cost of a formal wedding in the United States—including a dinner and bar for 200, engagement and wedding rings, a gown, menswear, a band, a photographer, a florist, invitations, bridal consultant, and all the extras—costs approximately $18,000 to $30,000 depending in what area of the country you live.

Setting a Realistic Budget

The *wedding budget* is probably the biggest area of turmoil for most couples. No one—I repeat, no one—wants to talk about the cost of the wedding. But ultimately, you do have to broach the subject, and the earlier you begin talking about it the better.

Now comes the real issue. Just how much is this whole affair going to cost? Well, it's not going to be cheap, but I firmly believe that you don't have to mortgage the farm for your wedding.

Cost Comparison

Turn to Appendix B and glance at the "Cost Comparison Worksheet," which lists all possible wedding expenses. The purpose of this worksheet is to find the norm for your market area and to determine what sets each estimate apart. It won't help you one bit if I quote you the cost of hiring a photographer in Indiana if you live in Boston. You have some homework to do here, but it will pay off in the end (literally).

This groom waits for his bride to come down the aisle while the maid of honor watches him. Notice her two-piece gown. *(Photo by Colter Photography)*

Now is the time to begin reviewing those names of possible vendors you have gathered from bridal shows, your family, your friends, and maybe from your bridal consultant. Call at least three vendors under each entry to determine where their prices fall, then record the information on this worksheet (use a pencil in case you have to make changes!). Make sure you ask the same questions of each vendor so you can compare "apples to apples."

Putting Your Budget on Paper

When you've finished the "Cost Comparison Worksheet," turn to the "Wedding Budget Worksheet" in Appendix B. Using your completed "Cost Comparison Worksheet," run down the list of service providers.

Continue to do the same with each entry on the budget worksheet, and then add everything up and see what ballpark you're in. You may be way, way out of the park, or you could be right on target.

The next step is compromise. If you want a dinner reception for 650 of your closest friends but you just can't figure out how you can afford it, see where else you can cut costs to make up the difference. Maybe you can serve less elaborate food for the reception, have fewer flowers, or cut your guest list a little. You have to be willing to give and take. Unless you have unlimited resources or Uncle Ralph died and left you a huge inheritance, you have to be cost-conscious in your thinking. If you're set on having that top-rated photographer in your area who costs $5,000 just to book him, think about ways to decrease your flower bill, or go with a DJ rather than a band. Give and take—that's the name of the game.

Teddy's Tips

The more open you are to compromising with the budget, the less stress over money matters you are likely to have later. You're also less likely to be disappointed because your budget cannot accommodate your dreams.

Getting Everyone Involved

When determining your wedding budget, be sure to include all members of the wedding finance committee. That may include the bride and groom, all parents, grandparents, and others. Sit down in a relaxed atmosphere, and talk about the expenses of this wedding. Most of all, think positive and be willing to give and take.

This wedding photo is a take-off of the famous "Family Reunion" photo created by Norma Edelman. This was a very informal wedding with a Hawaiian theme. Notice the leis around everyone's necks.
(Photo by Monique Feil)

The groom does have a responsibility for some parts of the wedding costs. Traditionally, the groom and his family cover the bride's bouquet, the flowers for the groomsmen, the rehearsal dinner, and the flowers for the mothers. Sometimes, the groom's parents also may offer to pay for part of the cost of the reception, the photography, or the floral bill. Etiquette dictates that the bride or her parents cannot ask the groom's parents to help with the expenses. If they offer, however, the bride's parents may choose to take them up on it. After all, it's their son's wedding, too, and they may want to feel as though they're contributing a part.

Who Pays for What?

Weddings are considered traditional ceremonies of a life passage. As customs and traditions have changed during the years, so have the rules for who pays for what. Traditionally, the bride's family has paid for the majority of the wedding costs. However, that is changing, and more couples are coming up with creative ways to meet their financial obligations. Today, it's not uncommon for the couple to pay all their expenses or for a combination of contributors to give funds for the wedding, including both sets of parents, grandparents, and even close friends.

Wedding Woes

Never leave key players out of the budget discussion. If you don't have the financial resources to spring for this wedding on your own, you need backing from family. Play it smart.

The "Who Pays for What Worksheet" in Appendix B gives you an idea of the traditional items in a wedding budget. But this worksheet is only a guide. This is the twenty-first century, and there are many ways to divide wedding expenses. Find the way that works best for you.

The Least You Need to Know

◆ Determining the level of formality early on lets you decide what's important. It also enables you to establish a realistic budget.

◆ There are no hard-and-fast rules concerning the levels of formality. These are suggestions. Find a starting point, even if the wedding you want seems to cross a couple formality levels.

◆ Use cost comparison to determine prices in your area. You can't begin putting together a budget if you don't have an idea of the going rate for services in your area.

◆ Sit down in a relaxed atmosphere with everyone who needs to be involved with the wedding finances. Be realistic in what you want and what you can afford. When you have established your budget, do your best to work within it.

◆ Think positive, and be willing to give and take!

In This Part

First Things First

This part of the book talks about what you need to reserve first and how far before the big day you need to make the reservations. Although it might not seem like it now, there is a method to all this madness. It covers areas like reserving the reception and the church or ceremony site. I'll talk about asking friends to be part of this wonderful day, discuss your wedding party, and finish up with talking about the rehearsal dinner and the all-important honeymoon.

Be patient. We're just getting started. The big day will be here before you know it—and you'll be ready!

In This Chapter

- What to consider when choosing a date
- Selecting a site for the ceremony
- Questions to ask when choosing a site
- Cultivating a good relationship with the officiant

Chapter 3

Get Me a Church on Time!

Probably some of the most obvious duties to cover at the beginning of your wedding planning are what I fondly call the "biggies": setting a date, finding a place, and making the arrangements for someone to perform the service.

These tasks are not as time-consuming as meeting with the caterer or visiting the reception facility, but they need to be done first. After all, if you don't have a date, how can you plan anything else?

Setting the Date

Before you can reserve a reception site, of course, you need to determine a date for the occasion. When choosing a date for your wedding, keep in mind family commitments (birthdays and other anniversaries), holidays, how far guests will have to travel, special events and tourist activities taking place in the area, and likely weather conditions.

Plan Around Big Events

Planning a May wedding in Indianapolis around the time of the Indianapolis 500 is probably not a wise move. In fact, it would likely be a very expensive proposition. Hotels and motels double their room prices, crowds swell the city beyond imagination, and many of the ideal reception spots are booked years in advance for race activities.

Likewise, a wedding in New Orleans during Mardi Gras is not a wise idea. Again, you would have to deal with loads of tourists and inflated prices, in addition to the difficulty of booking a reception site. Save yourself a lot of planning nightmares by checking out the tourist trends in your area. Then try your best to avoid scheduling your wedding at the same time as a popular special event.

> **Teddy's Tips**
>
> Set your date with the church and the reception site as early as possible. Sometimes you have to juggle the date to coordinate both facilities.

This wedding is taking place at a country club. The couple used a tent for the ceremony and then guests celebrated in the clubhouse. *(Photo by Colter Photography)*

Other dates that you should try to avoid—mainly because of floral difficulties—are Mother's Day weekend and Valentine's Day weekend. Both of these times are extremely busy for florists; some florists will not even accept a Mother's Day weekend wedding because they find it too difficult to handle the pressures of a wedding along with holiday floral orders. Just as important for you, flowers almost triple in price during these holidays.

> **Teddy's Tips**
>
> Be sure to refer to the planning checklist in Appendix C to help you remember what to do in the months leading up to the big event.

Also check with the local convention and visitors bureau to make sure there are no really big conventions in town that will take up many hotel rooms and reception sites.

This couple was married on the floor of the state house. It is free, but everything else must be rented and brought in. Here the couple shares a quiet moment before guests arrive. *(Photo by Wyant Photography)*

Holidays: Pressure Cookers or Money Savers?

Holiday weddings, especially during the Christmas season, can be stressful given the hectic nature of the season, but they also can be money savers. Most facilities are already decked out for the holidays, which means you can save big bucks on decorations. The cost savings doesn't come without a price, however. We all know the kind of stress that can accompany the holidays in everyday life; add the task of planning a wedding, and you compound that stress many times over. However, if you love Christmas and can handle the added pressure, you can save substantially on your decorating costs.

One of the prettiest Christmas weddings I can remember included 500 white poinsettias, candles on every aisle, red ribbons and fresh greenery at the entrance, and a large Christmas tree in the lobby area. The church congregation had already decorated for the season, and it was breathtaking. The best part was that the couple didn't spend a dime on any of it!

If you want to save money on decorations, a holiday wedding is a good way to go. This couple was married in a traditional church service at Christmas. *(Photo by Wyant Photography)*

Waltzing with the Weather

Be sure to take the area's weather into consideration for the time of year you're planning your wedding. It will affect not only the drive to the church and reception site, but your out-of-town guests who may be driving or flying in. For my own January wedding in 1971, I never even considered the weather as a factor. Now, because I'm from Indiana, I should have known better. It snowed eight inches on the day of the wedding. Lucky for us, the snow came straight down, it didn't really drift much, and everyone was able to drive to the church.

Of course, eight inches of snow is probably a pleasure compared to temperatures climbing into the 90s and high humidity! You can't control the weather (although at times, I sure wish I could), so if you live in an area where bad weather conditions tend to be a problem, try to take the weather into consideration when you set the date.

This couple chose fall for their wedding. The leaves scattered on the grounds of the country club add a nice seasonal touch. *(Photo by Wyant Photography)*

These gentlemen in the wedding party enjoy some time on the golf course before the ceremony begins. *(Photo by Colter Photography)*

Consider holding a summer wedding on an outdoor patio. This couple's ceremony featured a tropical theme. *(Photo by Wyant Photography)*

Consider Other Commitments

Family commitments also make a difference in setting a date. Make a list of those commitments before you pick a day. You can say to Aunt Martha, "We're thinking about sometime next May for our wedding. Can you think of any dates that you and Uncle Fred may not be able to attend?" You don't have to do this with all your relatives—and unless you have a very small family, you can't—but try to consider the schedules of those people whose presence is especially important to you.

If you and your groom (or your guests) have school commitments or careers that are affected by the time of year, take those commitments into account as well. And if you're an accountant, setting a wedding date in the weeks leading up to April 15 is probably not wise planning!

If you take some time now to plan around other family commitments, your local traditions (festivals, large sporting events, and so on), the holiday schedule, your own work or school

schedules, and your local weather conditions, you will please more of your guests in the long run and make life a little easier. In the end, though, you and your partner need to be happy with the date.

This Jewish ceremony is being performed in a temple. The covering over their heads is called a chuppah. These can be simple, like this one, or very elaborate, with flowers and ribbons. *(Photo by Wyant Photography)*

Teddy's Tips

One simple thing that can easily sneak up on you is remembering to apply for the marriage license. Each state has different requirements and policies, including the length of the waiting period, the ages of both parties, blood tests (or other medical examination), identification requirements, and how much the license costs. Within each state, each county may have its own set of rules. Your first step should be to call the office of the marriage clerk or county clerk in your county seat and ask how to proceed. You should investigate the requirements several months before your wedding date. Many counties now make allowances for long-distance couples, but you should find out well in advance of your wedding day.

Selecting the Ceremony Site

Okay, you have a date in mind. After you've determined how formal you want this wedding to be and when to have it, you need to find a place for the ceremony.

In this ceremony, which takes place in an auditorium, the drapes are pulled back on either side to show all the candles in the back. Also notice how long the bride's veil is. This is another example of a cathedral-length veil. *(Photo by Wyant Photography)*

The place you choose for your wedding ceremony can be as unique as you and your partner. Your options include the following:

- A church
- Cathedral
- Chapel
- Temple
- A hall
- A private home
- A garden or other outdoor setting
- Private club
- Restaurant or resort facility
- Judge's chambers

This couple chose a downtown location for their wedding and afterward strolled down the empty street by the state capitol. *(Photo by Wyant Photography)*

A lovely bride steals a precious moment with her flower girl in this simple yet stately church. *(Photo by Wyant Photography)*

A city park was the setting for this couple's ceremony. The ivy-covered columns and pink flowering bushes add a nice touch. *(Photo by Wyant Photography)*

This couple chose a beautifully decorated park shelter for their wedding. *(Photo by Wyant Photography)*

Some couples have expressed their personalities by choosing unique venues:

- Hot air balloon
- Underwater
- Roller coaster
- On horseback
- Beach
- Barn or ranch
- Boat (be sure to check your state's regulations regarding marriage licenses and weddings on water!)

Golf is a favorite pastime for this bride and groom! *(Photo by Stephanie Cristalli)*

For cooling off on a hot summer day, this fountain was just too inviting to pass up! *(Photo by Wyant Photography)*

A bagpiper is bringing in the bride in this Scottish-theme wedding. *(Photo by Colter Photography)*

Examine the Facility Firsthand

Whether it's your home church or a rented space, be sure to visit the facility. Here are some questions to ask:

◆ How many guests can it seat?

◆ What kind of musical equipment comes with it (if any)?

◆ What are the restrictions with the music?

◆ Is there a room for the bride to get dressed in, if that's necessary?

◆ Is there ample parking, and is it close by the facility?

◆ Does the facility have air conditioning (important if you're planning a late spring or summer wedding!)

◆ Are there adequate restroom facilities?

◆ Is there a wedding policy booklet available?

◆ Are there restrictions on vendor delivery times, such as for flowers?

◆ Can you bring your own clergy or officiant to perform the ceremony?

◆ How much time will you be allowed for the wedding? Does that include taking pictures?

◆ Is the room where the actual ceremony will take place large enough to accommodate your wedding party size?

A hotel ballroom, with its impressive dome and aisle pieces, makes a beautiful site for this ceremony. *(Photo by Garbo Productions)*

Understand the Fees and Policies

Be sure to ask about fees. Yes, a church is a business, and many churches charge for the use of the facility, and some of these fees can be quite steep. Ask what the fee includes. Churches that charge a single fee that includes all the necessary services (musicians, janitor, officiant, and rent) probably offer the best deal. You're going to have to pay for those services anyway, so if you can line them all up with one stop, that's not a bad option.

Use the "Ceremony Site Worksheet" in Appendix B to ensure that you've asked all the right questions and have thoroughly investigated a facility before you actually write the check to reserve it.

Wedding Woes

Make sure you read and fully understand the church or other facility's wedding policies before your wedding day. If you can't work with its rules, look elsewhere. If there are restrictions on certain parts of the church rental, be sure to inform those who will be affected, such as your vendors.

Last but certainly not least, make sure you have copies of the contract or letter of agreement (a simpler form of a contract) from the ceremony site. Don't rely on "I'll put you down for that date" from the church secretary. A written contract reserving your date with the facility is best.

This couple chose an interesting place for their ceremony—one in which they could look "down" on the world. *(Photo by Wyant Photography)*

Working with the Officiant

Someone has to perform your service—that's a given. Whether the officiant is a justice of the peace, a judge, a priest, a rabbi, or a minister, someone with the legal authority allowed by the state must preside at your marriage. My best advice when working with this person is to make him or her your friend, not your enemy. Strive for an amiable relationship. After all, the officiant is going to perform a very important ceremony in your life, and you want fond memories of this event.

The officiant is your link to the legal aspects of your wedding. Without his or her consent and cooperation, the wedding may take place, but if the officiant doesn't complete the legal paperwork to validate the marriage in the state, the union won't be legal. So although you may have different ideas about what you want to include in your service, it's wise to have a good relationship with your officiant. Meet with him or her. Ask for opinions and advice. Get the officiant on your side first, and then talk about the particulars of your service.

Notice the placement of the priest in this Catholic church service; he is standing in front of the couple so that when they say their vows they will be facing the congregation. *(Photo by Wyant Photography)*

Unlike a priest, the minister in this Protestant church service is dressed in a suit (priests always wear robes). With an altar area this large, you either spend a fortune in decorations or keep it simple and use your money in other places. *(Photo by Stephanie Cristalli)*

This couple looks on as the priest offers communion at their wedding. *(Photo by Colter Photography)*

Bouquet Toss

I once coordinated a wedding in which the officiant refused to marry the couple just two weeks before the wedding. It wasn't that the officiant was concerned about the marriage itself—he just didn't like the way in which the couple answered a question he posed to them. He called the bride's mother two weeks before the wedding (invitations had been out for weeks at that time, the reception was arranged, and all systems were go) and told her to find another officiant. This was not an easy task, given the particulars of that wedding!

Certainly, most officiants are pleasant and friendly and want to help make your wedding day memorable. A little common respect and courtesy can go a long way toward making the officiant a friend.

The Least You Need to Know

◆ Consider weather conditions, family commitments, and local special events and celebrations when choosing your wedding date.

◆ There are many options available when choosing a site for the ceremony. Pick one that best suits your needs and your personalities.

◆ Visit the site in person to check out location, layout, the number of guests it will hold, and parking—and be sure to understand all fees and policies.

◆ Treat the officiant with respect. Try your best to work with him or her to ensure a smooth road both to the church and down the aisle.

In This Chapter

◆ Making sure you get what you pay for in your reception facility

◆ What to consider when reserving the reception site

◆ How to find a good caterer

◆ Understanding your responsibilities when serving liquor

Chapter 4

Seeking Your Soirée

Okay, folks, it's time to talk about the reception, quite possibly the biggest party you will ever throw. It takes careful, timely planning and lots of research to get the party you want.

The reception can be the most costly item in your wedding budget. In addition to finding and reserving the reception site, you need to know what to look for in a good catering facility and in the caterer, and you need to make the big decision: whether or not to serve liquor. I'll hit the high points here and give you the details in Chapter 8. So let's party on!

The Reception Site—Getting What You Pay For

The reception (facility rental and catering costs) will account for about 40 percent of your total wedding bill. When planning your wedding reception, make sure you pay close attention to all the details so that you get your money's worth. Remember to book early; the prime reception sites will be reserved as far as 18 to 24 months in advance in larger cities. (Be sure to turn to the "Reception Site Worksheet" in Appendix B for help in choosing the site.)

One Size Doesn't Fit All

Your biggest consideration in choosing a site is whether the facility is large enough to accommodate your number of guests. Here are a few questions to start with:

◆ Can it comfortably accommodate your guests as well as the activities you want to include, like dancing and a band or disc jockey?

◆ Is there room to introduce the wedding party?

◆ Is there room for a receiving line?

This hotel ballroom features a long table with seating on both sides for either guests or the wedding party—a popular trend these days, instead of the one-sided head table. *(Photo by Jeff Hawkins Photography)*

This Victorian house has been turned into a reception facility. Notice the tall, elegant centerpieces. *(Photo by Wyant Photography)*

This open-air space is located in San Diego, where it's sunny most of the time. Notice the unique centerpiece filled with sliced fruits and flowers. *(Photo by Monique Feil Photography)*

Deal With the Details

Make doubly sure that you get what the facility will and will not provide *in writing*. Here are some other questions you'll want to ask:

◆ Are linens included (tablecloths, table skirting, chair covers, napkins, and so on)?

◆ Do you have a choice of colors with linens?

Most reception sites provide those items as part of their contract, but that is not always the case. Just know what you're getting when you pay your deposit.

Ask questions of the manager. If the manager's only comment is "We can't do that," see if you can find another facility that is more accommodating. The manager works for you, not the other way around.

Adorning a chair with an elegant chair cover and matching tulle bow makes the room look more complete. *(Photo by Jeff Hawkins Photography)*

Most wedding gifts should be sent to the home, but because we are such a scattered society, many gifts are brought to the reception. This gift table is set up at a hotel. Always keep the gift table out of the main traffic flow. *(Photo by Jeff Hawkins Photography)*

- ◆ Are microphones, speakers, and other equipment included?
- ◆ Is there a dance floor? Can it be moved?
- ◆ Does the site provide security guards?
- ◆ Are there ample restrooms?
- ◆ Are there considerations for guests with disabilities?
- ◆ Is there adequate parking for guests?

Reserving the Reception Site

Many reception sites—whether a private club, a hall, the church's social hall, a restaurant, or the civic center—will accept early reservations. You can reserve many of the prime reception sites at least a year in advance. In larger cities you can book some sites at much at 18 months in advance.

This reception is being held in a small private dining room of a private club. *(Photo by Jeff Hawkins Photography)*

Ask friends, family members, and certainly recently married couples where they had their reception. That's a good starting point. Also, check in the Yellow Pages (under headings such as "Banquet Facilities," "Halls and Auditoriums," and "Party Centers") for sites you might not have thought about.

Don't be afraid to consider more offbeat sites! This old warehouse has been transformed into a unique and attractive space. Notice the open-concept ceilings with lighting. *(Photo by Jeff Hawkins Photography)*

Teddy's Tips _____

Book the reception site early! Get the details in writing of the items that the facility provides, and make sure that you feel comfortable with the manager.

Possible reception sites include the following:

- Private clubs
- Hotels
- Catering halls
- University or college facilities
- Victorian homes or mansions
- Art museums
- Historical society buildings
- Gardens
- Parks
- Tents
- Private homes

This lovely tented reception features a unique lighting system—Japanese lanterns hanging from the tent walls. Can you see the lake in the background? *(Photo by C. B. Bell, III)*

Traffic Jam

The traffic flow inside the facility is an important factor that shouldn't be overlooked. Your reception manager should be able to make suggestions, based on past experience, for the best traffic pattern for a wedding reception at that facility. Also check floor plans.

What About Services and Restrictions?

Check with the manager about the restrictions the facility has for food and beverages. Can you bring in an *outside caterer* of your choice, or do you have to use the facility's *in-house caterer?*

> **Nuptial Notes**
>
> An **outside caterer** is a person or organization not associated with the facility who comes to the facility to prepare the food. An **in-house caterer** is the person or organization responsible for that facility's food service.

Look at the "Choosing the Reception Site Worksheet" in Appendix B for more help in selecting a site.

> **Bouquet Toss**
>
> The largest wedding dish ever prepared was a roasted camel. The camel was prepared in the following manner: Eggs were stuffed into fish, fish were stuffed into chickens, chickens were stuffed into a roasted lamb, and the lamb was stuffed inside the whole camel. The entire camel was then roasted and served to the wedding guests.
>
> —*Guinness Book of World Records*

Who's in Charge Here?

Try to gauge whether you will be able to work with the reception manager. As I mentioned earlier, you don't want to hear, "That can't be done." Instead, "Let me see what we can do" is the response you want. You're going to be spending a lot of time (and money) with these people, and you want it to be a pleasant experience. After all, it is not the reception manager's wedding reception. You are the client, and his or her only job for that day is to make you look good. If you look good and are happy, the reception manager (and the facility) looks good!

Choosing a Caterer

After you select a reception site, the next step is to find a caterer. If the reception facility you reserved provides an in-house catering service, you have no choice. Most of the larger facilities, such as hotels, country clubs, colleges, or universities, provide in-house catering.

Notice how the chef has arranged the cheese slices on this hors d'oeuvres station to resemble stacks of wood. Presentation is everything! *(Photo by Colter Photography)*

If you decide to hold your reception in a hall, art museum, home, church social hall, or outdoor setting, you must arrange for a caterer to provide the food. If the choice of caterer is up to you, shop around and find someone who can give you the food choices you want at a price you can afford.

Friends, family, and recently married couples are your best bet when discussing possible caterers. Ask the reception facility manager, too. Sometimes facilities limit which caterers may come into their facility. They may give you their preferred caterer list and ask you to choose a caterer from that list. This usually means that those caterers are competent, provide quality work, and take care of the facility so that the reception manager doesn't have to worry about damage from the caterers.

Be sure to check the "Choosing the Caterer Worksheet" in Appendix B for help on selecting a caterer. Chapter 8 also contains detailed information about caterers.

May I Serve You?

Traditional etiquette says that the only thing you must offer your guests at the wedding reception is something to eat and something to drink, so cake and punch will do the trick. Indeed, the simplest type of wedding reception is a cake-and-punch reception, with some mints and nuts thrown in for good measure, if you so desire. Anything else is icing on the cake (pardon the pun!).

You might want to move up one step and serve hors d'oeuvres and a limited bar. A limited bar means just that: You limit the selection of liquor, perhaps opting for wine or beer and soft drinks. One step up from this would be an open bar and hors d'oeuvres. (There's more about serving liquor in Chapter 8.)

Then there is the simple buffet for guests. A simple buffet includes one entrée, plus other side dishes. You can expand this into a more elaborate buffet by simply adding more entrées and other side dish choices.

The most elaborate reception meal you can offer would be a five- or six-course dinner served to guests, including a selection of wines with the meal. If you choose this option, consider hiring extra wait staff. If the facility's price normally includes one waiter for every two tables (20 guests), consider adding enough to have two waiters for every three tables (30 guests). This will speed the service and make the guests feel more special.

This stir-fry station comes complete with a chef to do some of the cooking. *(Photo by Jeff Hawkins Photography)*

Wedding Woes

Be wary of caterers who refuse to deviate from their standard menu. Good caterers will be willing to take your favorite recipes and price them out for your reception. This is great if you have some foods you particularly like or that are family traditions (such as Aunt Eileen's traditional Irish soda bread).

This server is pouring the champagne for the toast. Most champagne is served these days, instead of bottles being left on the tables. The large white plate with the emblem in the middle is a charger plate, which is used in very formal dinners. The salad or first-course plate will be served on it and then, after the guest is finished with that course, the whole plate will be removed. *(Photo by Jeff Hawkins Photography)*

This New Orleans–themed station features all kinds of southern goodies. *(Photo by Jeff Hawkins Photography)*

So What Will It Cost?

After you decide on the kind of meal you want to serve, start getting price estimates. Most caterers figure their prices per person, except for hors d'oeuvres, which sometimes are figured per dozen. Unless you have your heart set on particular food items, it often works well to give the caterer a price range or amount you do not want to go over and let him or her be creative. The caterer can choose the food, subject to your approval, based on seasonal availability.

Ask about the caterer's policy on guaranteed numbers. This is an important concept for you to understand before you begin contacting caterers. If you plan to serve major food items, you must have an accurate guest count. The caterer obviously isn't providing this food just for the pure pleasure of it; it comes with a price tag, and that's why you need to provide an accurate count. Check with the caterer about the policy on what percentage of food he or she will prepare over your guarantee. The usual is between 5 and 10 percent. So if you give the caterer a count of 100 and 105 people show up, it will be all right. If 130 show up, then you're in trouble.

Be sure to build in some extra time for checking out caterers and reception sites. This is one area of wedding planning that can carry a heavy price tag, and you want to find a facility and a caterer that offer you the best value for your wedding dollars. Also, get the catering details in writing. This can save you a great deal of grief later as you try to remember exactly what was quoted, including the 5 or 10 percent window above and below the guaranteed number. (See Chapter 8 for more information.)

Liquor: To Drink or Not To Drink?

The decision of whether to serve alcohol to your guests is solely a personal one. If you're going to offer alcohol at your reception, you need to engage either a caterer with a liquor license or a liquor-licensed dealer. This is a wise move, considering the liability issues presently in focus in the country. Many states now make the host liable for accidents involving guests at a party. (Direct any concerns about local laws regarding alcohol to the liquor-licensed dealer.)

Licensed bartenders are included in the contract. If the catering facility has a liquor license or if the caterer contracts the liquor out to a licensed liquor dealer, it will provide the bartenders. There is usually an extra charge for bartenders, but it is well worth the cost.

A hotel has its bar set up and ready to go. *(Photo by Jeff Hawkins Photography)*

Although all caterers are supposed to ensure that their bartenders comply with local laws, it may be wise to brief them (or have the wedding consultant do it) on specific guests they should watch for and to ensure that they know when and how to cut people off tactfully. (I'll talk specifically about designated drivers in Chapter 20.) If you're planning to serve champagne, also provide nonalcoholic sparkling grape juice so that those who do not wish to (or can't) drink can have something bubbly for the toasts.

> **Bouquet Toss**
>
> The word *bridal* comes from the old English term *bride-ale*, which refers to the mead drink (a fermented beverage made of water, honey, malt, and yeast) consumed for 30 days following the marriage.

The Least You Need to Know

◆ Be sure to ask lots of questions about the physical layout of the reception site. Make sure the facility can accommodate the number of guests you're inviting. Also check whether parking is adequate.

◆ The reception facility should have a good traffic flow pattern. Too little room to comfortably allow for the number of guests you expect can be frustrating for everyone involved.

◆ Make a list of questions for the caterer before you meet with him or her. Get all details in writing of what the caterer will provide.

◆ Understand your legal responsibilities if you decide to serve alcohol at the reception.

In This Chapter

- ◆ Determining the size of your wedding party
- ◆ Deciding who to include
- ◆ Children in the wedding party
- ◆ Asking friends to help in other ways
- ◆ Getting by with help from your friends?

Chapter 5

The Wedding Party: A Circle of Friends

One of the best parts of planning your wedding is telling your friends the good news and asking them to share this wonderful time with you. Most people consider it an honor to be asked to be part of a dear friend or family member's wedding.

Because you're asking someone to stand with you on one of the most significant days of your life, be sure to put careful thought into choosing your wedding party. Also, think about asking other friends to help with the other wedding duties, such as being the guest book attendant. All these folks play a huge part in keeping your wedding running smoothly.

Wedding Party Size

A complaint I hear frequently is, "My groom wants to ask 14 guys to be groomsmen. I have only eight friends for bridesmaids. Where can I get some more maids?" Well, it's probably not a good idea to rent-a-bridesmaid, although sometimes it may seem like the only option you have left. You don't need an even number of bridesmaids and groomsmen. Figure out exactly how many people the two of you want to stand up with you, and then figure out which other jobs you can delegate to friends.

This wedding party is enjoying a little time down by the tracks! *(Photo by Jeff Hawkins Photography)*

Don't you just love the sign that says "BRIDE XING"? This wedding party in San Diego looks like they're enjoying their walk from the ceremony to the reception. *(Photo by Norma Edelman, the creator of the sign)*

If the ceremony site has a large enough altar area to have 40 of your best friends lined up to be in the wedding party, then go for it. However, if the area will accommodate only a total of 12 people (that's the 2 of you, plus 5 bridesmaids and five groomsmen), you're going to have to prioritize who you want to do the honors. You need to coordinate the size of your ceremony area with the size of your wedding party.

Size probably doesn't matter as much as your feelings for the family and friends you're about to ask to be part of one of the most wonderful days of your life. These should be people you feel especially close to and really want to participate in this occasion.

Sometimes the smallest members of the wedding party can steal the show. *(Photo by Jeff Hawkins Photography)*

Teddy's Tips

Talk with parents or older relatives about their wedding party. How many of the friends they "just had to have" are still friends? Do they even know where some of them are today? How close are some of those "best friends"? Twenty years from now, will you look at the wedding pic-

Finalizing the List

Your wedding party will consist of several groups of people. The first people you will ask will be the maid or matron of honor and the best man. You may refer to these people as the honor attendants; however, in current use, an honor attendant refers to a male maid of honor or a female best man.

The special honor of maid or matron of honor may go to a sister, a cousin, or a very close friend. You even can choose to have both a maid and a matron of honor. Just be sure to decide before the ceremony which duties each will perform. Maybe the maid of honor will hold the groom's ring, while the matron of honor will help arrange the bridal gown's train. Both can help with some of the preliminary duties, such as running errands, being a good listener, and organizing some parties. Of course, this all depends on whether the honor attendants live in your area.

This maid of honor is trying to keep the bride's veil from blowing—one of the hazards of taking pictures outside. *(Photo by Colter Photography)*

Traditionally, the bridesmaids are young women who are close to the bride. These may include sisters, cousins, the groom's sisters, and good friends. Bridesmaids have no official function in the wedding party but are there to be supportive.

The gals all get together for this formal shot at the altar. *(Photo by Wyant Photography)*

Likewise, the groom chooses a best man. He can decide to have two best men, although this is not as common as having both a maid and a matron of honor. The groom might even ask his father to be his best man. (What an honor for any father!) The best man helps the groom prepare for the wedding, making sure he arrives at the ceremony site on time. He holds the bride's ring during the service and offers the first toast to the new couple during the reception.

Bouquet Toss

Choosing a best man keeps with the ancient custom of finding a good friend, most likely a tribal warrior, to help shield the bride from abductors known to prowl around the ceremony site.

The groom then chooses men to serve as his groomsmen. These can be brothers, the bride's brothers, cousins, or good friends. Like bridesmaids, groomsmen have no official function in the wedding party. They generally are not ushers, but simply are friends chosen to stand up with the groom and help witness the ceremony.

The remaining members of the main wedding party include the ushers, usually one usher for every 50 guests. Sometimes, the groomsmen double as ushers. There usually isn't a problem with this system, although it helps to have at least one usher in the back of the church to help with late arrivals or unexpected happenings.

If one of your attendants drops out of the wedding plans because of illness or other circumstances, you have a couple choices. You can ask someone else to step in if that person is agreeable and if (for the women) the dress fits the new attendant. Or you can just go as is and not worry about having even pairs. As I mentioned before, you don't need to have matching numbers of attendants.

Other attendants making up the wedding party may include the flower girl and ring bearer, candle lighters, train bearers, Bible bearers, junior groomsmen, junior bridesmaids, and pages. You may give these assignments to children or young adults.

These two young ones are just taking it all in. The flower girl isn't quite sure she wants to wear this thing in her hair and from the looks of it, might not. *(Photo by Colter Photography)*

"All right, already. Let's get moving!" This little guy seems like he's had enough of the mushy stuff. *(Photo by Jeff Hawkins Photography)*

Using Children as Attendants

Children as members of the wedding can add joy to the day. They represent innocence and remind us of the circle of life we all share. They also can detract more than you think from the wedding ceremony. You need to remember that children in wedding parties are still kids—they're not little adults in children's suits. They think like children, they behave like children, and they will be unpredictable like children. With children in the wedding party, my best advice is to just go with the flow. If that little flower girl doesn't want to walk down the aisle in front of 400 unfamiliar faces, don't bribe,

beg, or force her. She is a child and those 400 faces are scaring her. If you want everything absolutely perfect (there is no such thing), you might not want to include children in your wedding party. Above all, with children involved, always keep your sense of humor handy!

Ah, children at weddings. There should be a book written about what they will do. This young lady is very carefully placing these petals—and *not* on the white cloth. *(Photo by Wyant Photography)*

Now what makes me think these two might be up to something? You be the judge. *(Photo by Colter Photography)*

Bouquet Toss

I coordinated a large wedding last summer where the best man and ring bearer were father and son. When I sent the flower girl and ring bearer down the aisle, as the little girl dropped the petals, the ring bearer kept reaching down and putting them back in her basket. She didn't know what to think of this pesky boy who kept messing with her petals, and he was equally frustrated that someone so cute could be so messy. Finally, he stopped halfway down the aisle and yelled to his dad, "*Daaaaaaaad,* she keeps dropping these flowers!" The father calmly answered that it was okay for her to drop the petals on the floor.

Here are some jobs you might consider assigning to special young people you want to honor:

◆ Ring bearer (age 3 to 6)

I call this photo the reluctant ring bearer, and I think it speaks volumes. Children are just that, children. Don't put 5-year-old Junior in a tux and expect him to act 22. He's just a kid. *(Photo by Wyant Photography)*

◆ Flower girl (age 3 to 6)

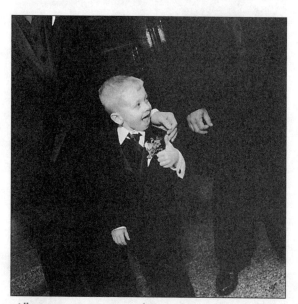

All systems are go according to this ring bearer. He's giving the thumbs-up sign to the priest that it's time to get the show on the road. *(Photo by Colter Photography)*

This little princess is looking most angelic in her flower girl dress. Notice the ball of flowers she is carrying. *(Photo by Wyant Photography)*

These two look like they're on their best behavior. *(Photo by Colter Photography)*

Doesn't this little guy look so proud! *(Photo by Colter Photography)*

◆ Train bearer (age 4 to 8)

◆ Guest book attendant (age 12 and up)

◆ Program attendant (age 12 and up)

◆ Coat checker (age 10 and up)

◆ Gift attendant (age 13 and up)

◆ Candle lighter (age 10 and up)

◆ Altar boy or girl (Catholic service; age 10 to 15)

These tasks are all very important and can be used to show special attention to those whom you can't include in your immediate wedding party.

I'm not sure what this ring bearer just told the flower girl, but they are having just too much fun. *(Photo by Wyant Photography)*

Other Ways to Include Friends and Family

Jobs for other adults or young person (14 and up) include the following:

◆ **Guest book attendant.** This person, male or female, greets guests as they enter the ceremony site or reception site (depending on where you want the guest book placed) and asks guests to sign the guest book.

◆ **Birdseed, petal, or bubble attendants.** These are the folks who will distribute birdseed, flower petals, or small bottles of bubbles to guests so that the bride and groom can be showered with them as they exit.

Wedding Woes

Traditionally, newly married couples were showered with rice, but it has been found to be harmful to the birds that later ingest it. Instead, shower couples with a more environmentally friendly alternative such as birdseed, flower petals, or wedding bubbles. Be aware that many facilities are limiting what you can toss at the new couple. Be sure to check with the facility to make sure they don't charge a cleanup fee!

- **Program attendant.** This person usually stands by the guest book and distributes the wedding programs; this person also acts as a greeter.
- **Readers (both scripture and poetry).** During the service, you may have several readings. This is a responsible job for the right person.
- **Gift bearer.** During a Catholic service, the gift bearer brings the bread and wine to the priest.
- **Personal attendant.** This is a close friend of the bride who is there to help, run errands, and be supportive.
- **Gift attendant.** At the reception, this person is in charge of taking gifts from the guests and placing them in the appropriate spot (either a gift table or a locked room).
- **Reception assistants.** These folks, usually ladies, are asked to help with the reception foods, mostly cutting and serving the wedding cake.

Getting a Little Help from Your Friends

Over the years, I've heard statements like these from time to time: "Aunt Shirley is going to cater my wedding." "My friend Ellen is doing the flowers." "Jennifer, my sorority sister, is going to coordinate my wedding." "Uncle Harvey likes to tinker with a camera and will be taking the pictures." All these examples have two common elements: The couple thinks they're saving money, and they expect a professional job. They most likely will be disappointed on both counts.

There's nothing wrong with asking your friend Ellen to take care of your floral needs. She's a good friend, and you know she'll do her best. The problem comes when she

doesn't—or can't—deliver what you expect. When those flowers arrive, you may find out too late that Ellen wasn't really right for this task. The colors are all wrong, the arrangement doesn't look anything like the picture you showed her, and she forgot the main centerpiece for the head table at the reception.

The bottom line? Don't assume that just because someone is your friend or a family member, he or she has the expertise to handle a particular task. Even with their best efforts, these jobs may be too much for friends or family to take on. Unless your friend or family member is a florist, photographer, or caterer by trade, it's best to leave these tasks to the professionals.

Sometimes barefoot is the way to go. *(Photo by Jeff Hawkins Photography)*

A little quality time with her attendants, and this bride's ready to head down the aisle. *(Photo by Colter Photography)*

The Least You Need to Know

◆ Make sure the church or other ceremony site can comfortably fit the wedding party you're planning.

◆ Wedding party members should be those individuals you feel close to and want to include as a special part of your day.

◆ Use good judgment and common sense when you choose to include children in your wedding party. Remember, children will almost always act like children. That can make for some unpredictable moments.

◆ There are several important tasks you can allocate to friends and family members so that they are included in your wedding day.

◆ Be very careful when asking family and friends to do some tasks for your wedding that would be better left to the pros.

In This Chapter

- ◆ The purpose of the rehearsal dinner
- ◆ Determining who to invite
- ◆ Incorporating your own personal style
- ◆ What to include on the agenda

Mr. and Mrs. William Scott cordially invite you to the Rehearsal Dinner honoring Robert and Susan

Chapter 6

Cast Party: Arranging the Rehearsal Dinner

The rehearsal dinner is another wedding tradition that has evolved over time. Its main purpose is to invite guests—usually family and the wedding party—to gather after the wedding rehearsal and have fun. It serves several other purposes as well, including sometimes introducing family members for the first time, letting everyone involved with the wedding ceremony have a chance to meet each other, and generally celebrating the start of the wedding festivities.

Read on to learn all you need to know about planning a rehearsal dinner, and be sure to use the "Rehearsal Dinner Worksheet" in Appendix B as a guide.

Why Have a Rehearsal Dinner?

After you've reserved the church, reception site, and some of the fundamental elements of the wedding day (such as photographer, florist, and musicians), you should begin thinking about a place to hold the rehearsal dinner. Usually, the rehearsal dinner immediately follows the wedding rehearsal, although it can be held just before the rehearsal or even on an entirely different day.

Because the rehearsal dinner is usually held the night before the ceremony, it's a good time to get friends and family members together to relax, to get to know one another, and to celebrate this wonderful occasion. In some cases, a family member or close friend might even offer to host the rehearsal dinner.

Mom, Dad, and the bride practice their entrance at this casual rehearsal. *(Photo by Colter Photography)*

Notice the chuppah that the men are holding over the couple in this rehearsal of a Jewish ceremony. *(Photo by Colter Photography)*

Wedding Woes

Check with all the players involved with the rehearsal dinner to make sure no one is accidentally left off the guest list. Usually, the bride's family submits a guest list to the groom's family.

Getting to Know You

Because today it's not as common as it once was to marry the boy or girl next door, the rehearsal dinner has become a very important part of the wedding activities. Many times, this is the first opportunity for the bride and groom's families to meet each other. It isn't unusual for the two sets of parents to live on opposite sides of the country, and getting them together before the actual wedding isn't always feasible. The rehearsal dinner is a time when you can bring everyone together to meet and get to know each other in a relaxed setting, before the formality and pressures of the wedding day.

Even though the groom or his family traditionally hosts the rehearsal dinner, some planning—and conferring with the bride—is in order. Because it's so important for all guests to feel comfortable, the setting for this dinner is an important factor—especially when your families come from different backgrounds. If the couple wants a very simple, casual rehearsal dinner, that should be how the event unfolds. The couple needs to understand that this is a party the groom's mother may plan, so let her have some freedom, too.

Here are some location ideas for rehearsal dinner. It is limited only by your imagination:

◆ Hotel

◆ Restaurant

◆ Beach

◆ Park

◆ Home/backyard

◆ Boat (obviously large enough to comfortably accommodate all of your guests)

◆ Church social hall

◆ Private club

◆ University or college setting

"Whew ... glad that's over with. Let's party!" *(Photo by Colter Photography)*

Rehearsals are a good way to bring family and friends together. Looks like someone just told a good joke! *(Photo by Colter Photography)*

Who to Invite

Your guest list for the rehearsal dinner should include all the key players who normally would attend the wedding rehearsal. That may include:

◆ The wedding party, including their spouses or dates

◆ Parents of the bride and groom

◆ Grandparents of the bride and groom

◆ Out-of-town family members who arrive for the wedding

◆ The officiant and his or her spouse

◆ The musicians who will be performing at the wedding and reception

◆ The parents of the flower girls and ring bearers (if these children are older, you may want to include them at the dinner along with their parents)

◆ Soloists or readers

◆ Anyone else you would like to attend, within reason (While it is a nice gesture to invite the entire 30-voice choir to the dinner, it is probably not practical or necessary!)

If one side has more guests than the other, who makes the call? Technically speaking, the person(s) who are hosting the rehearsal dinner make that determination but should *always* consult with bride and groom. If, say, the bride's side has 75 names on the guest list and the groom's side only has 25 and doesn't want to pay for more than 50 guests total, then if possible, offer to pay the difference.

Many couples choose to send invitations for their rehearsal dinner. As long as the invitation is not more formal than the wedding invitation, you can do what you please. Maybe a phone call inviting guests is enough for you, or maybe you've seen some wonderful informal invitations that go with the wedding theme. Some companies also offer some great rehearsal dinner invitations. Being a mother of two sons, I have envisioned different kinds of invitations to our sons' rehearsal dinners. We'll just have to wait and see what the two future Mrs. Lendermans think.

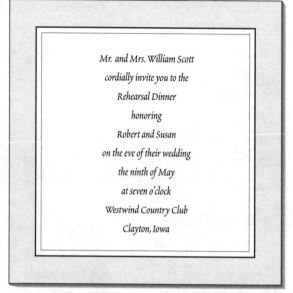

Mr. and Mrs. William Scott
cordially invite you to the
Rehearsal Dinner
honoring
Robert and Susan
on the eve of their wedding
the ninth of May
at seven o'clock
Westwind Country Club
Clayton, Iowa

This invitation has a more formal feel.

Basically, your guest list depends on what your budget will allow and the size of the facility you choose for this function. There are large guest lists for rehearsal dinners, and there are small, intimate guest lists. The choice of how large or small the guest list can be is ultimately the hosts'.

Giving It Style

The rehearsal dinner does not have to be a formal, sit-down affair. Some of the more successful rehearsal dinners that I've heard about have been very relaxed and informal. Brides and grooms sometimes choose to have picnics, pizza parties, cookouts, or even carry-in suppers instead of a formal dinner. Remember, the primary purpose of the rehearsal dinner is to get newly merging family members together in a relaxed, informal setting.

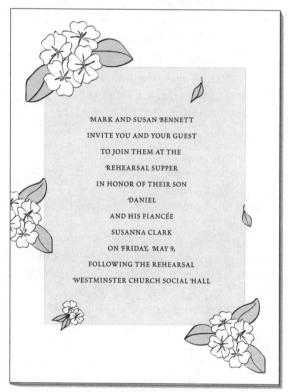

MARK AND SUSAN BENNETT
INVITE YOU AND YOUR GUEST
TO JOIN THEM AT THE
REHEARSAL SUPPER
IN HONOR OF THEIR SON
DANIEL
AND HIS FIANCÉE
SUSANNA CLARK
ON FRIDAY, MAY 9,
FOLLOWING THE REHEARSAL
WESTMINSTER CHURCH SOCIAL HALL

A semiformal invitation might feature graphics like these.

Teddy's Tips

Unless there is a tight budget for the rehearsal dinner, out-of-town family—especially close family members such as aunts and uncles—should be invited to the rehearsal dinner.

Have It Your Way

Some couples go with a theme for the rehearsal dinner. One couple opted for an old-fashioned, Midwestern picnic supper on their lakefront property and finished the evening with a dramatic display of fireworks. To dress up this rehearsal dinner, they used red-and-white gingham-checked tablecloths and napkins, real china, and real silverware. Although they served hamburgers and hot dogs, the fine dinnerware made the event seem more special than if they had used paper plates.

Come One! Come All!
Susan Jones
and
Robert Small
invite you to help in the
celebration
at their rehearsal picnic
Friday, May 9,
Falls State Park
1500 South State Road 46
Dayton, Ohio

The fun begins following the rehearsal at 5:00 P.M.
at Holy Rosary Church
(see map). Casual dress.

Here's an example of an informal invitation to a rehearsal dinner (which is actually a rehearsal picnic).

Other ideas include the following:

◆ A beach party rehearsal dinner complete with volleyball

◆ A riverboat rehearsal theme (throw in some "play" money and gamble the night away)

◆ An informal night of pizza, beer, and soft drinks at home

◆ A family carry-in at the church social hall

◆ Hors d'oeuvres and simple cocktails at a club (use tall cocktail tables instead of seating guests to encourage mingling)

◆ A formal dinner at a country club

◆ A restaurant theme dinner (Italian, German, Greek—celebrate your heritage)

◆ A pool party, complete with beach balls and barbecue

◆ Carry-in supper from your favorite restaurant to either your home or the church

◆ An autumn theme complete with hot dogs, toasted marshmallows, hayride, and bonfire

Because this wedding took place around the Fourth of July, the bride used red-and-white checked material to add some flair to her casual picnic theme.
(Photo from the author's collection)

Notice how the silverware is wrapped in napkins and tied with the same red-and-white material. Little details like this can add a lot to the casual rehearsal dinner. *(Photo from the author's collection)*

Whatever you decide to do, just make it enjoyable for your guests. Make your guests feel relaxed, welcomed, and special. They are all nervous about meeting the other side, so try to put them at ease. You might want to assign a host or hostess to each table at the rehearsal dinner to help keep the conversation moving and to make sure guests are cared for. Another way to help avoid some extra stress for your guests is to assign them a seat for the meal. That way, you can put who you want next to crazy Cousin Cindy (every family has one, you know) and not worry about your future mother-in-law sitting next to her.

What's on the Agenda?

Several points need to be made during the evening at your rehearsal dinner.

◆ First and foremost, always take time to introduce your guests. The bride can introduce her side and the groom his and get the ball rolling with introductions.

◆ Thank your parents, family, and friends for their love, encouragement, and support.

◆ Give your wedding party their gifts.

This bride hands out gifts to her attendants at the rehearsal dinner. *(Photo by Colter Photography)*

◆ Take time for toasts. The father of the groom or the host offers the first toast to the bride. The second toast by the host is always to the couple. After those two toasts the floor is open to anyone else who would like to make a toast.

Wedding Woes

The rehearsal dinner should never be more formal or more elaborate than the wedding reception.

The Least You Need to Know

◆ The rehearsal dinner should be a time when family and friends—the special people in your lives—come together in a comfortable setting to meet each other and to help you launch your new life together.

◆ Include all members of the wedding party and their spouses or dates. It's not mandatory to invite very young children from the wedding party, but do include their parents.

◆ Rehearsal dinners do not have to be formal. Make it whatever you want—sit-down dinner, picnic, carry-in supper—just make it a setting in which both families will feel comfortable.

◆ Use the rehearsal dinner as a chance to introduce everyone, say thank you, and to give your gifts to the wedding party.

In This Chapter

- ◆ Deciding what type of honeymoon you want
- ◆ A look at some popular honeymoon spots
- ◆ Determining the best place for you
- ◆ Tips for hassle-free traveling

Chapter 7

Romance and Roses: Planning Your Honeymoon

Although it may be easy to overlook in the hustle and bustle of planning for the wedding itself, making your honeymoon reservations is one more thing you need to consider early in the planning stages. Depending on where you plan to take your honeymoon, you need to arrange reservations and details as early as possible.

In this chapter, I'll talk about the type of honeymoon you want, explore some popular spots, and help you figure out your perfect honeymoon site.

Finally, Some Time Alone …

Ah, the honeymoon! Finally, you and your brand-new spouse will be able to get away and be alone. The wedding and reception will be behind you, and your wedding day will be only fond memories and warm fuzzies. With all the pre-wedding parties, checklists, and appointments, the two of you won't have much time together. You're definitely going to be ready for some quality time alone.

This couple seems ready to start the honeymoon. Ah, young love ... *(Photo by Wyant Photography)*

Communication Is the Key

So now you're planning for this wonderful time away, alone together for the first time as husband and wife. Where do you start? First, talk to each other and decide what your options are, how much time and money you have, and what your ideal honeymoon is. It's very important to discuss openly and honestly with each other what you want to do on the honeymoon.

Teddy's Tips

While on your honeymoon you will be likely be exhausted from the wedding activities and the hectic months leading up to the wedding. Don't let anyone else convince you otherwise. Make sure your honeymoon plans include plenty of time for rest and rejuvenation!

Whatever you choose for your honeymoon, whether it's a two-week cruise down the California coast, a week at a luxury resort in the Hawaiian Islands, or a weekend in the big city, make it special. It doesn't have to cost you a

bundle, either. Talk with your partner early on about the amount you realistically have to spend on this honeymoon. Stay within your budget. There is no reason to overspend on the honeymoon. Remember, you are in control of all pricing, including your honeymoon expenses.

The bottom line on your honeymoon is to make it special for both of you. Plan early, and find a good travel agent who knows what your budget is and will help you stick to it. Be sure to ask about special packages, especially those made just for honeymooners. (If you *don't* want to be identified as honeymooners, don't pick a honeymoon package or go to one of the traditional honeymoon locations.) Make sure you get all details ironed out before you leave. (The "Honeymoon Worksheet" in Appendix B can help you get them down on paper.)

Your honeymoon doesn't have to be elaborate, just enjoyable for both of you, such as spending the weekend at a favorite hotel. It looks like this couple is having a good time already! *(Photo by Wyant Photography)*

> **Bouquet Toss** _____
>
> The word honeymoon comes from the days of marriage-by-capture. A man would see a woman he liked, capture her (many times against her will), and hide out for a moon (30 days—one full moon to another full moon), or a month. During that time they would drink a concoction sweetened with honey—thus, honeymoon.

Get Thee to Paradise

As with any trip or vacation, deciding where to go on your honeymoon is a very personal decision for the two of you to make. You've probably heard about some of the traditional honeymoon spots, however, and you may want to give them some consideration. According to Virginia Pfrommer of I.T. Travel (www.ittravel.com), the top three most popular honeymoon spots are:

◆ **All-inclusive resorts**, including the popular Sandals Resorts. Probably one of the most popular types of honeymoon couples are attracted to is the "All-Inclusive Resort" type. At these resorts, you pay one price and that includes absolutely everything. Even alcohol consumption is included. You know well ahead of time what it will cost and there are usually no extras. Sandals are located in the Bahamas, Jamaica, Antigua, and St. Lucia. Jamaica is the most popular.

◆ **Hawaiian Islands.** All the islands offer the right weather with the right atmosphere for some very romantic times. These islands are about as close to Eden as you can get. The islanders have that "hang loose," "don't worry," "it's going to be okay" attitude that makes you feel so welcomed and relaxed.

Watch for specials during the fall and in early January. This is an affordable vacation spot for lots of couples. If you watch for a price war on airfares, you can get some pretty good rates.

◆ **Cruise ships.** Many couples feel that an ocean cruise is the ultimate honeymoon idea. One price gets you all kinds of entertainment and endless eating (alcoholic beverages are usually extra). You can go for a romantic walk on the deck in the moonlight. Dozens of activities can fill your day, including the sights and sounds of the neighboring islands (when in dock), swimming, sunning, taking exercise classes, gambling, dancing, and taking in cabaret shows. Other activities may include board games, basketball, skeet shooting, Ping-Pong, saunas, country-and-western nights, a piano bar, a library, beauty shops, arts-and-crafts classes, massages, laundry services, midnight buffets, room service, and duty-free shopping.

> **Teddy's Tips** _____
>
> When packing for a cruise, consider shorts or slacks with elastic waistbands—with all the food available around the clock, you may need some room to grow!

Here are some points to consider if you're thinking about a honeymoon cruise:

Age group. The age of passengers varies, not only on ship but also by area of the world. For example, travelers on cruises in the Caribbean usually are younger than those traveling in the Alaskan waters or the Baltic seas.

Ship size. The size of the vessel will help determine what kind of cruise you want. Those carrying more than 1,200 passengers will offer more activities than the smaller ships.

Price. Prices vary. Check with a travel agent who specializes in cruise ships. He or she should be able to offer you all the information and help you to determine which line and what size ship is right for you and your budget.

Departure days. Most cruise lines depart on a Saturday. A few sail on a Sunday, however, to accommodate the honeymooners who are married on a Saturday.

Cabin accommodations. Be sure to check with your travel agent about the cabin accommodations. If you want a king- or queen-size bed in your cabin, understand that not all cruise ships offer that option.

Shore excursions. Check about shore excursions before you sail. In many places, these can be an unnecessary purchase. (Strolling through the local village market can be fun on your own; you might not want to go on-shore in a group.) In some cases, though, the excursion may catch your eye (hiking through a rain forest, riding horses on the beach, or snorkeling in clear blue waters). Ask your cruise travel agent for a list of ports where it would be better to go solo for sights and those ports where you will need a group tour.

Other spots requested for honeymoons include the following:

♦ **The Poconos.** This "honeymoon capital of the world" includes four counties located in northeastern Pennsylvania and consists of 2,400 square miles of majestic mountains, wonderful views, rivers and streams, and beautiful forests. There are many resorts to choose from in this region, and any of the four seasons are perfect for a stay in these resorts, which feature all types of activities: winter sports, water-skiing in the summer, and walking along mountain paths in the fall foliage. They offer both earthy pleasures and fantastic accommodations. If you dream of a heart-shaped bathtub in your private cabin, then one of the resorts in the Poconos might be just right for you. If you've always wanted to spend the night in a 1900s farmhouse, a charming country inn, or a French chateau, then a resort in the Poconos may be just the ticket.

♦ **Caribbean Islands.** Located on the eastern side of the United States and running from south of Miami to South America, the Caribbean holds many islands to choose from. Watch for specials during the low season (April to October); it rains more at this time of year, so prices run about 30 percent lower than the high season, which is November to April. Cruise several islands, or fly off to a remote island. They call this paradise, and there's a reason for that. With their gorgeous beaches, clear waters, and fun nightlife, many of the islands bid for the honeymooner business.

Teddy's Tips

Just as the Association of Bridal Consultants can provide names of consultants in your area, they also can provide names of destination and honeymoon travel specialists who are also members. Call 860-355-0464 or e-mail them at BridalAssn@aol.com for information.

◆ **Mexican Riviera.** South of the western United States, the Mexican Riviera boasts 2,000 miles of white-sand beaches. Some favorite honeymoon spots here include Acapulco, Cancun, and Puerto Vallarta. Again, they offer great nightlife and fantastic resorts.

◆ **Hilton Head, South Carolina.** This romantic city by the sea is fast becoming a popular honeymoon site. With a variety of condos and hotel prices to choose from, almost any couple can spend some time here walking along the beach, sipping a cool drink on the hotel balcony, or hitting one of the many golf courses.

◆ **Las Vegas, Nevada.** Las Vegas not only represents a wedding ceremony site for many couples, but it also offers some excitement for honeymooners. You can find some of the most famous hotels in the world on "The Strip." The city's off-season is November to January. Some sites around the area include Death Valley, Grand Canyon West, Hoover Dam, and Lake Mead.

◆ **San Diego, California.** This city, which lies just north of the Mexican border, was once a remote Spanish mission. Famous must-see sites include Balboa Park and the San Diego Zoo. San Diego is full of history and has a near perfect year-round climate. Many people want to retire here, but don't let that stop you from considering it for a honeymoon spot—it has action, too.

◆ **Breckenridge, Colorado.** If it's snowy weather and skiing you dream of for your honeymoon, then you should venture to Breckenridge. The city actually got its start in 1859 with a gold rush discovery. Since then, the town has enjoyed activities for all seasons. There are many historical buildings in Breckenridge, and its Victorian charm lures honeymooners from all over.

◆ **Disney World.** If you want to feel like a child again, head south to Orlando for a time of fun and excitement amid the king of entertainment, Mickey Mouse. The various hotels in the area are geared to offer all the extras for the honeymooners, and you shouldn't be bored for lack of something to do.

Wedding Woes

Many of these honeymoon spots are also popular with the college crowd for spring break. If you don't want to spend your honeymoon with 20,000 college kids on the same beach, avoid the traditional March and early April vacation times.

Hints for Honeymooners

Here are some tips to help you take some of the worry out of your honeymoon travels:

◆ Remember that since the September 11, 2001, terrorist attacks, security at airports around the world is very tight. Be prepared to have your bags inspected. Don't forget to bring two forms of ID, one a photo ID such as a driver's license.

◆ Allow plenty of time for checking in at the airport (at least two hours for domestic flights and three hours for international flights). If you are leaving on a Sunday morning, be sure to factor in some extra time. Sunday mornings are busy at airports.

◆ Don't lock your suitcases (either checked or carry-on bags). Because of high security, they will be opened and checked at will.

◆ Make sure you don't carry anything that might be construed as a weapon. That includes items like metal nail files and pocketknives. (On a recent flight, my car keys were taken because they were on a ring that the agent thought looked like it could be a weapon.)

◆ Do not draw attention to yourself. Be polite and courteous in public places and stay alert, especially if you are traveling overseas.

◆ Cooperate at inspections. Airports now do random inspections and you could be pulled out of line and asked to open your bags.

◆ Take most of your money in traveler's checks. Be sure to get some in smaller denominations ($20) because some areas will not honor larger amounts ($50 and higher).

◆ Keep a list of your traveler's checks' numbers, credit card numbers, and checking account numbers separate from where you keep the checks and cards themselves. Also take the phone numbers for these companies with you. In case any of these items are lost or stolen, you can get help much faster if you have phone numbers and account information.

◆ If traveling overseas, convert some cash to the foreign currency to cover initial expenses (transportation, tips, and more) before you leave. You really don't want to go out on your wedding night to convert currency!

◆ Overseas, it's best to use a credit card for purchases. The conversion rate usually is better than what you'll get at a bank, which is much better than what you'll get in stores and hotels. I traveled to London this year and can tell you firsthand this is very true!

Teddy's Tips

Make sure you take $1 bills with you if you go to other countries. Many times you will find yourself wanting to purchase items that street vendors are selling and have to barter with them. American dollars are the best way to pay.

◆ Label luggage both inside and outside with your name, address, and phone number. Keep a list of luggage contents (for claims, if your luggage is lost).

◆ If you're traveling by air, pack any medications, valuables such as jewelry, and important papers such as passports in a carry-on bag.

- Rental car companies require a major credit card and have age restrictions. Check ahead of time.

- Make sure you have homeowner's or renter's insurance on your wedding gifts before you leave home.

- When making airline reservations, do not make the bride's ticket in her married name. Use the name she will have ID for, because you will have to provide it to security at check-in.

Wedding Woes

If you travel to a sunny climate or to a climate with sun and lots of snow, be sure to take and use your sunscreen. Nothing can ruin a romantic getaway faster than a painful sunburn.

The Least You Need to Know

- It takes a good travel agent and advance planning to get the best prices and accommodations, so plan your honeymoon early.

- Be realistic about what you both want and what you can actually afford. Don't overstep your budget.

- Put a lot of thought into how you want to spend your first days as husband and wife. Choose a location you are both comfortable with, and then pick activities that you both enjoy.

- You can keep your travel plans running smoothly by following some common-sense tips.

In This Part

Part 3

Putting It All Together

In this part, you'll learn more about selecting the right vendor for the rest of your wedding details. I'll lead you on the right path for talking with caterers and understanding your liquor obligations. I'll show you some new ways to use flowers and what to look for in good musicians. There is a chapter on gowns—both yours and your maids—plus the men's formalwear. There are invitations, favors, and programs to learn about, and finally, I'll show you some ways to cut costs and still have the wedding you want.

In This Chapter

- How to work with the caterer and still stick to your budget

- Deciding on what to serve

- Understanding guaranteed numbers

- Choosing the wedding cake and groom's cake you've always wanted

- What you need to know about serving liquor

Chapter 8

Eat, Drink, and Be Married

Regardless of how simple or elaborate you want your reception to be, menu planning takes time. I keep stressing *time* because the wise wedding consumer allows enough time to shop for comparisons.

In Chapter 4, I gave you some tips on choosing a caterer and understanding your responsibilities when it comes to serving alcohol at the reception. In this chapter, we'll explore these topics in more detail. This is a big part of your overall budget and you can't be too careful or detailed when it comes to planning the reception.

Working with the Caterer

As you'll recall from Chapter 4, in-house refers to a caterer that provides the food for functions within a particular facility. An outside caterer is an independent caterer you hire on your own, from outside the facility. Whether the facility provides an in-house caterer for you to work with or you bring in someone of your choice, what's your next step?

When working with either the in-house or outside caterer, go into the first consultation with some notion of what kind of reception you are looking for. You should have some idea whether you're thinking a formal seated affair or food stations. Have some plan in mind. Then let the caterer guide you with what works best in his facility. Don't let him tell you it can't be done—ask questions to see if it can be. If something you've had your heart set on is a "No" in his book, ask why. But please, ask "Why?" respectfully. You are going to be spending not only time but also money with this person and you want to be on the best terms possible.

The bride's name is Dinkel, so we found some Dinkel Beer and had it served at the reception. Personalization is the name of the game. *(Photo by Colter Photography)*

There is really no difference in dealing with either the in-house caterer or the outside caterer. The only difference is that the in-house caterer knows the property like the back of his hand and the outside caterer has to move from reception site to reception site. Most facilities that do not provide catering will provide a list of approved caterers their facility will allow to work the event. There is a reason they are approved. They've done a good job before and the facility wants them back.

What's on the Menu?

After you've decided which caterer you'll be working with, choose your menu carefully. Make good use of your food choices. If you're on a limited budget for the reception (and who isn't?), make sure you thoroughly consider the time of day you choose for your wedding and reception. The time of day your reception occurs has much to do with what your menu will be and can help determine how much money it's going to cost you. (Review Chapter 2 for budgeting strategies.)

Bouquet Toss

The custom of serving food at a wedding reception dates back to the ancient Greeks; they had the bride and groom share a quince (fruit). The Greeks thought that by having the couple eat this fruit, which has a bitter and sweet taste, the bride and groom were accepting the good and bad times that come with marriage. Other cultures have used the tradition of consuming food on the wedding day as a prerequisite to a good marriage. In ancient Britain, couples drank "marriage ale" for 30 days following the wedding. Those native to the South Sea Islands feasted on fruits and flowers for 30 days, after which time the couple was considered married.

Here are some food and beverage ideas:

- Wedding cake and punch
- Wedding cake and punch, with champagne for the toasts
- Finger sandwiches, wedding cake and beverage
- Hors d'oeuvres and beverages
- Grazing stations and beverage stations (guests "graze" from station to station)
- Specialty food stations placed throughout the reception room offering a variety of choices (you might offer a pasta station or a seafood station, for example)
- Buffet meal with beverages
- Plated dinner (guests are served a preselected meal)

Be sure to check with the caterer about the reception site's floorplan if you want to use the food station concept. Traffic flow here is crucial. If your facility does not lend itself to this type of layout, you probably should stick to a more basic setup. You may opt for dividing up the food into two areas and offering the same items in both places. This helps move guests through the lines without so much delay.

Thinking Through Your Food Options

Suppose that you're going to have an hors d'oeuvres reception with a limited bar. Your test now is to make good use of your money as far as food selection goes. Offering liquor always means you must serve some substantial food. You don't have to serve meat and potatoes—especially for an hors d'oeuvres reception—but you do need to provide something filling so that guests don't drink on empty stomachs.

You might opt for some pita triangle sandwiches (pita bread cut into triangles and filled with various fillings). You could add a fruit tray with a yogurt dip. To that, you could add some water chestnuts wrapped in bacon and cooked in a brown sweet-and-sour sauce (mmmm, one of my favorites), and so on. The catering manager should sit down with you and find out what your favorite foods are and how to incorporate them into the menu. (Turn to the "Catering Worksheet" in Appendix B for help on planning the food for your reception.)

Bouquet Toss

One of the most well-known champagnes in the world is Dom Perignon. Champagne was discovered by a monk in a northeastern region of France called Champagne. This monk found that sealing wine in a bottle for several years would cause the wine to ferment and sparkle. That monk's name was Dom Perignon. Today, Dom Perignon is a very expensive addition to your wedding reception.

Here are some questions to ask the caterer:

◆ Will the caterer prepare family recipes to serve at the reception? This is especially nice with buffets where you can place a sign that says "Aunt Emma's potato casserole."

◆ Check about add-ons? Are linens included?

◆ What about votive candles or colored napkins?

◆ How much are gratuities and other service charges?

◆ Will the caterer prepare a "tasting" for you where you and your groom can go into the facility and actually taste the items you will serve for the reception? Some facilities will, while others might charge you. It's worth it.

◆ Can you see photos of past receptions?

◆ Do they use good presentation with their food displays? Do they add greenery, flowers, and so on to make the food look inviting?

Playing the Numbers Game

As I mentioned in Chapter 4, you'll also need to talk with the caterer about what the guaranteed numbers mean. Find out what percentage the caterer will go under and above the guest count that you provide. Make sure that you understand how this process works and what it means for your reception.

At a recent wedding reception I coordinated, the mother of the bride had given the caterer a guaranteed number of 125. She guesstimated the number of expected guests. When the guests at the church numbered only 70, I was concerned that her count was high and that we would have many extra places at the reception. I was right. She was very upset that guests hadn't shown up when she thought they would. And she was stuck with a bill for 50 extra guests (at $25 per person) because she had not taken the time to get an accurate response count.

This story illustrates how important it is to have an accurate count for the caterer. *Do not guess.* So many times brides will say, "Oh, I know they're coming to the wedding," or, "I think we'll have about 150 people." Save your guesses for the lottery or the racetrack. "I think" and "I guess" are two phrases you don't want to use when it comes to guaranteeing your guest total for the caterer. This number equates to money—at times, *lots* of money.

That Fantasy Creation: The Cake

Perhaps one of the creations given the most thought during the wedding planning stages is the wedding cake. Maybe you've dreamed about a five-tier creation with fountains and lights or a simple, stately, stacked cake with fresh flowers adding the only color. When you're shopping for your wedding cake, be sure to ask for suggestions and recommendations from family and friends who have recently married. The caterer you're working with also might offer a wedding cake service, or he may be glad to provide you with names of competent bakers if you just ask.

An icing ribbon accents the top of this beautiful square cake. *(Photo by Wyant Photography)*

No, your eyes are not playing tricks on you! This couple has a great sense of humor and wanted their cake built upside down. And no, it's not magic—just a really good baker. *(Photo by Curtis Rhodes Photography)*

Here's another couple with a wonderful sense of humor and a very talented baker. This cake is like this on purpose. You have to admit, it's a conversation piece! *(Photo by Craig Larsen Photography)*

So Many Choices ...

You can select a wedding cake in a variety of flavors and fillings—another way to make a particular wedding unique. Wedding cakes today are as varied as the couples who order them. We no longer rely just on white cake. Some popular favors are:

- ◆ Carrot cake
- ◆ Chocolate with various fillings (raspberry is popular)
- ◆ Lemon
- ◆ Poppy seed with cream cheese frosting
- ◆ Red velvet
- ◆ Italian cream
- ◆ German chocolate
- ◆ Cheesecakes with a variety of toppings

This simple stacked cake is iced with rolled fondant icing and topped with fresh flowers. The icing is actually rolled out and placed around the cake and then smoothed. It is a very popular look today.
(Photo by Colter Photography)

> **Bouquet Toss** ___
>
> The first wedding cake goes back to ancient times, when the cake was actually a mixture of sesame seed meal and honey. Then, as Western Europe developed, the cake consisted of a small, unleavened biscuit. In the 1600s, a French chef tried an experiment with small cakes he stacked together and held in place with a white sugar icing. And before the Civil War in this country, the wedding cake was actually a fruitcake.

This classic tiered cake with fresh roses between each layer is a delicate beauty. *(Photo by Stephanie Cristalli)*

Bargaining with the Baker

Just as important as any vendor on your wedding list is the baker. Here are some questions to ask as you make your decisions:

◆ **Fresh or frozen?** Ask whether the baker bakes fresh or works from frozen cakes. Some bakers bake early in the week and then freeze their cakes and decorate them on Friday, with finishing touches the day of the wedding. I prefer fresh because I think the cake tastes better, but that's something you will have to decide for yourself. Get all the information; it never hurts to ask questions.

◆ **Pricing?** Wedding cakes usually are priced per person (meaning how many people the cake will feed), and your locale determines what that per-person charge will be.

◆ **Delivery?** Ask whether the baker will deliver the cake or whether you must arrange to pick it up. Is there an extra charge for delivery to the reception site? Most bakers will deliver; they may charge for that service, but it's probably worth it. They are pros at handling finished cakes; you don't want to take the chance of something happening to the cake when you pick it up.

◆ **Deposit and return?** Ask the baker if there is a deposit on the cake stands and pillars. Also, check how the wedding cake pieces (plastic pillars, the layer pieces holding the cake together) are to be returned. Find out whether the caterer will take care of that for you or whether you are responsible. You don't want to have to play with icing and cake pieces as you're trying to leave for your honeymoon, so take care of this item before your wedding day arrives. Designate a family member or friend to help.

◆ **Cutting the cake?** Finally, ask if the caterer will cut and serve the cake for you. Again, there may be a charge for that, but cutting a wedding cake is an art. If the baker doesn't offer that service, the catering people most likely will.

Turn to the "Wedding Cake Worksheet" in Appendix B when planning your cake.

Too often we're so impressed by a cake's splendor that we hardly notice the inside—in this case, a delicious chocolate. *(Photo by Colter Photography)*

This gorgeous five-tier cake with hydrangeas filling in between the layers is absolutely breathtaking. *(Photo from the author's collection)*

This stacked cake is nestled on mounds of fabric and surrounded by candles. *(Photo by Wyant Photography)*

Bouquet Toss

The wedding cake chosen by Lyndon Johnson's daughter, Luci Baines Johnson, and Patrick Nugent in 1966 weighed a whopping 300 pounds and was 14 tiers high. The icing posed a problem as the couple tried to cut the first piece: They couldn't cut through it. Finally, the president himself had to step in and make a stab at it.

The Groom's Cake

The groom's cake has become an important part of the wedding reception. These days groom's cakes come in all kinds of shapes, sizes, flavors, and themes. Grooms have used basketball and football themes. One groom who loved to play bridge had his groom's cake designed like a huge hand of cards. And remember the red velvet armadillo in the movie *Steel Magnolias*? That was an original (if not odd) groom's cake. You're only limited by your imagination!

This handsome couple stands next to their wedding cake and the groom's cake. It's the giant carrot on the right. (There must be a story here ...) *(Photo by Henderson Designer Portraits)*

Chocolate seems to be a very popular flavor with grooms, but I've also seen cheesecakes served with luscious fruit toppings as a groom's cake. Experiment and have fun with this. If your budget will allow it and you want a creative way to express yourselves, consider having a groom's cake.

Those Luscious Libations

Traditional etiquette says only that you must offer your guests something to eat and something to drink at the reception. If that something to drink is alcohol, that's your choice, and yours alone. Nonalcoholic beverages are certainly appropriate and should be included. The bottom line is that the choice is yours. Just make sure you understand your responsibilities to your guests when serving alcohol (as I discussed in Chapter 4; see also Chapter 20 for dealing with guests who have overindulged).

If you're considering offering liquor at your reception, become familiar with the terminology now so that you can ask your vendor intelligent questions. For help on planning your options, see the "Liquor Worksheet" in Appendix B.

Time for the champagne toast! Be sure to provide sparkling grape juice or other nonalcoholic beverage for underage guests and others who don't drink alcohol. *(Photo by Colter Photography)*

Let's take a look at your options:

- **Limited bar.** You limit what is served to the guests. This is your choice. If you want to offer only wine and something nonalcoholic, that's fine. Often a limited bar will feature both wine and beer, plus soft drinks or maybe punch.

- **A limited time bar.** You limit the time the bar remains open. For example, if your reception is scheduled to start with cocktails at 6:30 and dinner is served at 7:30, you may decide to have the bar open from 6:30 to 7:30, close it from 7:30 until 9, and then open it again at 9 until a half hour before the reception ends. You pay the bill with a limited bar.

- **Open bar.** You can offer a full bar outfitted with the liquor you choose. Here again, you want to make sure you provide nonalcoholic beverages. The bar consists of mixed drinks, wine, beer, and soft drinks. You also can choose to serve some after-dinner liquors. With an open bar, you pay the bill.

- **Cash bar.** If you offer a cash bar at your reception, guests pay for their own drinks. You may offer wine and soft drinks, and then if guests want something else in the way of liquor, they can buy it from the bartender. Many people feel that a cash bar is insulting to their guests. You wouldn't make your guests pay for a drink in your home, so why make them pay for one at your reception? The other side of the coin is that if guests are paying for their own drinks, they may not be as free with the liquor and will watch their consumption. It's your call.

Pricing for liquor at receptions can vary. You want to know what system the caterer uses to arrive at the figure that appears on your bill. There are several methods; you just need to know what system the caterer uses:

- **Per-drink charge.** The bartender literally keeps tabs on how many drinks are served to each guest.
- **Open bottle method.** Open and empty bottles of liquor are counted at the end of the event.
- **Per-person cost.** A cost per person for liquor at your reception is included in your contract. With this system, you are charged a set price for each guest. It doesn't matter whether every guest drinks alcohol—you still pay a set price for each person. This system is supposed to strike a balance between those who drink and those who don't.

Teddy's Tips

Don't take your responsibilities lightly when serving liquor. Make sure you have a reputable liquor dealer serving the alcohol. Liability laws differ from state to state, and you or the host needs to be informed on what your liabilities are in your state.

The monogram on this couple's toast glasses is an elegant touch. *(Photo by Colter Photography)*

The Least You Need to Know

- It's possible to work with the caterer without blowing your budget; be sure to go into the initial consultation with a good idea of the kind of reception you want.
- Choose your menu items carefully with an eye for what your budget will allow: anything from simple cake and punch to a full sit-down dinner.
- Always give an accurate count to the caterer; never guess at numbers for your guaranteed count. Be sure to discuss guaranteed numbers with the caterer.
- There are nearly as many choices in wedding and groom's cakes as there are brides and grooms!
- If you decide to serve liquor at your reception, become familiar with your options so you can make an educated choice.

In This Chapter

- ◆ Making sure you have the flowers you want and that they fit your budget

- ◆ Creating the "look" you want for your wedding

- ◆ Centerpiece ideas

- ◆ Understanding the musical choices for your wedding

- ◆ Finding the right musician for your tastes

Chapter 9

Snapdragons and Song

In this chapter, I will focus on two important aspects of your wedding: the flowers and the music. Both items are filled with choices. I'm going to talk about what you need to include in your floral order, from bouquets to centerpieces; give you hints on how to get the best value for your wedding floral dollars; and give you some extra tips on how to spice up the reception site.

I'll also look at your options for the music for your wonderful celebration. Music can really set the mood, and you want to make sure it's not only the mood you want, but a mood well spent!

Working with a Florist

Under normal circumstances, you don't really have to decide on flowers until two or three months before the wedding. If you're being married in a prime wedding season (May, June, or August), or if you're being married around a holiday (Christmas, Valentine's Day, or Mother's Day weekend), however, it's wise to go ahead and reserve your florist early for your wedding day. Some florists will service only one or two weddings a weekend during the peak seasons because weddings are such labor-intensive productions.

This beautiful cluster of various shades of white and pink roses has ribbon encircling the whole stem and a classic French wired ribbon bow. *(Photo by Wyant Photography)*

A handheld stemmed bouquet with a single band of ribbon. Notice the pearl pins on the ribbon. *(Photo by Wyant Photography)*

Bouquet Toss

The very first types of bridal bouquets included not only flowers, but also herbs and spices. Especially popular were strong-scented ones, such as garlic, to ward off evil spirits. Various kinds of flowers have different meanings. Ivy represents fidelity, lily of the valley represents purity, red roses mean love, violets represent modesty, forget-me-nots mean true love, orange blossoms represent fertility and happiness, and myrtle is the symbol of virginity.

Here are some suggestions for working with the florist:

- Ask if they are familiar with the ceremony and reception site before you meet with them. If they are not, ask if they could visit the site so they know how it looks so they can better assist you.

- Take pictures with you from magazines or other weddings so the florist has an idea of your likes.

- Ask if he uses a contract (some small-town florists don't) and if he will do an estimate for you.

- Ask if there is a delivery and set-up fee or if that is built into the floral charge.

- Ask if he will transport the ceremony flowers from the church to the reception site. Get your money's worth out of your floral bill!

This beautiful large floral decoration might have been used at the ceremony site and then taken to the reception site. Always try to get use of your ceremony flowers at the reception. *(Photo by Jeff Hawkins Photography)*

◆ If you are using silk flowers, ask to see and smell the silk flowers. Some silk flowers have a distinct odor to them.

◆ Make sure the florist knows if you or your groom has any floral allergies.

A good florist will do the following:

◆ Assist you in determining what flowers will work for your wedding, given the time of year and your wedding style

◆ Offer suggestions and ideas

◆ Stay within your floral budget

◆ Ask for a picture of your gown, the maids gowns, and color swatches

◆ Explain their pricing system, including if they require a deposit

◆ Provide references if requested

◆ Label corsages so you know who gets what

These ladies pose for a candid shot right before they head down the aisle. Instead of a veil the bride is wearing a flower band in her head piece. *(Photo by Colter Photography)*

Teddy's Tips

Petals, either fresh or dried, are a wonderful alternative to birdseed when showering the couple as they leave the ceremony. They don't get caught in your clothes and hair, and they smell wonderful. They are natural as well, so you don't have to worry about the environment. Check with your florist.

This lovely October bride chose to incorporate wheat stocks for her bouquets. Add to that the seasonal assortment of mums and you have a very pretty yet stately bouquet. *(Photo by Colter Photography)*

Buds of Beauty

Flowers used during the ceremony are divided into two sections. One set is referred to as "body flowers" and are the bouquets, boutonnieres, and corsages. We're going to find some ways to make the body flowers something you want to carry or hold, not something you saw in a bride's magazine that doesn't even begin to go with your total look. The second set is the flowers used at the sites, both ceremony and reception.

Bouquets and "Boots"

The two main body flowers for weddings are the bouquets and the *boutonnieres*, or as they're more fondly referred to, "boots." The first thing you should consider is the bouquet style and colors you want your maids to carry. Tell the florist your overall theme. Be sure to show him samples of fabrics, a picture of the dresses, and describe to him what you envision. Bold color in bouquets is very big; we have moved away from pastels and are adding brightly colored flowers to bouquets. Even bride's bouquets which were once thought to be only white are now featuring bold colors. Look at some of the floral pictures in this book and you will see how bold the color for flowers can get. Some sample styles of bouquets for your maids are nosegays, small crescent shape, arm bouquet (simply put, it lays in the crook of your arm), or a single, long-stemmed flower, maybe tied with an elegant ribbon. Let the florist help you with your decisions. Ask for his advice. That's what you're paying him for. Hand-tied bouquets are very popular now. But remember, because they are "hand-tied" (which means more labor-intensive), they are more expensive.

A simple round bouquet of roses is always elegant. *(Photo by Wyant Photography)*

This bouquet is what I refer to as a "hand-tied" bouquet. Notice the ribbon covering the stems. Each stem is individually wrapped and then wrapped again in ribbon. *(Photo by Wyant Photography)*

For your bouquet, there will be several things the florist will need to keep in mind as he designs your arrangement. First of all, he will note your physical size. I am 5 foot 9 and wear a size 10 dress. I can carry a long, cascading bouquet. My assistant Jean is about 5 foot and can't weigh more than 90 pounds soaking wet. She would be much better suited to carry a small nosegay type bouquet or something equally proportioned to her size. You don't want a bridal bouquet that you find yourself dragging down the aisle. The next thing the florist will want to see is a picture of your gown. The bouquet is meant to accent the gown, not take away from it. He can also tell from the lines of the gown how the lines in the bouquet should run. Remember, this is an art form, and it takes a good, experienced florist to pull the total look of a wedding together.

Nuptial Notes

A **boutonniere** is a small flower worn by the men in the wedding. Tradition says that the groom's boutonniere should be taken from the bride's bouquet. Today we don't pull flowers from the bride's bouquet and pin them on the groom, but his flower should match the bride's.

You need boutonnieres for the men in your wedding party, including the fathers, ushers, groomsmen, ring bearer (make his small!), and, of course, the groom. The groom's should be different from the others. Tradition suggests that his boutonniere be made of some of the flowers from the bride's bouquet.

In this natural-look bouquet, the stems are not wrapped but left free so it looks as though the bride just picked them out of her garden. *(Photo by Wyant Photography)*

Seal it with a kiss. The groom has on a single rose boutonniere with a sprig of babies breath. *(Photo by Colter Photography)*

The final body flowers you need to consider are corsages or something for the mothers and grandmothers to wear. Many mothers today opt for something other than a corsage. They prefer to carry a long stemmed flower down the aisle than to have something pinned to the dress that they just paid a fortune for and don't want pinholes in it. Grandmothers usually prefer corsages.

What a beautiful bride and a lovely bouquet made just for her. Bouquets are meant to accent you and the gown, not detract from either. *(Photo by Jeff Hawkins Photography)*

Petals and More

The flowers you choose to use at your ceremony site will depend on many factors. First, the all-important budget. Second, consider if the site is really in need of a lot of décor. Many churches are lovely just by themselves. Adding small amounts of flowers, such as some pew pieces, or some candles might be all you need. In Jewish ceremonies, it is popular to put flowers in the chuppah. It all depends on your site, your personal preference, and your budget.

Whatever you decide to do with flowers at the ceremony site, be sure they can be moved to the reception site. Whatever flowers you choose, you will be spending some bucks here, and you might as well get the most use out of those dollars.

This wedding party gathers for a quick pose. The flower girl does not have the traditional basket but instead is carrying a smaller version of the maids' bouquets. *(Photo by Wyant Photography)*

From Simple to Sensational: Centerpiece Ideas

For any type of reception besides a cake-and-punch reception, you will need to provide tables for your guests during the event. The layout of your facility, the time of day and style of the reception, the table size, and the number of guests you want to seat are all things you must consider before you decide what to use for centerpieces.

Here are some ideas and illustrations for centerpieces:

◆ For a simple, inexpensive idea, use some votive candles and greenery and sprinkle some glitter on the table. If you're on a tight budget, ask some good friends to set this up for you.

Votive candle with assortment of greenery placed around candles.

◆ Rent some table candelabras and have the florist arrange some flowers at the base.

Five-branch table candelabra with flowers intertwined.

◆ Rent tall pedestal centerpieces (the stem is about 36 inches) and have the florist put flowers in the top container. This works well in a large room with very high ceilings. Also, this can be mixed with low centerpieces, less elaborate on every other or every third table.

◆ Group several different size vases with a simple arrangement in each and add some votive candles.

A variety of vase sizes with three or four stems in each.

◆ Wrap empty boxes in Christmas paper and stack them in the middle of the table. Perfect for a Christmas wedding!

Boxes wrapped like Christmas presents stacked in the center of each table.

A large glass bowl filled with Christmas ornaments for guests to take as favors. The ornaments have the couple's names and their wedding date engraved.

◆ Use individual wedding cakes as your centerpiece at each table. Have the baker make a simple 9-inch-round cake, ice it like the wedding cake, and place it on a pedestal to use as the centerpiece. When you cut your first piece from your wedding cake, your guests can follow suit at their tables. (You can use a much smaller wedding cake for the formal one.)

Guests serve themselves from individual cakes at the tables.

◆ Wide colored ribbon can be laid down the center of the table with candles and glitter.

◆ Balloon bouquets or clusters are still popular. Just make sure they are tall enough they don't interfere with sight lines.

◆ Add things like a decorative napkin fold (such as a fan fold) or other unusual napkin placement to make the tables unique.

◆ A favor can add to the overall table décor.

◆ Use a variety of candles, some tapers, some pillars and of different heights to create a warm glow at the table.

A variety of pillar candles with rose petals scattered at the bases.

The same idea, only using polished rocks and shells (which the couple has collected) around the base.

◆ Bowls with goldfish are popular; surround the bowls with votive candles for a warm glow.

A fish bowl surrounded by votive candles.

◆ Hurricane globes with either tapers or pillar candles.

Hurricane globe with a taper candle tied with ribbon and greenery at the base.

◆ Hurricane globes laid on their sides with flowers spilling from both open ends makes an interesting centerpiece.

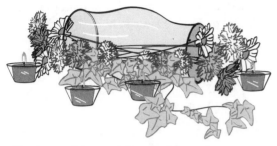

Hurricane globe turned on its side resting on greenery. The flowers spill from both open ends and votive candles surround the globe.

◆ Hurricane globes with taper and flowers packed tightly inside the base of the globe is still another idea.

Hurricane globe with taper candle flowers are packed inside the bottom of the globe, with three votive candles around the base.

◆ Polished rocks mixed with a variety of candles.

◆ A rose bowl with a single open rose in the bottom of the bowl

These delicate table lamps have been incorporated into the floral arrangement at this table setting.
(Photo by Jeff Hawkins Photography)

Be sure to check the "Floral Worksheet" in Appendix B for help in organizing your floral needs.

Making Beautiful Music

You must reserve wedding music early, both for the ceremony and the reception. Music completes your wedding atmosphere. Because it stays in the background, music is also one aspect of wedding planning that's easy to overlook, especially for the ceremony.

Waltzing Down the Aisle

First of all, the music for your wedding ceremony needs the approval of the church or the officiant performing the service. Always check with the ceremony site before you make plans. Most places welcome all types of musical instruments, but some are very strict. What do you and your groom like in music? Is an organ what you had in mind, or would you prefer something like a harp or a guitar? There are all kinds of ways to make music a fun and meaningful part of your wedding ceremony.

For your ceremony typical instruments and vocal includes the following:

- Organ
- Piano
- Violin
- String quartet
- Flute
- Harp
- Trumpet
- Small chamber orchestra
- Choir
- Soloist
- Duet

Wedding Woes

Try to use live musicians for your wedding ceremony. Using taped music may save you money, but it can also be risky. Just make sure you have someone reliable to run your CD player. I still remember the 14-year-old young man who was supposed to hit the Play button on the CD player and got so excited that he not only hit the Play button, but he also knocked over the candelabra, which burned a hole in the church's carpet!

A string quartet plays for this wedding ceremony instead of the traditional organ or piano. *(Photo by Colter Photography)*

Other musical suggestions include the following:

- A choir adds a nice touch for the wedding service. One couple who were both members of a professional choir hired the group to sing several songs during the prelude, but college or high school choirs will do as well. Perhaps a donation to their scholarship fund will be all that's needed to book them.

- Singing to each other. Couples (you have to be really comfortable with this idea) have sung to each other as part of the ceremony. Don't try this unless you are certain you can accomplish this task and have the talent to carry it off. (You might want to ask a friend for an objective opinion.)

Visit the musician in charge of your ceremony music. If you're having the ceremony in a religious setting, that person will most likely be the Minister of Music, the Director of Music, or the organist or pianist. Talk with this person about your likes and dislikes and what you would like to hear on your wedding day. Ask for ideas as well. Many times, if you meet in the facility, the musician can play a few bars of a certain piece so that you can hear the music. If you don't have access to a musician who can accommodate you, visit your local music store and purchase some tapes of wedding music. I have several tapes I loan to brides so they can be more active in choosing their wedding music.

Some popular choices for ceremony music are …

◆ **Processionals.** "Bridal Chorus," by Lohengrin ("Here Comes the Bride"); "The Wedding March," from Mendelssohn's *A Midsummer Night's Dream*; "Rondo," the *Masterpiece Theatre* theme, by Mouret; "Prince of Denmark's March," by Clarke; "Fanfare," from *The Triumphant*, by Couperin; "Sarabande," from *Suite No. 11*, by Handel; "Theme from *Love Story*," by Sigman and Lai; "Trumpet Tune," by Purcell; "Trumpet Voluntary," by Clarke; "Water Music," by Handel; The Wedding March from the "Sound of Music" by Rogers and Hammerstein.

◆ **Ceremony music.** "Jesu, Joy of Man's Desiring," by Bach; "Canon in D Minor," by Pachebel; "A Wedding Prayer," by Williams; "Wedding Song," by Stookey; "One Hand, One Heart," from *West Side Story*, by Bernstein and Sondheim; "Somewhere," from *West Side Story*, by Bernstein and Sondheim; "Theme from *Romeo and Juliet*," by Roto and Kusik; "Sunrise, Sunset," from *Fiddler on the Roof*, by Harnick and Bock; "Evergreen," by Barbra Streisand; "The Hawaiian Wedding Song," by Williams; "Theme from *Ice Castles*," by Melissa Manchester; "On the Wings of Love," by Jeffrey Osborne; "The Hands of Time (Brian's Song)," by Michel LeGrand; and "The Lord's Prayer," by Malotte.

Party Music

Although certainly not mandatory, music is a nice addition to the reception. This can be as simple or as elaborate as your budget and tastes dictate. A pianist playing soft background music is nice for the simple cake-and-punch reception, or you might choose to have a 20-piece orchestra in the ballroom playing the sounds of Glenn Miller for a formal dinner and dance reception. It goes back to your personal tastes and what style of wedding you want. Ask family and friends who have used a particular musician or group before for their recommendations.

They say a picture is worth a thousand words, and the look on this father's face says it all. *(Photo by Colter Photography)*

I guess this bride just got swept off her feet! *(Photo by Colter Photography)*

Here are a few things to keep in mind when you discuss your reception music with the vendor:

- What are their rates? Do they require a deposit?

- Ask for a tape of the musician or group if you're unfamiliar with the music.

- Check the contracts. How many breaks do the musicians require, and how often do they take those breaks? Do they have access to taped music to play during those breaks? It's nice for the guests to hear some soft music playing in the background rather than dead silence.

- Will they announce you or help with the garter and bouquet toss?

- How long will they play? Will they stay past their end time if you request them to do so, and how much will the extra time cost?

- If a style of music isn't working, will they try something different? Your dance floor should be active most of the evening, which is usually a sign of a good reception. In order for that to happen, a band must be able to "read" the crowd.

Teddy's Tips

Try to arrange to see the musician or group perform live at another venue before deciding to book them for your wedding. You'll also be able to judge their

- Ask if they carry liability insurance. Most facilities require this of all vendors, but especially the musicians.

- Ask if the band offers a song list from which you can make selections. Will they play a special song if asked?

- The musicians should be in tune (bad pun!) with the volume level during the reception. Tactfully ask about how they regulate the volume control. If you ask them to turn down the volume, will they cooperate? Some guests prefer to sit at their tables and chat with family and friends. If they cannot carry on a conversation over the music, it's too loud. You want the volume loud enough for those on the dance floor to appreciate, but not so loud as to make other guests shout to each other at their tables.

A DJ (short for disc jockey) is another avenue for your reception music. I've seen good DJs, and I've seen bad ones. Any form of music makers at your reception can make or break the party. Make sure you've seen a DJ's performance and understand what he will do and what he won't do. Read the contract carefully. Note how long he will play and how many breaks he will take. Check out whether he will need any extra electricity at the reception. Make sure he will be dressed appropriately as well.

Music can add a wonderful aspect to both your ceremony and your reception. Make wise musical choices for both situations. Your choices can frame your wedding day and set the mood for all to enjoy! Remember to check the "Musicians Worksheet" in Appendix B for help.

The Least You Need to Know

◆ Allow the florist some freedom in designing what will work best for your budget and your overall expectations.

◆ Flowers used during the ceremony include bouquets, boutonnieres, and corsages; flowers used at the ceremony and reception sites include centerpieces and other decorative arrangements.

◆ Centerpieces can be as simple or as elaborate as your taste and budget dictates.

◆ When choosing music for your ceremony and reception, consider all options.

◆ Music is a special part of any wedding, so consider what you and your partner like—and book early!

In This Chapter

◆ Shopping for the wedding gown and accessories

◆ Family gowns: to wear or not to wear?

◆ Check the care label

◆ Dressing the bridesmaids

◆ Decking out the men in your wedding party

◆ Creative ideas for your wedding transportation

Chapter 10

All Dressed Up and Somewhere to Go

Finding the right gown for the bride and then trying to outfit the bridesmaids can sometimes seem like an insurmountable task. It doesn't have to be, though, if you take it one step at a time. This chapter will guide you down the aisles of bridal shops to help you find your dream gown, accessories, and complementary dresses for the bridal party.

Also in this chapter, I'll be helping the men in your wedding party choose their attire, and I'll give you some creative ideas for wedding transportation.

Cinderella for a Day

Your wedding day is an opportunity for you to become a princess—to be the center of attention; to be *oohed* and *ahhed* at; and, of course, to wear the most magnificent dress you'll ever own: the dress of your dreams. Now, although the bride dons this dress for only one day of her life, it is important that it's just perfect. You don't want to look at those wedding photos a few years from now and proclaim, "Why in the world did I wear that?"

Wedding Woes

It's not a wise move to order your gown from a shop advertising that it's going out of business. If you can buy the gown off the rack, that's fine. But don't put down a deposit and allow the store to order your gown. One bride I worked with learned this lesson the hard way. The shop called and said that the gown was in. When the bride went to get her gown, the shop had "lost" the gown and couldn't reorder. What really happened was that the shop had sold that gown to another customer for more money.

This downtown couple appears ready for their big day. The spaghetti straps on the bride's gown can be removed if she wishes to wear the gown strapless. *(Photo by Wyant Photography)*

Before you begin your shopping, ask yourself the following:

◆ What gown might flatter you the most?

◆ What style of gown will help set the mood or theme of the wedding?

◆ How formal will the wedding be?

◆ What time of year are you getting married?

◆ Do you feel comfortable with the bridal salon and its staff?

◆ How important is comfort to you? This one you really need to think about once you have a few gowns to choose from.

Simple sleeveless gowns for the brides and the flower girls are always in style. *(Photo by Wyant Photography)*

Thinking Ahead

You should order your gown at least six months before the wedding. It doesn't take six months for your gown to arrive at the shop, but with delays in shipping, manufacturing problems, and alterations, it's best to be on the safe side. If you don't have six months' lead time, make sure you mention that to the shop. Several bridal gown companies specialize in short order times.

Bouquet Toss

The traditional color of a bridal gown is white, but that wasn't always the case. In ancient times, red and other bright colors were favored. In the mid-nineteenth century, Empress Eugenie, wife of Napoleon III, broke the medieval tradition of wearing a brightly colored wedding gown and chose white. In the Victorian period in this country, brides from affluent families began wearing white gowns to show that they could afford to have a special dress they would wear only one time. Most women simply wore the best dress they had at the time. A white gown did not come to represent purity until the twentieth century.

This bride chose a wedding gown with an unusual red-beaded bodice. Her groom is dressed in a classic tux with the new tie look. *(Photo by Wyant Photography)*

By Appointment Only

Make sure you check with the bridal shops to see if you need to make an appointment before your visit. This makes you appear more serious about buying, and if they know you're coming, they can give you the time and attention you deserve. If the shop doesn't accept appointments, ask for the best time to shop. Saturdays, for example, are often very busy days for bridal shops; try to shop on another day of the week.

Oh, It's *So* You!

When shopping for your wedding gown, look at many different styles of dresses. You might be really surprised to find that a gown style you thought would not complement you really does. You'll have several options in terms of style, cut, fabric, and adornments. On your first shopping trip, try on a few different styles to get a feel for what works for you. Perhaps you look best with off-the-shoulder, or you realize you're too petite for a train. Or the dress you fell in love with in that magazine makes you look like a marshmallow. If you're not familiar with the different types of silk, ask the salesperson—and that person should be very knowledgeable because that's what she's there for!

Strapless gowns are another elegant look for both the bride and her attendants. *(Photo by Wyant Photography)*

This bride waits for her groom in a strapless gown accented by a full cathedral train and tiara. *(Photo by Morris Fine Art Photography)*

Notice the embroidery on the train of this elaborate gown. The bride's cathedral-length veil flows over the chapel-length train. *(Photo by Wyant Photography)*

Here's some additional advice when shopping for a gown:

◆ Shop with an open mind. Just because you have your heart set on a sheath gown with a detachable train, don't be afraid to try on the gown with the flowing skirt and cowl neckline.

◆ A second (or third) opinion is always a good idea. Many mothers dream of the day they can take their daughters wedding-dress shopping. So take one or two people with you when you shop. But know that too many opinions also make it harder for you to choose the dress that's right for you.

◆ Don't think all stores are the same—shop around. You might even find the same or similar dress elsewhere but realize you like the service or location of a particular shop better.

◆ Look through bridal magazines to see the latest styles and trends (see Appendix A for a list of bridal magazines).

◆ Get referrals from recent brides.

For help in shopping wisely, turn to the "Wedding Gown and Bridesmaids' Dresses Worksheet" in Appendix B.

Teddy's Tips

If you don't dress up for this wonderful occasion, at least take a pair of dress shoes with you. Have your hair fixed appropriately, and add a little makeup. It's really hard to judge how you might look on your wedding day if you're wearing tennis shoes with your hair in a ponytail. Time spent checking hair and makeup and having the right shoes along will make a big difference in what you see in the mirror.

Don't Veil the Truth

It's wise to wait until you've decided on a gown before you begin picking out your veil or other headpiece. You wouldn't want an unflattering veil to overpower the beauty of the dress.

You might be surprised at all of the options you have with a veil—different weights of fabric, choices of trimmings, and, of course, length. All these decisions will be based not only on what works best for you, but also what works best with the gown.

You have the following choices in veil lengths:

♦ **Fingertip veil.** Just brushes the shoulders and frames the face.

♦ **Elbow-length veil.** Brushes the elbows.

♦ **Chapel-length veil.** Measures three yards long (nine feet).

♦ **Cathedral-length veil.** Measures four yards long (12 feet).

A cathedral-length veil is the longest possible veil a bride can wear. These ladies are taking time to spread it out fully before this bride and her dad take that long walk. *(Photo by Colter Photography)*

If your gown doesn't have a long train (or a train at all), you might want to consider having a longer veil to act as a train. Try on different styles to be sure that you get the best match for both your gown and your hairstyle.

> **Bouquet Toss**
>
> Before the sixteenth century, veils were worn by unmarried women as a sign of modesty, and by married women to show that they were submissive to their husbands. My, how things change!

This couple stands at the altar for their formal portrait. Her gown features a chapel-length train. The groom has on a white full-length tie with his tux.
(Photo by Wyant Photography)

You don't have to wear a veil at all. It depends on the formality of the wedding and your personal preference. Some brides opt for flowers in their hair or decorative hair ornaments. Others wear a veil for the ceremony and then remove the veiling for the reception, leaving the headpiece on.

The Glass Slippers

You might think that shoes are not something you need to devote much time to—who's going to see them anyway? But think about how many hours you're going to be on your feet! I can't emphasize this enough: Make sure the shoes are comfortable!

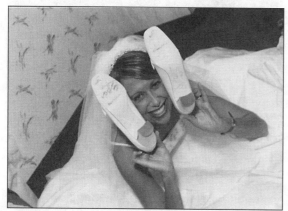

This pretty bride chose a low-heeled shoe to wear for her wedding and had her bridesmaids auto-graph the bottoms. Supposedly, the last signature left after all the dancing gets good luck for a year. *(Photo by Colter Photography)*

Brides often choose a lovely pair of formal shoes for the ceremony and then slip on a pair of ballet slippers for the reception. Their feet are exceptionally appreciative.

Also popular are tennis shoes trimmed with ribbons and lace to dress them up. These can be purchased at many bridal shops or through catalogs and can help the bride dance all night.

The Final Touches

Here are some added final touches to consider:

◆ Jewelry, just the right piece to accent the gown

◆ Long gloves if your gown is strapless

◆ A small matching clutch bag for the reception

◆ A shawl in warmer climates for cool evenings

◆ A warm wrap, either velvet or fake-fur for the winter climates

A lovely bride poses in the center aisle of her church. Notice the shawl wrap over her shoulders. Wraps are very much in style. The white lights lining both sides of the aisle add a nice touch. *(Photo by Wyant Photography)*

Underneath It All

What goes underneath your gown is just as important as all your other accessories. The type of bra and slip you choose to wear with your gown should be well thought-out. Most bridal shops carry these undergarments. First, you want a bra that is comfortable and that gives you the support you need with your particular gown. The slip helps give you the proper shape, whether your gown is a sheath or a southern belle–style gown. If your gown is a slim sheath, you might decide not to wear a slip. Make sure, however, that you cannot see panty lines through your gown—you should show smile lines, but not panty lines!

Service with a Smile

If you know others who have used a certain shop, ask those brides how they were treated.

- ◆ Were all their questions answered satisfactorily?

- ◆ How did the gown look when it was ready to be picked up or when it arrived at the ceremony site? Were the sleeves stuffed with tissue?

- ◆ Was a *bodice form* used? Was the train tied up or draped over the hanger?

- ◆ Did the shop explain how to bustle the gown?

- ◆ Are alterations included or an extra cost? This is a very important and potentially costly question.

- ◆ Make sure the shop takes your measurements for the ordering of your gown. Formalwear runs small so don't be surprised if you require a large sizer than you wear in ready-wear clothing.

Nuptial Notes

A **bodice form** is a piece of cardboard shaped like a woman's upper body that the shop places in the bodice of your gown to keep it wrinkle-free and looking fresh. This protects the gown during travel time from the shop to your home or ceremony site.

If It Was Good Enough for Mom ...

Sally Lorensen Conant, Ph.D., president of Orange Restoration Labs in Orange, Connecticut, offers the following advice and ideas if you're considering wearing a family gown—either your mother's, your grandmother's, your sister's, or even a friend's gown:

For the bride who values tradition and sentiment, a family gown may be just right. Family gowns come in all sizes and shapes, and they can be fitted to all sizes and shapes. In fact, we know a bridal shop that can make a gown as many as 12 sizes larger! Always make the decision to wear a family gown, whether it belongs to your mother or your favorite aunt or even a close family friend, based on the meaning the gown has for you and whether the style suits you—not on the way it fits or its condition. A specialist can restore even a yellowed, badly stained gown to the true color, and a talented dressmaker can reshape almost any gown to your size.

You can also update a gown by changing the sleeves, the neckline, or the shape of the skirt. Three sisters in one family remodeled their mother's gown so extensively that it looked completely different at each of the three weddings. Some brides add lace and beading such as pearls, sequins, or crystals, but these days brides more often choose to wear a family gown because they like the simplicity of the cut and the beauty of the fabric. Simply cut, unembellished gowns today are often the most expensive gowns on the market, and a bride may look just as elegant in a family gown at far less cost.

This beautiful bride was married in 1945 and wears a lovely gown of chiffon.
(Photo from the author's collection)

This pretty bride was married in 1975 and wears the same gown. Yep, they are mother and daughter, and the only thing the daughter did differently was to wear a hat with tulling and fresh flowers instead of a veil. I'm rather fond of these ladies. One's my mom and the other is my little sister. *(Photo by Wayne Manuel)*

Several companies offer gown restoration services, which can make your mother's or grandmother's yellowed gown beautiful again. Call the Wedding Gown Specialists Association at 1-800-501-5005 for a cleaner/preservation specialist in your area.

Wedding Woes

Alterations can be very expensive; always know up front what the shop will charge for the service. Your best bet is to try to remain approximately the size you were when you ordered your gown. If you're expecting a large weight loss, either have your gown made locally or wait until you're closer to the desired weight before you order. Never order a gown in a smaller size expecting that you'll lose the extra pounds. It's much easier to take the gown in than let the seams out!

See Reverse for Care

Whether you choose a gown off the rack, have one ordered, or decide to wear Mama's gown, Sally Lorensen Conant again offers this advice:

Beware the unserviceable gown! Before you actually purchase a dress, look at the care label. Federal law requires manufacturers to put labels into clothing describing the proper care for the garment. Some labels actually say "Do Not Wash" *and* "Do Not Dry Clean." Unless you have absolutely no interest in what happens to your gown after the wedding, better pass up a dress with these labels.

Also look carefully at the decorations on the gown. Something like dried rosebuds will not survive cleaning, no matter what the care label says, and the gown will have to be taken apart before it can be cleaned. Are the beads sewn onto the gown, or are they glued?

Some glues dissolve in water, and others dissolve in dry cleaning, so either way you lose. Beads that are sewn can be a problem, too. Some manufacturers knot the thread very infrequently so that when one thread breaks, many, many beads fall off. Others use beads that melt in the dry-cleaning process. You can test for loose beads by pulling at one or two of them, but without special chemicals, you can't very well test the bead's serviceability. That makes it even more important to read the care label; the manufacturer has to stand behind the recommended care. If there is no label, better ask the shop about the care recommended by the manufacturer.

Pretty Maids All in a Row

Shopping for your bridesmaids' dresses should be a pleasant experience. Let me offer these words of wisdom to help guide you:

◆ Shop only with your maid of honor and your mother or another close friend.

◆ Take into account the physical sizes of your maids so that the style you pick works for all of the girls.

◆ Try to choose something the girls can wear another time. Manufactures are making this task easier on brides these days by offering dresses that have separate tops and skirts and a variety of different styles that can be worn for other occasions.

◆ Use your best judgment and try to choose something with a reasonable price tag.

◆ A trend now is having the bride choose the fabric and ask each bridesmaid to chose a pattern that is complimentary to her and have their dresses made. While you still have the same fabric, each maid gets to wear a dress that compliments her figure.

The wedding party is dressed in black and white with accents of red. The bride's gown features three-quarter length sleeves and a scoop neckline. The children on the right of the picture are dressed as miniature versions of the bride and groom.
(Photo by Wyant Photography)

Dressed to Kill: Formal Wear for Men

The groom and his men want to look just as handsome as the bride and her attendants want to look beautiful. Take some time to look through bridal magazines to get a feel for what's available for the men in your wedding party. (Be sure to use the "Tuxedo Worksheet" in Appendix B.) There are hundreds of tuxedo styles, different ties, shirts, vests, and colors from which to choose. The sky is the limit with tuxedo choices.

The groom may choose the traditional cutaway coat with gray-striped trousers and an ascot. If your wedding leans more toward semiformal or informal, a nice dark suit and a white or pastel shirt is always a good choice.

Going with the Flow

Select the style and brand of tuxedo that will complement the wedding theme, the time of day, and what the bridesmaids are wearing.

Accent with Color

Prints, gold and silver threads on black vests, along with accents in ties and cummerbunds are appearing more frequently these days. We are also seeing the popular no-tie neckline for men. That style neckline comes with a type of broach that is worn at the neckline and thus no tie. White tie is still considered very formal and is a most appropriate look for a formal wedding after 6 o'clock in the evening. Many times, for a hint of color to coordinate with your brides-maids, the groom might choose to have col-ored handkerchiefs in the men's breast pockets.

Right Down to Their Feet

Make sure that the men have formal shoes. You don't want them dressed to the hilt in a wonder-ful tuxedo, yet wearing cowboy boots or tennis shoes. They need to have a pair of black or gray (depending on the color of tuxedo) leather or patent leather dress shoes. Also, white socks just don't complement the ensemble for some-one wearing a dark suit or tuxedo! Make sure that the groomsmen have black dress socks to go with their formal shoes.

Bouquet Toss

One ancient tradition was to dress the bridesmaids and groomsmen like the bride and groom so that the evil demons would be confused if they tried to put a curse on the couple.

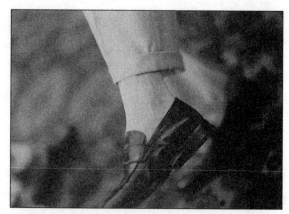

Even though this was an informal wedding, this groomsman forgot his socks. Unless you're getting married on a beach, socks are a must! *(Photo by Colter Photography)*

Getting the Suit on Time

The men should order their formal wear about two to three months before the wedding. Look in the Yellow Pages under "Wedding Services and Supplies" or "Formal Wear" for listings of retailers that offer tuxedos (formal wear) for rent. You can also purchase tuxedos, but they are expensive; unless you plan to use one extensively, it's cheaper to rent a tuxedo when you need it.

Buying in Bulk

Many stores offer some kind of special or dis-count on tuxedo rentals: "Rent six tuxedos, get the groom's free," or maybe, "Rent your tuxe-dos from us, and you receive your limousine rental free." Always ask about specials.

Your rented tuxedo is a package deal. In other words, you will receive the jacket, trousers, choice of shirt, tie, vest or cummerbund, studs, and cuff links for one price.

Shoes may be rented also, but that's usually an extra charge. Sometimes colored handker-chiefs are included to add color to the outfit (they go in the breast pocket, not the back pocket).

The Perfect Fit

Alterations are usually kept to a minimum. Jacket sleeve length and pant length can be altered, but unless you have a specific concern, shops try not to get bogged down with alterations.

Long-Distance Shopping

If you have out-of-town men in your wedding party, then the task of getting them fitted is relatively simple. When you go to the shop to select your formal wear, give the names of the men who need to be fitted to the shop. They will provide postcards with the brand name and style number of the tuxedo included. Send those postcards to your out-of-town men, and have them take the cards to their local tux shops. They will be measured and can try on the same brand of jacket to check for fitting. That shop will also take other measurements to ensure a correct fitting. Then, have your men return the cards to the local tux shop to have their tuxedo orders placed. When the men arrive in town for the wedding, have them go to the tux shop and try on their tuxedo completely (or, at least the jacket and trousers). Last-minute alterations can be made if something doesn't fit properly.

> **Teddy's Tips**
>
> It's a good idea to carry collar extenders in your emergency kit in case the shirt is too tight around the neck. This little contraption can add an inch or so to make your life—and breathing—a little easier.

Arriving in Style

The mode of transportation you plan to use for your wedding day is one detail that's easy to overlook. With a little planning, however, this item can add a unique flair to your special day. The "Special Transportation Worksheet" in Appendix B can help you in this area.

A classy sports car whisks you away in style. Notice, too, the sparklers for this couple's send-off. *(Photo by Wyant Photography)*

If a gorgeous classic car like this one is available, why not use it? *(Photo by Janet Klinger Photography)*

Many couples use special transportation to take them from the ceremony to the reception. Other couples use special forms of transportation from the home to the ceremony, and some couples use special types of transportation to take them from the reception to their wedding night destination. It's a personal choice; be creative, but stay within your budget.

Here are some ideas for your transportation desires:

◆ Limousine—elegant and classy, riding in a limousine can make you feel like a celebrity

◆ Rolls Royce

◆ Classic car—a convertible, for example

Make your exit in a classic car like this one. *(Photo by Wyant Photography)*

This couple sits atop this Rolls Royce ready to "roll" to their reception. *(Photo by Wyant Photography)*

This classic car awaits the couple outside a Seattle club. *(Photo by Janet Klinger Photography)*

◆ Horse and carriage

For an unusual twist on the horse-drawn carriage, consider the bicycle-drawn carriage! *(Photo by Norma Edelman, Wedding Casa)*

◆ Motorcycles (yes, I said motorcycles)

Well, I know they will figure out how to get her gown over the back end of this motorcycle. Have fun! *(Photo by Wyant Photography)*

◆ Trolley car (for the entire wedding party, too)

◆ Bus (again for the whole wedding party)

Most of these forms of transportation you can find in the Yellow Pages under "Car Rentals" or "Car Clubs." Maybe you have a friend who owns a classic car who would let you use it for your "getaway."

An antique car is the perfect exit for this newly married couple. *(Photo by Wyant Photography)*

Mother Nature strikes again—good thing this limo driver was prepared for rain. *(Photo by Colter Photography)*

This wedding party decided to make good use of the country club's golf carts for the trek from the tent to the clubhouse. *(Photo by Colter Photography)*

Be Creative!

Perhaps my trophy for the most unique mode of wedding transportation I have ever witnessed goes to a couple I worked with several years ago. They had a beautiful garden wedding followed by a lovely garden reception. The home was in the country, and we were surrounded by trees, flowers, and the beauty of nature. When I asked them if they were going to leave from the reception in any special form, they assured me that they had nothing in mind and would just leave in their car. When the time came, the bride's brother appeared with a small tractor (yes, I said tractor) that had a box on the back for hauling. The couple took one look at the tractor, hopped onboard, and off they rode into the sunset (or the field, or wherever their car was parked). The picture that scene created was fantastic and still remains in my mind today.

Just when I think I've seen it all ... this couple makes a memorable exit in a speedboat! *(Photo by Janet Klinger Photography)*

Parents of one bride surprised another couple with a helicopter ride from the reception to the airport. So be creative, and if possible, try to tie in the season, location, and your interests. Use your imagination. Make your grand exit in style, but make it in *your* style. As always, remember to ask many questions of the various vendors and to get referrals.

The Least You Need to Know

◆ Try to allow at least six months for ordering and receiving your wedding gown. If you don't have that much time, you may find that it will cost you a bit more.

◆ If you're considering wearing a family gown, check with a gown restoration service, which can make an old gown look beautiful again.

◆ Read the care label carefully before choosing your gown.

◆ When choosing bridesmaids' dresses, think about the attendants' physical attributes and coloring, as well as what they can reasonably afford.

◆ The groom's formal wear should complement the style of wedding you're planning as well as the bridal gown.

◆ Be creative when deciding on the transportation you will use for your wedding day. Use your imagination and have fun with this decision.

In This Chapter

- ◆ Considerations when choosing a photographer
- ◆ Different styles of wedding photography
- ◆ Understanding the contract
- ◆ Finding the right videographer
- ◆ Before or after? The best time to take pictures
- ◆ Making sure you get the shots you want

11

Pretty as a Picture: Photographers and Videographers

In this chapter, we take a look at the photography and video industry—what's out there and what choices you have. (Yes, despite everything you hear, *you* are in control and make the final choice—I'm writing this book to help you make *good* choices.) These two elements of your wedding day are so important. Don't take shortcuts here if they are a high priority for you. Shop wisely for these vendors.

Also in this chapter I'll talk about when to take those precious pictures and the options you do have. Finally, I'll let you in on how not to leave anyone out of the pictures.

Memories to Last a Lifetime

Photography is an expensive undertaking for most couples. You want good pictures that capture your special day, but that means you're going to have to spend some time investigating your choices now and to allow for enough money in your budget to accomplish that goal.

So Many Questions, So Little Time

When you meet with the photographer, you need to consider several items. The first thing you should look at is the quality of the photographer's work.

◆ Does the photographer's work capture the moment?

◆ Look through the display albums. Do the pictures express the romance of the day?

◆ What catches your eye? Are they straight shots? Do the pictures tell a story?

- Find out whether the photographer will take candid shots; many photographers will not.
- Is the photographer available on your wedding date? What is the fee?
- What kinds of packages does he offer?
- Are the photos you are viewing the work of the photographer you are actually hiring?

Wedding Woes

Be sure to find out what kind of contract the photographer uses and read it carefully. Does the contract include a time limit? You want to avoid having to pay overtime to your photographer; overtime can add up to big money very quickly.

As you're looking over the work displayed in the studio, be sure to ask whose work you're viewing. If Mr. Smith took the pictures they are showing you, but Ms. Jones will be the photographer shooting your wedding, ask to see Ms. Jones's work. Looking at the work of another photographer from that studio won't help you decide whether the photographer you are considering is right for the job.

It's a great photographer who can capture the fun and excitement of a large wedding party. *(Photo by Wyant Photography)*

Do You Get That Warm, Fuzzy Feeling?

One of the most important questions you have to ask is whether you both feel comfortable with this photographer. Be honest with yourselves. You will spend a lot of time on your wedding day with this person; if you don't like the person, for whatever reason, it will show in your pictures. Over the years, I have watched brides who were so obviously annoyed by their photographer that the only things that came across in the finished product were clenched teeth and forced smiles. Not good! It's important to have a good rapport with your photographer.

Teddy's Tips

Always take care of your support staff—photographer, videographer, DJ or band, and coordinators—by offering them food and a special place at the reception for them to regroup.

As long as there's no flash used, most officiants don't mind pictures being taken during the ceremony. *(Photo by Colter Photography)*

Well, it's all over but the party! *(Photo by Colter Photography)*

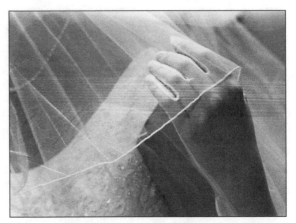

The simplest things can make the moment. See how graceful this bride's hands look in sheer gloves. *(Photo by Colter Photography)*

What's in a Picture?

You might encounter several different styles of wedding photography from which you will have to choose. The type of wedding photography that a particular photographer offers depends on his ability, experience, and personal choice, but you'll be better off if you at least know the differences and can understand the terminology.

Soft Focus

When we were married, I remember fondly the photographer pulling out these wonderfully romantic pictures from his samples and waving them tantalizingly in front of my eyes. They were dreamlike and romantic with soft lighting. That type of photography is called *soft focus*. The photographer uses a special lens to give a romantic look to the pictures. You wouldn't want your entire album in this style, however, because after a few shots, the romantic look loses its effectiveness.

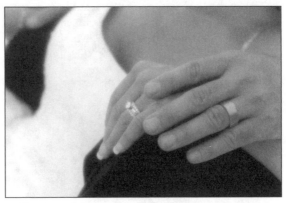

Here's a nice way to show off the beautiful rings. *(Photo by Janet Klinger Photography)*

Portraiture

Portraiture is probably one of the most common types of photography, although you might not know it by this name. This refers to the formal posed pictures at the ceremony site and reception. There isn't much spontaneity here, but the pictures can be almost perfect, depending on the photographer. The time element here is what you need to understand. Yes, your pictures can be quite lovely, but if it's going to take the photographer five hours to accomplish that task, maybe you should think of other alternatives.

This posed picture of a lovely bride also emphasizes the architectural beauty of the building. *(Photo by Janet Klinger Photography)*

A posed yet very interesting photo speaks volumes. *(Photo by Wyant Photography)*

Natural Light

This type of photography does not use artificial light. In other words, no flash is used with the camera. The photographer takes what light is available naturally and uses that to create the image. When done well, a *natural light* photograph reminds you of a fine work of art, but it's very difficult to arrange.

Looks like rain is holding off for this couple. Notice how the photographer uses offbeat settings besides the usual church. *(Photo by Janet Klinger Photography)*

This photographer used sunlight to add contrast to the photo. *(Photo by Morris Fine Art Photography)*

Photojournalistic

Wedding photography done in the *photojournalistic* style takes its technique from the news media. The photographer, through pictures, tells the story of your wedding on film. Instead of posing pictures trying to create a mood, the photographer follows the people and mood of the event and captures it on film as it unfolds. This can be a fantastic way to show emotions, highlights of the day that have special meaning, the people involved, and anything special you want to include. Examples of "capture the moment" photography are located in several places throughout this book. It is becoming more popular with couples all over the country, as well as the mixing of color photos with black-and-white images.

Look at the emotion on this groom's face (left) as he watches his bride come down the aisle. *(Photo by Colter Photography)*

The groom waits pensively for the minister and the start of his wedding ceremony. Moments like these are too precious not to capture. *(Photo by Colter Photography)*

Bouquet Toss

In one wedding I coordinated, the groom's mother had died just six months before the wedding. He wanted to do something special in her honor at the service. When the parents were to be seated, the groom appeared in the back of the church and walked by his father's side down the aisle. They went to the altar rail and lit a candle in memory of his mother. It was a very touching moment, and one which the photographer really couldn't pose. By using the photojournalistic approach, the photographer got a wonderful shot to capture this special moment.

Read the Fine Print: Understanding Contracts

It's very important to understand the kind of contract the photographer uses and exactly what the price includes. Make *sure* you understand this and don't be afraid to ask questions. Does the contract include albums? Does it include a charge for the proofs?

It's important to consider whether the contract includes a time limit. When you buy a package, is there a time limit on how long the photographer is available? Suppose your wedding is at 5 P.M. You don't want to see each other before the service, so the bride has some pictures taken with the bridesmaids and family. The groom has similar shots taken with his groomsmen, ushers, and family. The majority of the pictures, however, must be taken after the service. Before you know it, your time is up and you're into overtime with the photographer.

That's what you want to avoid, if at all possible. I've been quoted $200 per half hour overtime for photographers in the Midwest—that's a lot of money. So check whether the contract contains a time limit clause. It may be cheaper for you in the long run to get a package with more time than you think you'll need just to save you from paying overtime.

When All Is Said and Done

Good wedding photography is meant to last a lifetime. You want to choose a photographer who can help you capture on film all the wonderful emotions of your big day. You want someone who treats you with respect and sensitivity, and you want all this without even noticing that the photographer is in the room. Use the "Photography Worksheet" in Appendix B to determine your photographic needs.

"Okay, Dad, I'll try to remember," is what this bride seems to be thinking as she listens to her dad. *(Photo by Colter Photography)*

"Oh, honey, it was wonderful!" is what the mother of the groom seems to be saying to her new daughter-in-law. *(Photo by Colter Photography)*

You can't pose the romance and emotion that shines through in these pictures—two of my favorites.
(Photo by Colter Photography)

Hiring a Videographer

After you have hired a competent photographer to shoot the still pictures for your wedding, you also might want to consider booking a videographer. Videotaping by an experienced videographer can add so much life to your wedding memories that this is fast becoming a very popular wedding component. Some couples are even opting for a professional video in lieu of professional photography. With technology today, it's possible to pull still frames from a video or add animation to help create the video of your dreams.

Look at Samples

When you check out a video company, always ask to see a demo tape. This should give you an idea of the quality of work the company provides. Look for the following:

◆ Is there clarity both in film quality and in the coverage of events?

◆ Does the tape flow smoothly from one portion of the wedding to the next?

◆ Does the videographer use *fade-outs?*

Nuptial Notes _____

A **fade-out** is a technique where the film fades from one scene to another so the transition is smooth, giving the film a more professional quality.

Also make sure you understand whether the tape will be edited or unedited. Edited is what you would most likely prefer. Another tip: Ask to see a recent tape (not just the demo that will be the best one ever shot).

Home Video Quality

The biggest complaint I hear from brides who asked Uncle Henry to tape their wedding is, "I thought it would be just like TV." Well, it's not. For a videotape to have some of the major components of a TV show, you will need at least two cameras—and three would be better. Normally the videographer has several assistants helping operate the cameras.

Here are a few things you'll want to ask about:

◆ Ask the video company whether it can provide the groom with a wireless microphone to pick up the vows segment of the ceremony.

♦ Ask about including special effects, such as incorporating your baby pictures into the video or using animation.

♦ Ask whether the videographer will attend the rehearsal to get a feel for placement at the ceremony site and to meet the officiant. For help with this part of your wedding planning, turn to the "Videography Worksheet" in Appendix B.

Wedding Woes

Always check with the officiant to make sure you're permitted to have your ceremony videotaped. That's your responsibility, not the video company's. Nothing is more embarrassing than having the video company all set and ready to go when the officiant announces that his church or synagogue does not permit videotaping.

The Sound of Music

Is there music that will be added to your edited video? Will you have a choice in the selection of music? Most videographers consider themselves artists and in that regard, do not like having you pick the music (although they may ask what kind of music you prefer). Some videographers, however, will ask a couple to select a few meaningful songs to include, and then fill in with what they consider appropriate.

It's the little things that make the memories, such as this picture of sheet music for the "Wedding March."
(Photo by Colter Photography)

The Package Deal

Just as you would with any other aspect of planning your wedding, ask questions about price and what is available to you:

♦ Can you order extra tapes?

♦ Approximately how long after the wedding will you receive the tape?

♦ Does the videographer use a contract? (Most do.) Is there a time limit on his contract?

♦ Does he charge for overtime?

♦ What do the videographers wear for the wedding?

When to Take Those Pictures

One of the biggest dilemmas couples face today is how to work in time for the wedding pictures. The tradition of keeping the bride and groom apart before the wedding probably developed in the days of arranged marriages. That way, the groom would not see the bride and back out of the wedding if he didn't like what he saw. The question you and your groom have to answer is, "Do we want to see each other before the ceremony?" This is a personal choice, but before you make up your mind, let's talk about available alternatives. Basically, you can choose from three time periods for your wedding photography.

Before the Ceremony

This is my first choice of when photos should be taken. Most photographers will tell you that they not only get better pictures when they do everything beforehand, but it also relieves some of the pre-wedding tension. If you do everything before the service, you're more relaxed than if you take the pictures after the service, when you're wondering what's happening at the reception and if everything is okay.

Pretty as a picture. *(Photo by Colter Photography)*

Three pairs of shoes await three bridesmaids before the ceremony starts. *(Photo by Colter Photography)*

If all the pictures are taken beforehand, you're free to leave the ceremony site along with your guests. Couples tell me they enjoy the wedding and reception so much more because they aren't worried about pictures. Grooms tell me that there's still something very mystical, magical, and romantic about the moment when the organ goes into "Bridal Chorus" and the bride starts her walk down the aisle—and even if they have seen their bride before the ceremony, it's still a very moving moment.

One thing I do for my clients who want to take all the pictures beforehand is to find some private time for the couple to see each other in their wedding finery for the first time. The bride gets dressed in her gown and veil while the groom is putting on his tuxedo. I find a private room somewhere at the ceremony site, take the bride to the room, and then bring in the groom. Then I close the door and give them some private time. Some couples use this time to give each other their gifts or cards. I even had one groom who sang to his bride!

Teddy's Tips

Allow enough time to accomplish whatever photographic style you've chosen. It's always better to allot too much time for this than too little.

I've learned over the years that this private time might be the only quality time the couple will have the entire day until they get in the car to exit the reception. Some couples find this hard to believe, but experience wins out here. Once that ceremony starts, you're on a roll; things don't calm down much until later into the reception. You might want to gaze longingly at your groom as you walk down the aisle, but there's so much else going on that this usually isn't possible. Also, depending on the site, once you start down the aisle and the congregation stands (as they usually do), the groom's view of the bride—and the bride's view of him—is obstructed by the guests (unless, of course, you're both eight feet tall).

If you choose to have all your wedding pictures taken before the service, allow enough time to accomplish this task. Your photographer should give you a timeline for the picture schedule. For example, if you're taking all the pictures beforehand, the photographer might start taking pictures with just the bride and then bring in the groom. Your parents might be next in line. The photographer will build up the photography session so that she finishes with the entire wedding party. Thus, you don't have lots of people standing around with nothing to do but wait to have their pictures taken.

Try to build in some extra time for just relaxing after the pictures are completed. Posing for

pictures is work—don't let anyone tell you differently. If you can build some extra time into the day for just sitting back and maybe even slipping off your wedding attire and resting for a while, it can make all the difference in the world later.

"I think I'll just rest here a minute ..." (Photo by Janet Klinger Photography)

After the Ceremony

You might have to take pictures following the ceremony if you choose not to see each other until after the wedding, or you might be scheduled into a church where there just isn't time to take pictures beforehand. If you're having a Catholic wedding at 6:30 in a church in which Mass is scheduled for 5, for example, the only way you can have pictures taken before the ceremony is to go to the church very early in the afternoon and take them at that time.

In most cases, the photographer should be willing to come in and do some candid shots, perhaps in the dressing room or at your home while you're adjusting your veil, or maybe take a picture of you and your mom. The bulk of your photos will be taken after the ceremony, however.

This bride wrapped in her veil is a stunning image.
(Photo by Jeff Hawkins Photography)

Lush, natural settings are a nice complement to the
formality of the bride. *(Photo by Janet Klinger
Photography)*

Wedding Woes

Trying to finish pictures without the entire wedding party is difficult. Make sure your wedding party knows when and where the pictures will be taken and who's expected to be photographed. Don't just assume they know what your plans are.

You need full cooperation from your wedding party. Let me repeat that: You need your wedding party, your parents, and anyone you want included in the photos to be cooperative with the photographer. Make sure everyone understands that pictures will be taken immediately following the ceremony and receiving line (if you're having one).

For pictures after the ceremony, the photographer probably will reverse the strategy and begin with the large group shots, working down to the shots of just the bride and groom. Sometimes, he may photograph the parents first so that they can leave and greet guests at the reception. Pictures taken following the wedding will take some time, but they don't need to take hours.

Before and After

Probably one of the most common ways to work in all the photos you want taken is to take some before and some after the ceremony. If you're determined not to see your partner before the wedding, this is probably the method you will choose for getting all the shots you want.

When you have some photographs taken before and others taken afterward, the photographer usually starts with the bride and then adds her parents, maybe the bridesmaids, and then perhaps the groomsmen. Then he'll do the same sort of routine with the groom. In other words, the photographer takes as many pictures as possible without you seeing each other before the ceremony.

> **Teddy's Tips**
>
> If you're truly not comfortable, for whatever reason, with seeing each other before the ceremony, do not let anyone—the photographer, your mother, your future mother-in-law, or the bridal consultant—talk you into going against your wishes. This is something that is definitely up to you.

Following the ceremony and your receiving line (if you're using one), you can do the larger pictures: the couple with the entire wedding party, the couple with the parents, and so on. It shouldn't take too long if you work with the photographer. She's not a magician, so get your wedding party there on time, let them know what to expect, and smile.

Don't Forget Anybody!

Most photographers have lists of favorite photo shots a couple might request. Be sure to look over the list and check those photos you want captured as your day unfolds. This will also help keep the photographer on top of the wedding photo scene. He needs to be in charge at this time. Too many requests from family or you at the last minute can eat up precious time on your wedding day.

If you have a large and extended family or if you have special people you want included in those pictures, your photographer needs a list of those people. Unless he is familiar with your family, he will need help getting those members rounded up. This can be a real chore, especially if the numbers are large. You might ask a family member to help the photographer locate those family members whose photo you want. He should also have a schedule of events or agenda of the reception so he can capture those special moments for you.

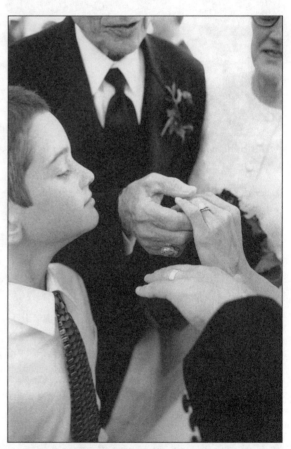

"So this is what all the fuss is about. Hold it down so I can see!" *(Photo by Janet Klinger Photography)*

Your wedding pictures are meant to last a lifetime. When everything is over, they are what you have left to remember this special time. Work with the photographer to help capture the very essence of your day.

The Least You Need to Know

◆ Make sure you feel comfortable with the photographer who will be taking your wedding pictures. You will be spending a significant amount of time together and need to have a good rapport.

◆ Wedding photographers may specialize in different styles such as soft focus or portraiture. Be sure you're familiar with the terminology.

◆ Read the photographer's contract thoroughly to understand exactly what you're paying for.

◆ Ask to see a demo tape of a videographer's work before you make a commitment.

◆ Pictures can be taken at different stages and different time periods during the wedding day. Make a decision early about when to have the photos taken.

◆ Work with the photographer to make sure you have plenty of time to complete all your pictures. Let members of your wedding party know when photographs will be taken, and ask them to be on time and to work with the photographer.

In This Chapter

- ◆ What to know when selecting your invitations
- ◆ Deciding on the wording
- ◆ What's included in an invitation
- ◆ Personalize it with save-the-date cards, wedding newsletters, and more
- ◆ Designing a wedding program

Chapter 12

Extra! Extra! Read All About It!

Isn't it exciting when you open your mailbox and find a wedding invitation? You can usually tell it's for a wedding immediately—the envelope is a different size and shape than other envelopes in the pile of mail, the quality paper is usually notably nicer, and sometimes it's even a different color than that of the same old white envelopes you see in there every day.

And stand out it should—the invitation is the first hint your guests will get of what your wedding will be like. In this chapter, I'll tell you all about invitations, a "save-the-date" card, wedding newsletters, welcome letters, and creating your unique wedding program.

Selecting Your Invitations

When it comes to buying your invitations, rule number 1 is: Never pay full retail price for invitations. There is so much competition out there for your invitation order that you should never have to pay full price. You can always get something at a discount.

You can find selections for your wedding invitations at any of the following places:

- Stationery stores
- Through a bridal consultant
- Party stores
- Card/gift stores
- Bridal or tux shops
- Websites

Your wedding invitation sets the tone for the wedding and the reception to follow. It also gives the guests the first glimpse of the type and formality of your wedding. Whether it's an engraved, ivory-colored, formal invitation, or a pair of kissing frogs or two toothbrushes nestled side by side (there really are such items), your invitation tells your guests what they can expect in terms of the mood of the big event.

Nuptial Notes

A typical wedding invitation "packet" might include the **invitation** itself, **reception card invitation, response card** and **return envelope** (so you know who can attend), an **inner envelope** containing all the these cards, and an **outer mailing envelope.**

You have a few things to consider when choosing your invitations—whether you want them engraved, what type of paper you like, and what size and shape you want the invitation to be. It's best that you familiarize yourself with some of the terminology of printing invitations before you go shopping. Here's a primer to give you a head start. (Be sure to turn to the "Invitations Worksheet" in Appendix B for more help with invitations.)

Putting Your Stamp on It

Engraved invitations involve a process in which the paper is stamped with a mold (or copper plate), leaving an indentation in the paper. The ink is added to fill in the indentation, and then the paper is pressed onto the plate. If you look on the back of an engraved invitation, you will see indentations. The copper plate is sent back to you as a keepsake.

Just keep in mind that it takes six to eight weeks after ordering to receive engraved invitations. Also be prepared for sticker shock—engraved invitations are much more expensive

than other printed types. Engraved invitations are considered to be the most formal.

Mr. and Mrs. Robert Smith
request the honour of your presence
at the marriage of their daughter
Deborah Ann
to
Paul Allen Wright
on Sunday, the fourth of May
Two thousand and three
at eleven o'clock in the morning
St. Mark's Church
123 Morris
Nashville, Tennessee

A sheer overlay and ribbon decorate this formal invitation, issued by the bride's parents.

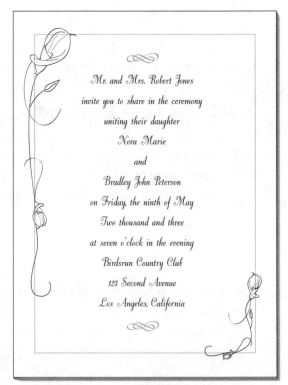

Mr. and Mrs. Robert Jones
invite you to share in the ceremony
uniting their daughter
Nora Marie
and
Bradley John Peterson
on Friday, the ninth of May
Two thousand and three
at seven o'clock in the evening
Birdsrun Country Club
123 Second Avenue
Los Angeles, California

Raised floral accents make this formal invitation stand out.

An informal invitation issued by the couple.

Rise to the Occasion

Thermography is a popular choice today. This is the opposite of engraving. In this process, the words are written out in glue, and the ink color is sprinkled over the glue. Then it's heated, so the lettering is raised. If you run your fingers over the invitation, you can feel the lettering. Thermography is much less expensive than engraving and still has an elegant look.

The Paper Chase

Once you decide which type of printing you want, you'll need to select the paper. The actual invitation paper is the only item in which "what you see is what you get." It cannot be changed to another color or have the pink flowers on it made lavendar (unless that is stated in the ordering process). Everything else that goes with the invitation is your choice. You can select:

◆ The color of ink(s)—companies are now starting to offer two-color inks on the same paper

◆ The format—the couple's names can be enlarged or set in a different font so that part stands out

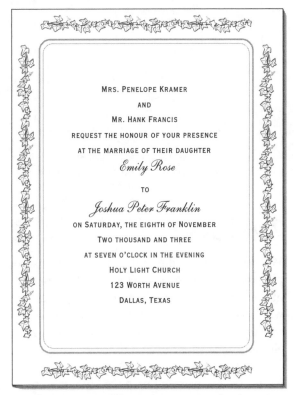

Notice the two different fonts used in this formal invitation, issued by the bride's divorced parents.

- Envelope lining
- And of course, your own wording

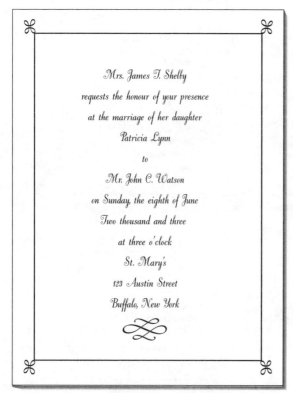

Mrs. James T. Shelby

requests the honour of your presence

at the marriage of her daughter

Patricia Lynn

to

Mr. John C. Watson

on Sunday, the eighth of June

Two thousand and three

at three o'clock

St. Mary's

123 Austin Street

Buffalo, New York

This formal invitation issued by the bride's widowed mother is elegantly simple.

Pure Poetry

Wording your wedding invitation can be a simple task, or it can be very complicated. Located in the front of most invitation books (from which you will select your invitations) are wording suggestions for almost every known circumstance. You can find the traditional, formal wedding invitation issued by the bride's parents to the wording used when Uncle Fred is sending the invitations for his niece's wedding. From those samples and from the samples you see in this chapter, you should have the help you need to make the wording for your wedding invitation an easy task. Most times, salespeople are standing by to help with details that are complex or unusual.

Wedding Woes _____

Never—I repeat, *never*—include a list of the stores where you're registered with your wedding invitation. You can spread the word through family and friends, but it should not go out with the invitation. That information can be included in shower invitations.

Those Little Extras

A formal wedding invitation when the reception is in a different location wouldn't be complete without additional little cards and stamped envelopes. Those include the following:

- Reception invitation card
- Response card and self-addressed, stamped envelope
- Map with written directions
- Within the ribbon card (for very formal weddings)

Let's take a closer look at each of these.

Now, Let's Party!

Sometimes, guests are invited only to the ceremony and not the reception. Usually, however, guests are invited to both. Most formal invitations include a reception card enclosure. Because the wedding invitation focuses on the ceremony, guests often need to be instructed as to where the reception is being held. That's where reception cards come in handy. Reception cards are enclosed with the invitation that invite the guest to the wedding reception, stating where it is and perhaps what kind of reception it is. For example, if you're having an hors-d'oeuvres-and-cocktail reception, your card may read, "Please join us following the ceremony at the country club for hors d'oeuvres and cocktails."

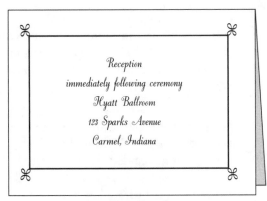

Reception
immediately following ceremony
Hyatt Ballroom
123 Sparks Avenue
Carmel, Indiana

Reception card.

RSVP

RSVP is an acronym for the French phrase *répondez s'il vous plaît* and means, simply, "please respond." When you see it written on an invitation, it means that you are to call the host or return a response card by the specified date to indicate whether you can attend the function. The response card and matching self-addressed envelope is always stamped.

Please respond on or before
March 15, 2003

M_____

Number of persons _____

Response card.

One formal way to word a response card might be:

> *The favour of a reply is requested by April 1, 2004.*
> *Name* _____
> _____ *will attend* _____ *will not attend*
> _____ *number attending*

A less formal response card could read:

> *Come join us in the celebration. Please respond by April 1, 2004.*
> *Name* _____
> _____ *will attend*   _____ *will not attend*
> _____ *number attending*

Wedding Woes

Be careful about the wording on your invitation if your wedding falls around a mealtime. For clarity, list on the reception card what type of reception this will be: "Hors D'oeuvres Reception" or "Dinner Reception." That way, guests know what type of food service to expect.

Map It Out

Map and direction cards are common in the wedding packet today because so many of your guests could be from out of town. The least-expensive way to do these cards is to print out one sheet on your handy PC and then make copies on nice paper.

Within-the-Ribbon Cards

Within-the-ribbon cards are enclosed with the invitation that give guests special seating "within-the-ribbon" or in a reserved spot. Within-the-ribbon cards are usually used for very large and formal weddings where many guests are expected and seating special family members is a must.

Order! Order!

You should order your invitations at least four months before the wedding, except for engraved invitations, which take much longer to produce (see the preceding section). That will give you one month for the order to be delivered (plenty of time), six weeks for you or the calligrapher to address them, and then you should get them in the mail five to six weeks before the wedding. Always allow more time than you think it will take. At holiday times or other busy times of the year, you may need to order your invitations even earlier. Just be sure that everything is solidly booked with the ceremony site and the reception facility before you place your order.

Teddy's Tips

Always order 25 more invitations and enclosures than you think you will need. It's much cheaper to order the extra 25 than to have to order more later.

Once you're ready to send them out, take the finished invitation to the post office and have it weighed to determine the correct postage for the weight *and* size of your invitation. You don't want all your invitations to come back stamped in red, "Return for postage." It's not a pretty sight!

Printed Accessories

Invitation companies offer all sorts of printed accessories to complement your wedding invitations, such as:

- **At-home cards.** An at-home card was used more in the early part of the twentieth century when couples took extended honeymoons and guests would be told

that "After January 8, Mr. and Mrs. Smith will be at home," meaning you could visit after January 8. Today, this information may appear on the back of the wedding program.

- **Scrolls.** These are small pieces of paper, usually a fine paper, with a verse or message from the couple printed on them. Scrolls can be handed out at the ceremony or saved and used as a favor at the reception. Tied with a lovely ribbon to match the wedding colors it makes a nice favor for guests.

- **Place cards.** Place cards are another little extra that can make your wedding more unique. Actually, place cards are used two different ways. The true place card is an individual card with the guest's name written on it and then placed at that guest's place setting at the table.

Ben and Elizabeth

August 10, 2003

Susan Jones

Place card.

- **Table assignment cards.** Table assignment cards are usually used at large formal weddings where all the guests have been assigned a table. The card can be a single card or enclosed in an envelope. It either stands or lies on a table outside of the banquet room and contains the name of the guest and his or her table number.

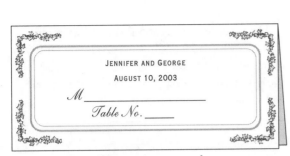

Table assignment card.

Other extras you may wish to include with the invitation include the following:

- Informal note cards and envelopes for general notes or as thank you notes
- Thank you cards specifically printed with the words "Thank You" on them
- Napkins with your names and wedding date or monogram printed on them to be used at the bar or cake tables
- Paper guest towels for the bathroom
- Personalized matches (as favors)
- Mini note pads (as favors)

Teddy's Tips

One suggestion I make to couples when ordering their napkins is to not print the wedding date on them. If they're not dated, you can use the extras in your new home when entertaining.

Personalize It!

By now you've covered the biggies, and the dollars are starting to add up. You still want your wedding to have a uniqueness, but how can you make your wedding unique when you're on a tight budget? Read on for several inexpensive ways you can incorporate paper accents to help make your wedding unique.

A printed menu card is a nice touch. *(Photo by Garbo Productions)*

Ladies and Gentlemen, Mark Your Calendars!

You might try a "save-the-date" card or letter to let guests know of the upcoming event. This can be as simple as a postcard with the couple's names, wedding date, and place. You can also do it in the form of a short letter. Its main purpose is to announce the wedding date. Put simply, it might say:

We've finally set the date, so please put it on your calendars. We want you to be able to share this wonderful weekend with us.

Saturday, May 20, 2005—New York, NY

Sally Winters and Tom Fox—you can visit our website at www.loveRus.net.

Some suggestions for ideas:

- One first grade teacher sent out a "chalk board" drawing on black paper with "stick figure" bride and groom which read "Dum, dum, de dum" on the front
- Valentine's cards to family and close friends announcing the date

- Sports theme
- "Newspaper headline" theme—"Ann and Jim announce big merger"

Start Spreadin' the News

Another relative of the "save-the-date" card is the wedding newsletter. Now this is where you can create your own flavor and entice the guest's curiosity. You might send one out early in the planning process to let guests know some of the activities you have lined up and to set a tentative agenda for the weekend. You might wait and send it only to the wedding party and close family and friends, especially those who will be coming from a distance. You can also do two separate newsletters: one to guests in general and one to the wedding party members and family.

Here are some details you might want to include in your newsletter:

- The weekend agenda
- Activities in the area for guests to do with free time
- Dress for the rehearsal dinner and other functions
- Directions to the hotel, ceremony, and reception sites
- Hotel check-in time
- Transportation options and phone numbers
- Information on local weather
- A contact phone number in case of emergencies
- Any other important information you need to let your guests know (such as any areas of construction, time zone differences)

For the newsletter to just the wedding party, include all these points but add the brief introduction of your wedding party (if they don't know each other). Also in this letter, make sure you tell when the rehearsal is and that you need everyone to be there on time.

Here's an example of a recent newsletter that went to the wedding party, all the family members, and a few close friends. The rest of the guests received a shorter version in their welcome baskets.

We've started the countdown: We have less than four weeks before the big day. We are so excited you will be with us. We thought we'd give you some updates on activities and times and, of course, directions. April in Iowa can be quite pleasant. You might need a light jacket for evening, but otherwise, you should be fine. No winter coats unless you hear we got hit with a blizzard!

Thursday, April 10: Early check-in at Hyatt

Meet in the Grill (lower level of hotel) for informal get-together at 8 P.M. Casual dress.

Friday, April 11: (the day before!)

Bridesmaids luncheon at 12:30 P.M., third floor of Hyatt, Room D. Dresses/pantsuits.

Guys to play golf at 11:30 A.M.—see John Smith for sign-up sheet, Room 1215.

Shopping in mall attached to hotel via walkway.

Historical museum across from the hotel; very interesting if you're a history buff.

Rehearsal at Century Church, 1256 N. Meridian Street. (for wedding party, readers, immediate family); meet in lobby at 5:30 P.M. for transportation. Rehearsal is at 6 P.M.

Rehearsal dinner: Canopy Club at 7:30 P.M.; 3500 N. Meridian Street—see map. Dressy attire. Those attending this event should have received an invitation from John's parents.

Saturday, April 12: The day!!

Ladies in wedding party meet in Suite 1245 for hair and makeup at 9:30 A.M. Breakfast breads, juice, and coffee served. Come with clean hair, clean face, and a smile.

Men in wedding party meet in Suite 1247 at 12 P.M. sharp for pictures. Please be on time.

Leave for church (all) at 2 P.M. Limos will pick us up outside the lobby entrance.

2:30 P.M. Begin pictures at church

4 P.M. Pictures finished (if we're on time)

Ushers need to be ready to greet guests

4:30 P.M. Here comes the bride …

Following the ceremony, we will be releasing the rows and greeting guests at each pew. When we finish, we will make our grand exit to the limo and meet you at the reception.

Let the party begin!

Sunday, April 13

12 P.M. Champagne brunch in the Porch Room. Everyone is invited, and we hope you come by and say hi.

The hotel has extended our guests' check-out time until 3 P.M.

If you have any questions or concerns—anything that we can do to help make your time with us go smoother—please call our bridal consultant, Teddy Lenderman. She is staying at the Hyatt also, in Room 1009. Please call her for any assistance you may need.

Have a safe trip home, and thank you again for sharing this weekend with us.

Love,
Susie and John

Teddy's Tips

I have had my name added to the wedding newsletter several times, and it does take pressure off the couple or the parents. One groom even put the information on his rehearsal dinner invitations because he didn't want his bride or himself to have to deal with questions.

One bride and groom even used the following newsletter to send to the men in the wedding party about getting their measurements for the tuxedos. It was titled "How Do You Measure Up?" which I thought was quite clever and yet got the point across.

BRIDAL UPDATE

Susie and Todd—October 2, 2005

To all Groomsmen, Ushers, Father of the Bride, and Father of the Groom:

How Do You Measure Up?

We are in need of your tuxedo measurements as soon as possible. The tuxedo rental company requested that you have your measurements taken by another tux shop and then phone or fax them in. They have found that measurements from tailors don't always provide a proper fit. And, of course, "looking good is half the battle!" Right?

Please phone or fax your measurements to:

Smith's Tuxedo Shop
123 Main Street
Toledo, OH 12345
123-555-1234
123-555-5678 (fax)

Mention the Miller/Stewart wedding.

Your tux can be picked up any time on Friday. The shop requests that you allow 15 to 20 minutes to try on the tux prior to leaving the shop.

We can't wait to see all of you. Please call with questions: 123-555-7896.

Love,
"The Bride" Susie

When the Masses Arrive

When guests check into the hotel, have a scaled-down copy of the weekend activities for everyone. List the following:

- Activities
- Attire for the occasion
- Time and place
- Directions
- Shuttle information
- Area activities
- City map
- A personal note from you, the couple

Just Follow Along, Please

Wedding programs make a nice addition to your wedding service. They can be simple or elaborate. The whole purpose of a wedding program is to enable the guests to participate in the ceremony by listing the order of the service and identifying the members of the wedding party. It's something like a playbill at the theater.

The silver bells that accompany these programs will be used to ring in the new couple. *(Photo by Jeff Hawkins Photography)*

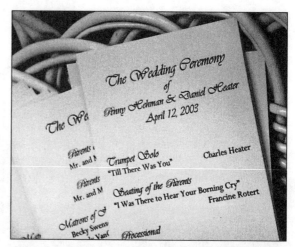

Notice the trumpet solo listed on this program. The groom's father played that piece right before the processional. It was very moving. *(Photo by Morris Fine Art Photography)*

Other points you might add to your program include the following:

- The relationship of the wedding party member to the bride or groom
- Interesting information about the family ("John and Susie are being married today on Susie's parents thirtieth wedding anniversary")
- A note of thanks and appreciation to family
- Your new address
- Parts of the service that some guests may not understand
- Wedding trivia
- Showing respect for a departed loved one ("The candle on the altar is in memory of John's father")
- Names of other participants in the wedding ceremony—readers, greeters, soloists, musicians, guest book attendant

Keep It Simple ... or Go to Extremes!

Programs can be as simple as a single sheet of colored paper printed on a computer and duplicated. Roll it up and tie it with a coordinating ribbon, and you have a simple, attractive, and inexpensive presentation. For an elaborate look, have your programs printed on several sheets of paper covered with a heavy outer paper, emboss or engrave monograms on the front, and then tie the paper with coordinating ribbons.

These programs have the couple's last initial embossed on the front—a classy touch. *(Photo by Colter Photography)*

This basket of programs features the couple's monogram on the front. They also continued the monogram theme with their napkins. *(Photo by Colter Photography)*

One of the most elaborate wedding programs is a *missal*. This includes, verbatim, everything the priest, rabbi, or officiant says. This type of program is especially nice when the majority of your guests are not of your faith. This type of program is more costly simply because of its length, but you still can produce it economically.

Wedding programs are used more today than in the past. They are just another way of treating your guests with a little extra care and making them feel right at home. Besides that, having a wedding program gives your guests something to read while they're waiting for the wedding to start.

The Least You Need to Know

◆ Always ask about getting a discount on invitations; you should never pay full price. Always order 25 more invitations than you think you will need.

◆ Consider sending a "save-the-date" card if your guests are scattered across the country and you think an advance notice would help.

◆ Use newsletters to keep your guests, wedding party, and family members informed about the wedding plans.

◆ Think about incorporating a wedding program into your ceremony.

In This Chapter

- ◆ Show you care with favors
- ◆ Lots of ideas for favors, from simple to sensational
- ◆ Choosing gifts for your attendants
- ◆ How to create a unique "welcome basket"

Do Yourself a Favor

In this chapter, I will talk about the use of favors at your wedding. I'll offer some advice on ideas to use for favors and how to create your own ideas. I'll also talk about what to give your wedding party members.

I'll also share some wonderful ways to incorporate welcome baskets (even on a tight budget) into your wedding package. Read on and let your imagination run wild.

Favoring Your Friends

Favors—those little gifts you give your guests as a thank-you for attending your wedding—are a big trend now. You can select expensive and elaborate favors or very inexpensive and simple favors. The idea is not to dazzle your guests with great favors, but to make them feel special and appreciated and to add a special touch to your wedding. For help in planning favors, use the "Favors Worksheet" in Appendix B.

Look over the following ideas for favors and let your imagination soar. Some are more expensive than others, but the bottom line of making your guests feel special is what counts. Some of the items listed call for personalization or imprinting names and dates, which can be done either by the company where the products are purchased or by your local printer. If the item is something that can't be imprinted, try having a small card printed with the information you want and then tie it to the item. The Internet is a great place to find favors and have them printed to make them more personal.

- Candy—in either an elegant box tied with ribbon or a cloth bag tied with ribbon or cording
- Candy bar imprinted with "Thank you for sharing our day"
- Individual small candles at each place setting
- Golf tees or golf balls imprinted with the couple's names
- A single silk or fresh flower, tied with a ribbon, at each female place setting
- A bottle of bubbles to blow as the bride and groom dance their first dance

- A small tulle bag or paper cone filled with rose petals or potpourri

A basket of paper cones filled with rose petals will be used later to shower the bride and groom. *(Photo by Colter Photography)*

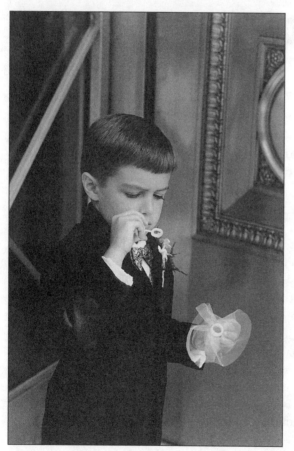

This young man prepares to shower the bride and groom with bubbles. He's certainly concentrating on his task! *(Photo by Wyant Photography)*

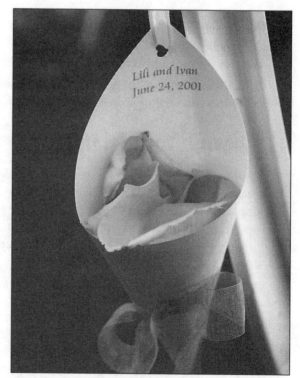

These paper cones were used first to decorate the pews during the ceremony, then removed so the petals can be tossed at the couple. *(Photo by Craig Larsen Photography)*

- A scroll paper printed with your favorite verse or poem

- Water bottles imprinted with the couple's names

- A huge glass jar filled with individually wrapped cookies and a note that reads "Sweet Dreams" (guests take a cookie as they leave the reception)

- A CD of the couple's favorite songs with their picture on the jacket covers (these can be wrapped in the wedding colors to add to the table décor)

- Individual half-splits of wine or champagne with the couple's picture on the bottle

These large jars of brightly decorated cookies were a huge success as guests left the reception. *(Photo by Colter Photography)*

Wine charms are a new idea in favors. The center charm is of a tractor, which is part of the family's farming heritage. Nice touch! *(Photo by Morris Fine Art Photography)*

- A printed card at each place letting guests know that a donation to a favorite charity was made in their honor

Wedding cake–shape cookies make clever favors. *(Photo by Craig Larsen Photography)*

One of my favorite ideas for a favor is to give to a charity in memory of family members. *(Photo by Colter Photography)*

- Sun block wrapped in bright paper for summer weddings
- Beach balls imprinted with the couple's names
- Candy corn in small natural baskets for autumn weddings
- Key chains imprinted with the couple's names
- Music boxes
- Gourmet jelly beans or mixed nuts in a decorative jar or canister
- Beer mugs or wine glasses etched with the couple's names
- Flower bulbs wrapped in spring shades of tulle
- Pears wrapped together with a small sign "The Perfect Pair"

- Packets of flower seeds imprinted with the couple's names
- Blank journals
- Imprinted note pads or matchbooks
- Tennis balls, visors, or other sports items imprinted with the couple's names
- Small picture frames

This handsome place setting includes a small picture frame for the guest's favor. *(Photo by Front Room Photography)*

The perfect "pair"! *(Photo by Colter Photography)*

Wedding Woes

Make sure you have plenty of favors to go around. Nothing would be worse than having more guests than favors and having to decide who gets one and who doesn't.

◆ Holiday ornaments or small Christmas wreaths for a December wedding

For a holiday wedding, this couple chose an ornament guests could take home and hang on their own trees. *(Photo by Colter Photography)*

Favors can make a place setting look extra-special. *(Photo by Garbo Productions)*

Teddy's Tips

Cluster your favors to make the table centerpiece. For example, small individual pots with flowers or plants arranged in a circle in the center of the table make a lovely focal point. You can even drape some tulle around the base of the circle or tie some ribbons around the pots. As guests leave, ask that they each take a pot with them.

◆ Small wicker baskets (check out some of the wholesale houses), with an arrangement of silk flowers, assorted candies, or decorative soaps tucked inside

Another favor idea: brass bells. These can be given out as guests leave the ceremony or placed on tables at the reception. What a wonderful way to greet the couple. *(Photo by Monique Feil Photography)*

This small brass bell tied with a coordinating ribbon adds a special touch to the napkin. *(Photo by Craig Larsen Photography)*

A crystal bell with the couple's names and wedding date on the ribbon is another nice idea. *(Photo by Colter Photography)*

◆ Heart-shape items or items that feature hearts on them, such as magnets, mugs, or candies (ideal for a Valentine's Day wedding)

◆ Small sombreros or piñatas for a Mexican-themed wedding, or floral leis for a Hawaiian-themed wedding

This elegant table setting is adorned with several favors. Notice the picture frame as a place card and the candy wrapped in clear paper on the plate. *(Photo by Front Room Photography)*

Wedding Woes

When ordering candy through the mail, be sure you know when it will be delivered so that you can arrange for someone to be at home to receive it. What an ugly mess it would be to find 300 chocolate bars melted all over your front porch because no one was there to accept the package. Not a pretty sight!

One couple decided to use this soap because the groom's last name is Leone. *(Photo by Colter Photography)*

These young men are taking full advantage of the disposable cameras included as favors. *(Photo by Colter Photography)*

Attending to Your Attendants

The gifts you choose to give to your attendants (a nice way of saying, "Thanks for putting up with my irrational behavior for the past six months") need to be custom-designed for your wedding party. I'm not saying go out and have something custom-designed for each and every member of your wedding party. I just mean that you should try to make the gift truly special.

Think about who they are and what they like. Nothing is carved in stone that says you must buy every bridesmaid and every groomsman the same thing. I know that's usually easier, but with a little planning, you can come up with some unique gift ideas for these special friends.

Have fun selecting these gifts. Here are some ideas:

- For the sports nut, a new racquet or membership to a health club
- For the traveler, an overnight bag or travel alarm clock
- For the new homeowner, wind chimes, a brass door knocker, or a stained-glass sun catcher
- Books
- A gift certificate to a favorite restaurant or store
- A figurine, like a Hummel or Precious Moments, or other collectible
- Beer steins
- Champagne or wine glasses
- Swiss army knives
- Shot glasses etched with the couple's monogram

Some other wedding party gift ideas include the following:

For men:

- Cuff links
- Monogrammed wallet
- Engraved money clip
- Travel kit
- Engraved calculator
- Basketball
- Football

For women:

- Jewelry box
- Basket with soaps or perfumes
- Charm bracelet
- Bud vase
- Music box
- Lingerie
- Book with personalized message
- Gift certificate for facial or massage

For children:

- Mug etched with name
- Charm bracelet
- Games (checkers, chess, backgammon)
- Stereo headset
- Classic book such as *Tom Sawyer* by Mark Twain
- Videotape of favorite movie
- T-shirt ("I was a ring bearer in Matt and Cathy's wedding")
- Stuffed animal (for the young child)

For either sex:

- Anything monogrammed in crystal or pewter
- Silver picture frame
- Personalized stationery
- Candle holder
- Pen and pencil set
- Bar set
- Crystal ice bucket

Welcome One and All!

With our society so scattered and family and friends all over the world, weddings have become more than just a way to spend a couple of hours on a Saturday afternoon. With that in mind, the idea of the welcome basket was born. Since guests come from all over, it's nice to offer them some goodies when they check into the hotel.

Welcome baskets or packages can come in all sizes and shapes. Even the tightest budget can accommodate a welcome basket for a few family members. The ideas for a welcome basket are endless and can only be limited by your budget or imagination. A lot of "baskets" are really fancy bags (you know, the colorful kind you can find in craft stores). You can fill them with anything you want. Some necessary items should include:

- A note from the couple
- An itinerary of the weekend
- A map showing the ceremony and reception sites
- Emergency phone numbers
- A small gift item, usually something to eat
- Something regional, like coffee if your wedding is in the northwest, cheese and crackers if the wedding is in Wisconsin, or Hershey kisses if the wedding is in Hershey, Pennsylvania
- Bottled water
- Wine or sparkling grape juice

Welcome baskets or bags, however simple or elaborate, are just a delightful way to say, "Glad you're here—have a great weekend."

The Least You Need to Know

◆ Say thank you to your guests for helping make your day so special by presenting them with favors.

◆ Favors don't have to be expensive; something as simple as Hershey kisses wrapped in pretty fabric and tied with a ribbon can be a nice touch.

◆ Try to choose gifts for your attendants that have some special or personal meaning. If possible, have the gifts personalized.

◆ If your budget will allow, try to have a welcome basket waiting at the hotel for those out-of-town guests.

In This Chapter

- ◆ Stretching your wedding dollars
- ◆ Cost-cutting ideas for saving on flowers, music, photography, and more
- ◆ Trimming reception costs
- ◆ The importance of understanding contracts and agreements

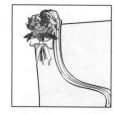

Chapter 14

Making the Most of Your Dollars

I've talked about budgets (I know—still not your favorite subject), and I've discussed questions to ask vendors to make sure you're getting what you pay for. Let's get some serious work done in this chapter and trim up that budget (in ways no one will recognize) and talk a little about contracts and agreements (I know, I know, more of that boring stuff, but nonetheless, *very* important). Keep in mind the wise wedding consumer's thoughts. A wedding is a product you are purchasing (now don't take me literally on that—but you do purchase flowers, invitations, church rental—you know what I mean). So you need to focus on where you are spending your dollars.

"Think before you spend" is a wise statement to keep in mind as you plan your wedding. There are lots of ways to cut costs and still have the wedding of your dreams!

Prioritizing Your Pennies

So far, I've suggested some questions for you to ask the vendors you're considering using. I've told you what to expect from these vendors, and you've started spending some of those precious wedding budget dollars. Before you blink and all those dollars have disappeared, let's look at ways you can trim some costs from your wedding bill.

Smart wedding shopping techniques begin with having patience and not being an impulsive buyer. Time is your friend when you're in the wedding market. As you shop with the various vendors, give yourself the time you need to make sure you're getting the best product for the best price. A lot depends on the importance you place on each. If that certain photographer is very important to you, figure out a way to incorporate his fee into your plans.

One couple on a limited budget decided they wanted their money to go toward the reception. Both sets of parents were divorced and remarried and not on the best of terms. So they decided one way to cut costs, keep tensions in check, and still have the reception they wanted was to have a small, private ceremony for only immediate family. We found a darling chapel on a university campus, which held about 40 guests. The chapel didn't cost anything since they were alumni of the university. The florist used some floral pieces that were later transferred to the reception site. They chose not to use programs, again because of the small guest list. Yet the ceremony was still very meaningful and lovely. The reception was wonderful, just what they had envisioned. Again, you need to decide what is best for you and go with your dreams, not the dreams of someone else.

Teddy's Tips

Don't ever be afraid to ask if an item can be discounted or rented. What more can someone say than "No"? Many times, you will find yourself pleasantly surprised by the answer. Just because you've never heard of doing it this way doesn't mean that it can't be done. Ask if the florist has suggestions on how something can be done less expensively.

The following sections give you some ideas of specific ways you can cut wedding expenses and stretch your wedding dollars.

Finding Ways to Cut Your Floral Bill

There are several ways to cut costs in the floral department:

- Check with the church to see if another wedding is scheduled on the same day as yours. If so, ask the other couple about sharing the expense for ceremony site flowers.

- At the ceremony, have the pew markers designed to double as centerpieces at the reception. This takes some coordination between the florist and reception facility, but I've had several brides use this cost-cutting technique.

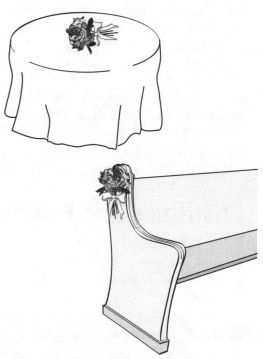

One of my favorite cost-saving tips is to have the pew pieces double as your reception pieces.

You can save money by using the same flowers for the ceremony and the reception. This bouquet is being used to decorate the head table. *(Photo by Colter Photography)*

This simple smaller bridal bouquet features fewer flowers and lots of ribbon and greenery. It's elegant but not overdone. *(Photo by Colter Photography)*

◆ If you're being married in the spring or summer, you can eliminate the cost of a large, expensive bridal bouquet by gathering wildflowers the morning of your wedding and tying them with a lovely ribbon to coordinate with your colors.

◆ If you live in a large metropolitan area, check to see if there is a local floral design school. Many times, students at these trade schools will gladly produce your wedding flowers for the cost of materials so that they can gain the experience and a letter of recommendation.

◆ Use balloons instead of flowers or greenery to cover blemishes on the walls (exposed pipes, marks on the walls). The balloons are cheaper, will cover more, add a festive party look, and can be assembled the morning of the wedding.

◆ Select flowers grown locally.

◆ Use only flowers in season.

◆ Instead of carrying a bouquet of roses, you can carry a single rose or a small floral arrangement on a family Bible or prayer book.

◆ Use lots of greenery (ferns, plants, palms) mixed with votive candles for a soft, lush, less expensive way to add some décor to the church.

◆ Check with your florist or a party rental store about the possibility of renting centerpieces. One couple on a tight budget had 20 tables to decorate for the reception. They found a florist whose daughter had recently married, and he rented his daughter's silk arrangements to them. The arrangements were lovely, and no one was the wiser.

◆ Place small vases on the head table and place the bridesmaids' bouquets in them to add color to the table.

A simple way to use bridesmaids' bouquets at the reception is to lay them around the base of the cake table. It looks pretty and is a great way to stretch your floral dollars.

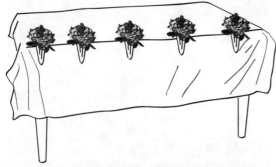

Another way to use bridesmaids' bouquets: Clip them to the head table using sturdy plastic holders that clamp onto the table. Space them out according to the number of bridesmaids' bouquets you have, and when the girls arrive at the reception, have someone gather the bouquets and place them in the holders.

Dressing for Less

If you are a very talented sewer or have access to a good seamstress, make your gown and veil. You can save some big bucks here. Some other ideas for trimming your budget in this area include:

- Check out the bridal discount stores, but be very careful! If you can buy a dress off the rack at one of these stores, you probably will come away with a bargain. If the store must order a gown for you, be sure that you understand the terms completely. With many stores of this type, the gown that arrives in the box is what you take home—rips, tears, stains, and all (and this happens, even with new gowns). The store usually will not send it back if it's damaged—it's yours! Just be sure you know what you're agreeing to.

- Look for a ready-to-wear tea-length gown that requires very little alteration.

- Look for sales at the bridal shops. You can often find truly lovely gowns on the sale rack for one-third to one-half off the original price.

Wedding Woes

All bridal discount stores are not created equal. Try to buy off the rack, because ordering from these establishments can be risky. Before you put down a deposit, make sure you understand what you're buying and what the store will do about flaws or mistakes.

- Consider wearing your mother's or even your grandmother's gown (see Chapter 10). Many times, these gowns from days gone by are actually back in style or will blend with the theme of your wedding. My sister, Kim, wanted to wear our mother's gown for her garden wedding. (Mother had also had a garden wedding.) The seamstress had to take a tuck here and there, but otherwise, it was perfect for Kim. Instead of wearing a veil as our mother had, Kim wore a garden hat with fresh flowers and veiling. My dad said there was a huge lump in his throat as he walked Kim down the aisle and thought about his bride of 30 years.

  A friend of mine used a Victorian theme for her wedding and wore her grandmother's gown. She even wore the high-buttoned shoes to match. Even if you can't physically get into the gown, see what can be done to remake it. You might be surprised at what a good seamstress can accomplish.

- Don't overlook resale shops. These stores are springing up all over the place in the Midwest. Many gowns that have been worn only once ("gently worn") find their way to these shops. You can pick up a lovely gown for a fraction of its original cost.

- Order your bridesmaids' dresses from national catalogs. One bride ordered all seven of her bridesmaids' gowns from a catalog and saved half of what she would have paid in a shop.

◆ Rent your gown and your bridesmaids' dresses. This is a great idea when you don't have a lot of planning time for your wedding. Some bridal shops will rent gowns. Check before you visit.

◆ Borrow shoes from a friend, or buy inexpensive ballet slippers. I wore white slippers that cost only $6.95 and no one knew the difference.

> **Teddy's Tips**
>
> If you're a craftsy person, why not buy a plain pair of slippers and decorate them yourself? Use sequins, pearls, buttons, or whatever you like to design a unique pair of slippers at a fraction of the

◆ With tuxedos, always look for package deals, such as, "Rent five, get the groom's tux free." (See Chapter 10 for more on outfitting the groom and groomsmen.)

◆ Try to rent the tuxedos from stores that have a local warehouse. Then if there are problems, you stand a much better chance at getting the problem resolved.

By taking some time to think carefully about what is important to you and your groom, you can prioritize those items where you want to spend the bucks. And as I've shown already, there are many ways to trim dollars from your expense sheet to make the best use of your wedding bucks!

Regulating Your Reception Expenses

Here are some tips to help trim those reception costs:

◆ Plan your reception for some other time than mealtime. You can save quite a bit of money by having a morning or early afternoon wedding and reception. Because the wedding doesn't fall within a mealtime (that is, 6 P.M.), you can get away with serving simple hors d'oeuvres or cake and punch.

◆ Watch for sales on liquor or paper goods. Ask about discounts when buying by the case.

◆ Use paper products instead of renting crystal or china.

◆ Use carafes of wine on the tables rather than bottles. Open wine bottles can be wasted, especially if the guests at a table do not drink alcohol.

◆ Rent a champagne fountain instead of using champagne bottles on the tables, or have individual glasses of champagne served to guests.

◆ Instead of offering an open bar, limit your guests' choices to only wine and/or beer, or serve a champagne punch instead of other liquor (see Chapter 8 for more about your options when serving liquor).

◆ Use only house brands of liquor. Most of your guests will not notice, and the cost difference between house brands and premiums is tremendous.

◆ Check local vocational schools for students or recent graduates in food service or decorating who would be willing to produce the food or decorations for your reception in exchange for the experience and the exposure. Many times, those just starting out will offer their services at a discount for a reference. You gotta start somewhere!

◆ Cut down the size of your guest list. Remember, the cost of the reception equals about 40 to 45 percent of your total budget. If you can't feed a crowd of 500 a sit-down dinner, try to cut that number to what you can handle. You can even do two receptions. Immediately following the service, have the cake and punch at the church social hall for the larger crowd. Then, later that day, offer your close friends and family the dinner-and-dancing reception.

◆ If you're having a do-it-yourself reception, accept all the offers you can from family and friends who volunteer to bring in items. Although this is risky because someone might not follow through on a promise (yes, it does happen), it can save you many dollars.

◆ Borrow as many items as you can. Don't rent or go out and buy a brand-new punch bowl, cake servers, or toasting glasses. Some friend or family member who has married recently might have these items. Ask to borrow them.

Don't buy a cake topper—use your toss bouquet instead!

◆ If you need extra help with serving, check with a local sorority or fraternity. Many times, for a donation to their philanthropy project, these groups will send several people to help serve your reception.

Managing Your Music Dollars

Music can add some large expenses to your wedding, but if you do your homework, there are a couple tricks you can use:

◆ Check into using local high school or college student musicians instead of paying more for experienced musicians. The students are often thrilled with the extra money and the added experience. Be sure to listen to them perform so you know what you are hiring. Like any other musical vendor, make sure they understand what they are expected to wear and how long you need them to play.

◆ Ask a reliable friend who has some experience and understanding of what makes a good DJ to play some CDs for you at the reception. He'll need a good sound system.

◆ Hire the musicians for a minimum amount of time.

Economizing on Those Extras

As I mentioned earlier, borrow any items you can. Don't buy a ring bearer's pillow, cake servers, or toasting glasses. Unless you get these items as gifts, there is little reason to spend extra money on something you'll use only once.

Here are a few more simple ways to trim costs:

◆ Don't have a date stamped on your wedding napkins. That way, you can use the extras in your new home after the wedding.

◆ Have the ring pillow made, or make it yourself. It's fairly simple and will mean even more to you.

◆ Make your favors and/or your attendants gifts (see Chapter 13).

◆ Buy things as you have the cash for them. For example, buy stamps for the invitations a couple of packs at a time.

◆ Get the families involved. You'd be surprised what talents are out there.

Bouquet Toss

One bride asked her grandmother to make some of the extras for her wedding. The grandmother felt so much more a part of the planning. She made the ring bearer's pillow, the bride's two garters (one to throw, one to keep), crocheted hankies for each bridesmaid to carry, and a table cover for the cake table with the couple's initials embroidered on it. She also crocheted pew bows for the ceremony. It meant so much to the bride that her grandmother was part of the wedding preparations, and the grandmother was so proud.

Paring Photography Costs

Because photography is such an important part of the wedding festivities, you want good photographs you can enjoy for years to come. Fortunately, there are a few ways you can trim some of these costs:

◆ Hire a professional photographer to shoot the formal wedding pictures (see Chapter 11), and then have a trusted friend who has some skill with a camera take the candid shots at the reception.

◆ Check out colleges and trade schools for an advanced photography student to shoot your wedding for a set fee and then give you the negatives for processing.

◆ Check out wedding magazines and websites for articles on saving on costs. Another source is *The Complete Idiot's Guide to Budgeting for Your Wedding* (see Appendix A).

Cutting Costs on Invitations

You can save money on invitations by including the reception information on the invitation instead of on a separate card. You can also save money by using a postcard for the response card. The card costs about the same as an enclosure card and envelope but you'll save on postage.

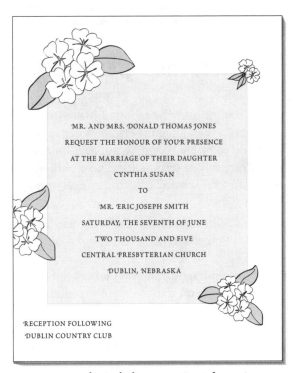

MR. AND MRS. DONALD THOMAS JONES
REQUEST THE HONOUR OF YOUR PRESENCE
AT THE MARRIAGE OF THEIR DAUGHTER
CYNTHIA SUSAN
TO
MR. ERIC JOSEPH SMITH
SATURDAY, THE SEVENTH OF JUNE
TWO THOUSAND AND FIVE
CENTRAL PRESBYTERIAN CHURCH
DUBLIN, NEBRASKA

RECEPTION FOLLOWING
DUBLIN COUNTRY CLUB

Save money by including reception information as corner copy on the invitation, as here, or as part of the main invitation.

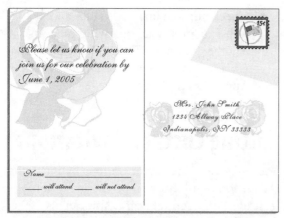

It's perfectly acceptable to send guests a pre-stamped, postcard-size response card with which to reply to your wedding. While the cost to print these is about the same as an enclosure and envelope, the big savings is in the postage. It's much less expensive to mail postcards than envelopes.

Contracts and Agreements

During the course of your wedding planning, you will most likely be required to sign several contracts or agreements with the various vendors you're hiring. If you're not accustomed to a contract and its terminology, take someone with you who is familiar with the legal mumbo jumbo.

Most contracts are written by an attorney who wasn't hired to make legal jargon understandable to the uninitiated. If you aren't sure what the contract means, if you need a point clarified, or if you want to be sure you understand what is required of you, ask the vendor to explain the contract in lay terms. If you're still not sure what it means, ask to take the contract out of the store to share with your family, with your attorney, or with someone else who can help you. Most vendors don't have a problem letting you take the contract—if they do, maybe you should wonder why. The contract is for both your protection and that of the vendor's. Although it can be confusing, it does have a legitimate purpose during the wedding planning.

If you use musicians from local schools, you might not have contracts with them. A letter of agreement from the sponsor of the student string quartet, for example, would do the trick. With the floral schools, a letter of what is expected and the supplies needed to complete the task is what would be expected here.

One couple I know didn't check their contract with the band. There was a requirement listed that stated the band must be fed a meal. It didn't say what the meal was to be; just that they were to be provided food during the evening. The band was not provided with anything and the couple got a surprise—the final billing from the band included a check to a local restaurant. When they called to question it, they were told they had asked for food during the reception and their request was denied so after the wedding, they got something to eat and billed the couple. Always read the fine print.

Wedding Woes

Never—I repeat, never—sign anything, whether it's a contract, agreement, or letter of intent, if you do not completely understand its meaning.

Always keep your contracts in a safe, easily accessible place. When you need to look at your contracts, you won't want to spend hours trying to find them.

The Least You Need to Know

- There are many ways to cut costs from your wedding budget.
- When it comes to stretching your wedding dollars, think creatively and read all you can about cutting costs.
- Never be afraid to ask for discounts or to inquire about renting items instead of buying them.
- Always make sure you understand what you're signing when you put your signature on a contract or agreement. If you don't understand the document, find someone who can explain it to you before you sign on the dotted line.

In This Part

Part 4

Help! My Family Is Driving Me Nuts!

Even if you're already well into planning your wedding, I recommend you read Part 4 from start to finish. It can make all the difference in your emotional state for the remainder of your planning. If you've turned to this part before you've begun any actual planning, you're taking a good first step toward having as stress-free a wedding as possible.

In this part, you'll learn what goes on emotionally—and mostly subconsciously—with some of the people around you as the process of planning a wedding unfolds. I'll talk about marriage as a rite of passage and why some decisions are so emotional for those involved. Then I'll offer some practical tips that might help smooth things over. I'll also tell you how to deal with wedding stress, how to work with divorced parents and blended families, where you can turn for help, and what you can do to help yourself. So strap yourself in tight, and get ready for the roller-coaster ride!

In This Chapter

- ◆ Understanding marriage as a rite of passage
- ◆ Knowing what to expect emotionally
- ◆ Winning the power struggle
- ◆ Dealing with tension between parents
- ◆ Practical tips to help you keep your sanity

Chapter **15**

And in This Corner ...

A marriage is a rite of passage. A marriage can be a very stressful event even under the best of circumstances. Understanding what goes on emotionally during this process can help curtail unnecessary emotional turmoil from invading your wedding bliss.

In this chapter and the next, I'll tell you why planning a wedding can be such a stressful time, and share with you some stress-busting strategies to help you relax and enjoy the process—and keep the peace in your families!

On a Personal Note

When I married at the age of 23, my mother did not like the idea of me getting married. She refused to help, thinking that I would give up and the wedding would not take place. I was totally unprepared for the confusing emotions my mother and I were about to experience. I didn't know that something as wonderful as making plans for my wedding could cause so much stress in a relatively normal family. None of the wedding planning books I bought mentioned anything about the emotional side of getting married.

I remember wondering why, if this was supposed to be the happiest time in my life, I was feeling so miserable. I would ask my mother a question or ask her opinion about some detail, and she would look at me and start crying. It began to feel more like I was planning my funeral instead of my wedding.

It wasn't that she objected to my fiancé. Neither my mom nor I really understood what was happening to us and why we were always arguing over the silliest things. We didn't sit down and talk about "it" because neither one of us knew what was really going on. It wasn't until I started working with couples that I put two and two together and figured out what was happening. Some good research on the subject proved I was on the right track. In the end, all turned out for the best, but it certainly was a bumpy road and one I wasn't expecting. I didn't see it at the time, but Mother's reluctance was actually due to the fact that she didn't want to believe she was old enough to have a daughter of marrying age. One of her babies was old enough to leave the nest. That is a traumatic moment in a mother's life, as I now know from personal experience. I myself am mother to a 29-year-old and a 22-year-old—both college graduates out on their own.

> **Teddy's Tips**
>
> Several books on the bridal market now deal with the emotional side of marriage—and it's about time! See Appendix A for a selection of books and other resources.

A Rite of Passage

Brides and their mothers sometimes disagree on many topics during the wedding planning stages, even the choice of mate. This was something I didn't understand when I got married, but that I have come to understand through my work with brides and their families: Marriage is a rite of passage. You're passing from one part of your life into a new part; you're leaving the primary role of child and taking on the new role of spouse. This universal rite demonstrates to a community that one of its own is old enough, responsible enough, and mature enough to take a mate.

There are three basic rites of passage: birth, marriage, and death. Of these three, marriage is the only one you choose. With this rite of passage comes a whole slew of emotions. These emotions are what fuel that roller-coaster ride you and your mother—and perhaps other members of the family—find yourselves on during the planning process.

"It's going to be just fine," is what this bride seems to be saying to her mom. *(Photo by Janet Klinger Photography)*

The Emotional Roller Coaster—What to Expect

Let's talk about your emotions for a minute. Keep in mind that most of what goes on with your emotions during this time is subconscious. You don't know why you feel the way you do; it's just how you feel. Right now you're engaged to a wonderful person. You're excited; you're scared; you're happy; you worry about how well your in-laws will like you; you wonder whether your parents will get along—all kinds of thoughts are running through your head. Now throw in the fact that your mother insists on beef for the entrée and that you and your fiancé both want chicken, or that she thinks pink is a terrible color for the bridesmaids' dresses while you've had your heart set on pink for years. You have the makings for some major fireworks, but what's really going on here? Is it about beef and chicken? Is it about the 10 different shades of pink you want to incorporate? I doubt it. It's about the bonds between parent and child, it's about power and control, and it's about growing up.

Never underestimate the power of a hug during these emotional times. *(Photo by Wyant Photography)*

Mother and Me

At this point in your life, you may be torn between yearning for independence and yet not being ready to leave the nest. You want to make your own choices and decisions, but you might be reluctant to give up the security of having someone take care of you. Even if you've been out on your own for a number of years, you're still your mother's child.

Your mother also might be feeling torn. She has reared you to be an independent person, but she's not really ready to lose her baby. She wants you to be strong, but she wants to make sure you make the right decisions (which often translates into the decisions *she* would make). Your mother is afraid that the marriage will break the bonds between the two of you, and that makes her sad. So while she might be perfectly willing to argue over beef or chicken, or your choice of colors, you can be fairly certain that's not really what she's upset about. She's afraid the marriage will change your relationship with her. She's afraid your new spouse will replace her, and you won't need her anymore.

She's also afraid of the aging process—you getting married means she's getting older. Again, she's afraid of losing her baby. She's afraid of many things, most of which she can't explain to you, nor does she understand. She wants to be your friend and let you have your way, but in doing so, she loses some of her control. Her mothering abilities are on display now, and she wants a great report card to show when all is said and done.

Bouquet Toss

One bride I worked with found her mother pulling away rather than becoming overly involved in the wedding plans. This was partly because the mother had read so many articles and heard so many complaints about overbearing mothers taking over the wedding that she went overboard the opposite way. Many times, she didn't offer any opinions and only said "That's nice, dear," when told about details. She offered little help with any of the plans. The mother never even discussed anything besides a general dollar figure, so the bride ended up feeling like her mother could have cared less that her daughter was getting married. In reality, the mother was trying too hard to let her daughter make her own decisions.

Don't be too hard on Mom. Had I understood what I know now about what *my* mother was really experiencing, I think we could have talked about it and made each other feel so much better. Try not to let these subconscious emotional issues get in the way of your planning, fun, and excitement.

Daddy's Little Girl

Much is written about the pre-wedding tension between mother and daughter. But what about daughter and dad? Where does he fit into the plan?

Fathers are generally very interesting creatures when it comes to making plans for their daughter's big day. Your dad is proud of the woman you've become, and he wants only the very best for you. On the other hand, he may be somewhat jealous of your groom, the man who is going to take you away. Dad has been your protector; now he's giving up that role, and he does so with a little sadness. It doesn't matter how he feels about your groom; his little girl is growing up. And here, too, it doesn't matter if you're a 30-year-old bride or a 22-year-old bride, you are still Daddy's little girl.

Dad also might feel left out of all the planning stages. At times, it does seem like a solely mother-daughter planning frenzy—kind of like a marathon of planning. If he seems grumpy or on edge from time to time, he might just want to be part of the process, too (other than writer of the checks), but he just doesn't know how to ask. When you ask if he would like to help, he may gruffly tell you that you and your mother are doing just fine with the planning, but he might not tell you that he feels better just that you had extended the offer.

Ask your dad how, or if, he wants to be involved in the wedding planning. If he gives the go-ahead, offer him some task that he will feel comfortable handling. Ask him to arrange for the limos for the day, or ask him to talk

with the bartender about the brands of liquor you plan to serve.

"Just remember all the things we did while I was growing up. I love you, Dad." *(Photo by Wyant Photography)*

Moments like this are priceless. *(Photo by Jeff Hawkins Photography)*

Always try to keep your dad informed about the decisions you've made. Try to ask his advice and counsel. This will make him feel close to you and needed. It wouldn't hurt to give him some extra hugs along the way, either.

This proud dad is moments away from walking his daughter down the aisle as they arrive at the ceremony. *(Photo by Colter Photography)*

Mama's Baby Boy

So you think this chapter is just for the bride and her family? Well, as a future mother of two grooms, I'm here to tell you that the emotional stress happens to the males, too. While it has always been associated with the female gender, grooms, along with their fathers, and of course, the mothers, all go through the same rite of passage as the bride and her family.

The best advice I can offer grooms is to get involved with the wedding plans (it's your wedding, too) and keep those lines of communication open with your family. Where you will pick up the stress and the emotions is from your mom. She is about to become the ill-fated "mother-in-law," and we all know that mothers-in-law are just these horrible creatures who prey on defenseless brides. (Can you imagine my daughter-in-law with fear in her eyes when my son tells her what I do for a living? I will be gentle.) You and your family are also experiencing the same emotions as your bride and her family. But because you are the man, it's just not talked about as much.

Here's one dad who seems to be all wrapped up in the wedding plans! *(Photo by Janet Klinger Photography)*

Your mom is thinking the same things as your fiancé's mom: Is she good enough for him, will she like us, should I ask if I can help? To help ease the tension and break the ice, involve your folks as much as they want to be involved and where they can be involved. If nothing else, keep them informed as to what is happening and where. You might suggest to your bride to ask her mom for her opinion on an item. Does she think you need to use a monogram or have the napkins printed with your names? If you ask simple questions and for opinion only, then you can take the advice or leave it. But the point is, you've asked and that's what matters.

Here's a happy groom-to-be and his mom at the rehearsal. *(Photo by Colter Photography)*

Here's the same groom and his mom as they begin their walk down the aisle. *(Photo by Colter Photography)*

Teddy's Tips

Parents feel left out when there is no communication taking place. Sometimes this can't be helped—perhaps because your parents live out of town—but most times keeping those lines of communication open can save everyone lots of heartache. (Be sure to tell your mom and dad you love them. That gesture always helps.)

Who's in Control Here?

One point of battle that might creep into your plans is the "Who's in charge?" theme. You see this wedding as your wedding, and rightly so—it should be. You know what you want and don't want for this day. You've taken every precaution to check out references with vendors. You've read articles, been to bridal shows, and interviewed many vendors. You know exactly what you want this day to include, right down to the favors on the table.

The only problem is that your mother might not have read the part that says *you're* in charge. Your mother may want to be in charge, too. Your mother might hold the checkbook, and the checkbook might have strings attached. It's her one last chance to show her stuff. Your mother may be having a tough time giving up her dominant role. She has taken care of you for all these years and made decisions with your best interests at heart. How could you not want her to make all the arrangements for your wedding, whether you like them or not? Control, power, whatever you want to call it—that's what this is all about. She's afraid of losing her power.

Another factor that might determine what kind of a role your mother wants to have in your wedding is how much control she had over her own wedding. So many times, the mother who had a small, simple wedding wants to give her daughter the grand wedding she never had. She wants the control she didn't have. Your invitations will be the ones she didn't have. Your gown will be the one she wanted. Your entrée choice will be beef because her own mother, or her circumstances at the time, did not allow her to serve the food she really wanted to serve. If your mother wants to make this the big production she never had, but you have a small, simple wedding in mind, you might have some big problems. If you can't go along with your mother's desire to have the wedding of the year, then be prepared for the fireworks—I can guarantee you that they'll be there.

> **Teddy's Tips**
>
> In planning the details of your wedding, patience is indeed a true virtue. Compromise and don't sweat the small stuff.

If this sounds like what you're going through, or what you think might happen, try talking to your mother. Sit down with her in a quiet setting; talk calmly and rationally about the wedding plans you have been planning. In your most adult, mature voice, let her know (very delicately) that this is your wedding, and while you want her help, it needs to be for items you as a couple want included. You'll find more practical tips later in this chapter.

Tension Between Parents

Something else that I have come to recognize (often on sight) is tension caused by two sets of parents vying for the couple's allegiance. You're no longer dealing with just *your* parents. All of a sudden, you've got another set of parents to worry about (and possibly stepparents thrown into the mix, which I'll discuss in Chapter 16).

The groom might want his parents' names on the invitation because they're paying for the liquor at the reception. The bride's mother, however, might refuse, saying that tradition dictates that only the bride's parents' names appear on the invitation.

Well, dear reader, your parents are battling out (subconsciously) their fear of losing your loyalty. How many times have you heard married friends say, "Oh, our parents are driving us nuts. They both want us to spend Christmas with them. How can we choose?" Well, you have to make a stand, and the sooner the better. It's nothing more than a power struggle over you, the new couple on the block. Your parents are arguing over who will have more control over you after the wedding. They want to make sure you still have allegiance to them.

> **Wedding Woes**
>
> As a couple your primary allegiance needs to be to each other and you need to present a united front. Avoid problems down the road by deciding early on what limits you will set as a couple regarding the expectations of your respective parents. Try to work things out with parents before you tie the knot, such as alternating holiday visits every other year.

Just remember that your parents aren't creating all this turmoil intentionally. Often, they don't understand why they behave like they do. Once you understand what's really going on, you can learn to work around it or work with it. How I wish someone would have told me some of this back when I got married. It certainly would have made my life a lot easier just understanding what my mother was experiencing. I know if we could have talked openly about the emotions we were both experiencing and the fears we shared, she and I would have had an easier time with my whole wedding process.

Practical Tips to Get Through It

The closer your wedding day gets, the thicker the tension can become. Here are some practical ideas that might help:

- Work on your attitude. Attitude makes all the difference in the world. Don't think of this wedding as solely *your* day—think of it more as a family affair. It's still your wedding, don't get me wrong, but if you can focus your attention away from yourself, you might be more open to others' suggestions and be willing to compromise.

- Remember, above all else, it's the marriage, not the wedding, that's really important. Which gowns are worn, flowers are carried, and entrées are eaten doesn't matter in the end. What matters is the marriage between two people who care, trust, love, and like each other enough to spend the rest of their earthly lives together. That's Commitment, folks, with a capital C.

- Put all your cards on the table. Know what you're dealing with and whom. As a united front, you as a couple should approach your families with your wedding desires. See what they are willing to contribute, and take it from there. At least you'll know where you stand. Trying to second-guess your parents is time-consuming and not at all practical. Many couples would rather know what amount of money they have to work with than to guess at what they think they might be working with. You need to know what's what.

- Decide which items about the wedding you must have control over and which items you could turn over to your mother or other family members. Don't let your mother feel left out. You want to prevent your mother from feeling insecure, if

possible. Insecurity sometimes leads to irrational behavior, and you sure don't need that now. The same advice goes for your partner's mother. One of the fastest ways to make an enemy of your future mother-in-law is to keep her guessing about the wedding plans. Unless she's helping financially, she doesn't have a real decision-making role, but asking her opinion, her advice, and which colors she likes best will help make your relationship stronger and make her feel more a part of the process. Keep her informed, and ask for advice.

Teddy's Tips

Take care of yourself! Try to get enough rest and exercise and eat properly during the wedding planning. Stress depletes the body's reserves. If you aren't physically able to handle all the ups and downs, you will be more stressed. You can't possibly keep up with the physical drain of wedding planning, plus all the raging emotions, if you're exhausted.

- If you and your mother have a huge argument and you hang up the phone or slam the door on her, take a deep breath, count to 100, and call back or walk back in the room. It might be very hard to do, but it will help you in the long haul. Explain that it's the wedding stress that has you bummed out, not her. Try to start fresh. Forgive and forget. In 10 years, no one will remember what the argument was about.

- Send your mother a card or flowers, and tell her you love her. Mothers love that mushy stuff—and please, make it sincere. So many times, mothers act the way they do just because they're mothers. (It's in the contracts we sign when our babies are

born—really, it is!) If she feels appreciated and loved, and still knows you care
about her, that will go a long way toward
mending fences.

Above all, try to stay calm and be patient with
each other. This is normally a stressful time,
just given the nature of all that goes on. Don't
let a disagreement ruin the fun and excitement
of planning for one of the most important days
of your life. If you argue, take a deep breath
and count to 10 or 100—or even to 1,000, if
necessary—and start over. Keep the lines of
communication open, and always be willing to
listen. Good luck!

The Least You Need to Know

◆ Marriage is one of the basic rites of passage. You're leaving a familiar role and
assuming a new role, and it's normal to
experience uncertainty and tension on
this journey.

◆ Try to take into consideration the emotions your parents may be experiencing.
They don't understand, at least con-
sciously, why they're acting as they are.

◆ Just understanding that arguments naturally happen during this planning process
(and that those arguments are normal)
might make this time easier to get
through.

◆ Keep the lines of communication open
among both sets of parents, and be sure
to tell them how much you love and
appreciate them.

◆ Remember that in the end, it's the marriage that counts, not the wedding. Don't
get so caught up in planning the details of
the wedding that you forget about the
marriage!

In This Chapter

- ◆ Understanding normal wedding stress
- ◆ Finding ways to control the stress
- ◆ Dealing with divorced parents and blended families
- ◆ Where to get help if you need it—and what to do to help yourself
- ◆ To prenup or not to prenup?

Chapter 16

I Think I'm Losing My Mind!

Stress—it's an everyday word in our society. There is good stress; there is bad stress. And no matter how hard and how well you plan, there is stress during your wedding planning months.

In this chapter, I'll expand on the previous chapter and talk about what's "normal" wedding stress. We'll talk about divorced and blended families (they're out there everywhere), and I'll give you some sage advice on how to deal with the stress caused by planning for the happiest day of your life.

Is This Normal?

"I'm stressed to the limit. I just can't take any more!" During the wedding planning stages, you may find yourself saying this more times than you can count. You may be saying it to family members, to friends, to yourself, and even to perfect strangers.

Yes, by their very nature, weddings are stress-producing events. The escalation of your emotions stemming from the added burdens and worries associated with wedding planning can cause prewedding stress. This is an emotional time. Much of the stress comes from all the details you have to be involved with, along with a sense of not having control over all that's going on. You might feel pulled in many directions as well; you have too many advice-givers and not enough supporters. At times, you might even wish that you and your partner had just chosen to elope. Relax—all these feelings and emotions are in the normal range of wedding stress.

Not every couple experiences prewedding stress. I've talked with some couples and their families who thoroughly enjoyed the wedding planning process. However, if you're like the majority of harried brides in the months before the wedding, you're likely to feel some added anxiety. Let's look at some of the reasons for this stress.

Take time out with your partner to stay connected.
(Photo by Tony Campbell, Indiana State University)

It Costs *How Much?*

Think back to Chapter 2, when I talked about the budget and helped you determine what's important to you as a couple and how much you have to spend. Remember when I suggested that you try to stick to that budget? Well, one very good reason for sticking to a budget is to help prevent all the negative emotions that can accompany spending more money than you've allotted.

Going over your budget is one of the biggest stress factors in wedding planning. It's like extending the limit on your credit cards. You buy something here and something there. You order your flowers, and when the estimate comes, it's twice your budget. What started out as a simple affair has now escalated into a complex and expensive event. Your wedding costs may resemble the national debt, and the price tag keeps right on climbing.

Then there are all the little extras: garter, guest book, welcome packages at the hotel, parking fees—the list goes on and on. Not expecting the add-on costs and not getting an accurate estimate for a service can leave you drained both financially and emotionally. This is why keeping your expectations reasonable and setting realistic goals is so important. (Turn to the "Wedding Budget" worksheet in Appendix B for help in figuring out a budget.)

Part of the planning stage involves working together to have the wedding you and your partner want and can afford. Listen to each other and then pick and choose what's really important to you. And don't forget the importance of compromise!
(Photo by Tony Campbell, Indiana State University)

Too Much Advice from Too Many People

When you become engaged, it's like you're suddenly wearing a sign that says, "Advice Needed Here!" You're deluged with all kinds of advice from all kinds of people. In Chapter 1, I suggested that you seek advice from those who had recently married. This is always a good idea, but be prepared for a lot more than you bargained for from other advice-givers. All of a sudden, you get to hear the details of every wedding horror story, the details of every wedding planning detail problem, and countless hours of "I did it this way." You will be filled to the limit with too much advice. Here's a scene that just might happen to you:

Scene: Coffee shop. You run into a friend you have not talked with for several months.

"Oh, Sally, good to see you."

"Say, Cindy, I heard you're getting married."

"Yes. Jim and I finally set the date."

"Well, tell me about your plans."

"Oh, we just want a simple wedding, nothing too fancy."

"Where did you get your gown?"

"At Bitsy's Bridal Boutique."

Silence. Then, "Bitsy's Bridal Boutique?"

"Yes, why?"

"Oh, nothing, it's just that they ruined Jane Owen's gown. Ruined it, I tell you. They didn't hem the dress, left a huge hole in the side seam, and then, would you believe it, the gown came back with a big pink stain on the front. They said they didn't do it, but who else did? I tell you, Cindy, you're a fool to work with them."

At this point in the conversation, you're sweating and your pulse is beginning to beat rapidly. You're starting to breathe heavily and your head is spinning. And you're wondering, "Did I do enough homework on Bitsy's Bridal Boutique? I checked with other friends who used them; they seemed happy with the outcome. So far, they're completely on schedule. Have I made a big mistake? I don't want pink stains on my wedding gown!"

Get a grip! Do a reality check! You've just experienced what I fondly refer to as listening to the "advice addict." If it happened, the advice addict knows it—this person knows why it happened, knows whom it happened to, and knows what to do about it. Take what that person has to say with a big grain of salt. Although you do need advice from many friends—especially those recently married—you eventually will reach a saturation point. You will become the proverbial sponge that can no longer soak up any more advice. Your cup will begin to overflow.

Wedding Woes

Don't get bogged down with too much advice from the advice addicts. Yes, they might have your best interests at heart, but if you've done your homework, you should be fine.

Relax! Take a deep breath. Let the advice addict's message go in one ear and out the other. Use what you can, and discard the rest. And remember: This, too, shall pass.

Take time out to recharge your batteries and discuss something other than the wedding! *(Photo by Tony Campbell, Indiana State University)*

Trying to Please Everyone

Another potential point of certain stress is trying to please everyone. "Everyone" means the entire Western Hemisphere. "Everyone" means both sets of parents, grandparents, aunts, uncles, cousins, second cousins, second cousins two times removed, all your friends, and your boss (you probably do still have to work for a living).

I've talked about this being *your* wedding. Don't lose sight of that now. You can't possibly please everyone. There will be someone, somewhere, who doesn't agree with what you're doing, the way in which you're doing it, or what you're serving, wearing, saying, singing, playing, or handing out. With weddings, it's just a given—you can never please everyone.

If you've done your homework, then just go with the flow. Worry about what you as a couple feel is necessary and what you want to include. Do take into consideration your family and their desires or wishes, but the bottom line here is that this is still *your* wedding. You will drive yourself nuts if you try to meet the demands of the entire family.

If you run into resistance from family members, be calm, be tactful, be diplomatic, and be firm. Talk it out. But don't alter your plans just to please someone else unless you can make the change without compromising your basic desires.

This bride and her mom are looking through wedding-related books and magazines for some ideas. Communication is always key when planning a wedding. *(Photo by Tony Campbell, Indiana State University)*

Divorced and Blended Families

Where do I begin on this topic? Divorce happens frequently in this country. It might have happened to your parents or your partner's parents or someone in your family. With divorce and remarriage of parents come *blended families*—you know, "yours, mine, and (sometimes) ours." If your parents are divorced and have remarried, you have a stepparent and probably some stepbrothers or stepsisters and extended aunts and uncles and grandparents. This is what we, in the wedding industry, refer to as a blended family. And the sheer numbers added to your family tree can provide plenty of additional stress.

> **Nuptial Notes**
>
> A **blended family** as I refer to it in this book is one in which the parents are divorced and have remarried. Most likely, the individuals bring their own children into the union, so you end up with stepbrothers and stepsisters, as well as grandparents, aunts, uncles, cousins … the whole nine yards!

Divorced family members don't automatically bring any additional problems to your wedding planning. If the divorce was particularly nasty, however, and the parties involved are still relatively hostile, you have the potential for some wedding fireworks. Some extra precautions could be in order.

When Divorced Parents Get Along

Perhaps your parents have been divorced for many years and are on good speaking terms with each other and you. Both have remarried, and you feel comfortable with your stepparents. When you announce your engagement and sit down to discuss plans, be sure to include both sets of parents—that is, both sets of your parents and your partner's parents. If there is physical distance separating all of you, make sure you keep both parties informed as to what you discuss and decide, and ask for opinions from all sides. Never put the two sides at odds with each other. Don't compare them to each other. Please don't say to your mother, "Well, Daddy's wife is going to take me to see Vera Wang about designing my gown." (Vera Wang is a big-time designer whose beautiful gowns come with very hefty price tags.) You'll only create a distance between parties that doesn't need to be there.

I know what it feels like to be a negotiator. I've been asked many times to make a stepmother who feels left out and wants to be included feel good about being involved in the wedding. It's not easy. So many times, having more open communication between the parents is all that's needed. You must make very sure that all your communication between your divorced parents is accurate and complete. Don't expect them to assume anything.

As for finances with divorced parents, let me offer this tip: Open a checking account to be used solely for wedding expenses. Have each contributor (your mother, your father, and so on) contribute equal amounts of money to the account. As the wedding bills are paid, each party contributes additional equal amounts to cover other costs. Any money left over might be given to the couple for a nest egg. This helps greatly in alleviating the "But I paid for this" syndrome.

It's also helpful to chart out who is going to be responsible for each aspect of the wedding expenses. Take a piece of paper and make several columns. One column is for the item and the others are for each set of contributors (you, your father, your mother, and so on). Then, go through the list and decide who will be responsible for what. Now you've got it in black and white. Give each contributor a copy of the plan.

Teddy's Tips

If your parents are divorced and not on friendly terms, never assume that they will put aside their differences long enough for you to walk down the aisle. Always use caution, courtesy, and compassion when you discuss your wedding plans with them and how you see their individual roles.

What I just described is the ultimate situation when dealing with divorced families. Unfortunately, there are more situations where we pray for peace among the parents just long enough to get through the day.

When Divorced Parents Don't Get Along

If your divorced parents want nothing to do with one another, accept that fact and work around it. For seating purposes, your mother should be seated in the first row and your father in the second. I have had brides request that their divorced parents be seated together in the first row. It's truly an unselfish act for divorced parents to put aside their anger and support their child, and it's not too much for a child to ask.

One wedding many years ago involved a wonderful couple who had extensively planned their wedding. We had spent time covering all the little details. The bride's parents were divorced, and her mother had remarried. When we had finished the final consultation a few days before the wedding, I asked the bride if there was anything else I should know. She paused and replied, "Have I mentioned that my father hasn't spoken to us in five years?" Well, no, I hadn't picked up on that. I asked her who was going to escort her down the aisle, and she informed me that she had asked her brother. So that's the way we practiced at the rehearsal.

I received a late phone call after the rehearsal was over. The bride was very upset and crying. Her father had called her and demanded that he be the one to walk her down the aisle. She didn't know what to do. We talked about options and decided that she should probably let him do the honors. He showed up right before the ceremony, appropriately dressed in a tuxedo. He was very uncomfortable standing in the church lobby. When the processional began, his daughter came up to him and took his arm. They marched down the aisle, and before she left him at the altar to go to her groom, she reached over and gave him a hug and a kiss. Here was a family who had not spoken to each other in five years. And with this one simple act, the ice had been broken. Since then, the other two sisters have married, and their dad has been at each of their weddings. While I'm sure that those parents are still not best buddies, they were able to put aside their differences long enough to give their children happy, peaceful wedding days.

Each wedding with divorced families has a different set of circumstances that must be addressed. You have to be sensitive, to a point, to the wishes of your divorced parents. Be supportive and try to be understanding. If you're faced with dealing with divorced parents and family members during your wedding, try to accommodate their requests. For example, don't put your mother at the same table with your father and his 22-year-old new wife. Even if they get along great, the fact that your new stepmother is younger than the bride might wear a bit on your mom. Use some common sense when dealing with divorced parents. They are still your parents. Hang in there, keep your chin up, and move forward.

Teddy's Tips

For additional help in dealing with divorced family members, you might find some helpful suggestions in *Planning a Wedding with Divorced Parents* (see Appendix A).

If both parents are so bitter that they cannot be trusted to behave themselves at the wedding, ask a neutral third party for advice—perhaps the bridal consultant (trust me, we've seen it all) or the clergy. Parents who declare, "Well, if she's coming then I won't!" may come around if you answer, "I'm sorry to hear that; we'll miss you." This day is about the two of you, not about parents who can't get along. And there's always the chance that despite your worst fears, everyone will get along famously.

Where to Get Help

All right, I'll admit it. Sometimes these delicate issues can cause some hairy situations. What do you do if you need some objective help and guidance? Several options are open to you.

◆ **The officiant.** One of the best places to gather some strength and advice is from your minister, priest, or rabbi. These trained professionals deal with all kinds of stressful situations.

◆ **Bridal consultant.** Many consultants feel that through our experiences, we should at least have earned our Ph.D. in human behavior. Given how close I am to the individual situations that arise with families, there are many times when I've felt as though I could easily hang out a shingle, "Dr. T. M. Lenderman." I've learned many things about human beings and what we can do if pushed hard enough.

◆ **Trusted family member or friend.** If you aren't comfortable discussing your problems relating to your divorced parents with an officiant or bridal consultant, seek out a trusted family member or a good friend.

Wedding Woes

If you choose to confide in a family member, be certain you can trust that person to be discreet and not share what you have confided.

What You Can Do to Help Yourself

Even if you don't feel the need to talk with a neutral third party, there are several things you and your future spouse can do to help yourselves during this stressful time:

◆ Get enough sleep and eat right (lots of fruits, veggies, water, and protein-rich foods).

◆ Get moving—an aerobics class, a walk in the park, swimming, a bike ride in the country … anything to help work off that stress.

Jogging, like any physical activity, is a natural stress reducer. *(Photo by Tony Campbell, Indiana State University)*

There's nothing like spending time together in the park on a beautiful sunny day to relieve some of that pre-wedding stress. *(Photo by Tony Campbell, Indiana State University)*

◆ Have fun doing some non-wedding-related things with each other. Take in a movie or sporting event. Get together with friends for a picnic or a night on the town. The only rule: No wedding talk!

◆ Work on communication skills both with each other and with your parents. Keep those lines of communication open.

◆ Learn to compromise—give and take.

◆ Don't lose sight of what is really important—your marriage.

Prenuptial Agreements

In our society today, we're faced daily with decisions that can be very difficult to make. In this decade, the prenuptial agreement is a reality, and more couples are being faced with this decision before they marry. This can add more stress than either of you thought possible. This is especially true when a family business is involved whose wealth has reached a point where a future divorce between the couple could be disastrous for the rest of the family. I know it's hard to think about this at a time when you're madly in love and think that nothing will ever part you, but sometimes, signing off on a prenuptial agreement is the only way you can say, "I do." You may want to check out the books *Don't Get Married Until You Read This* and *Premarital Agreements: When, Why, and How to Write Them* (see Appendix A for details).

The Least You Need to Know

◆ Don't be surprised if you feel over-whelmed and stressed during the planning stages of your wedding. These are normal reactions to this often hectic and emotion-filled time.

◆ Keep in mind that lots of folks out there are just waiting to give you some advice, whether or not you ask for it. Take what you can use, and let go of the rest.

◆ When working with divorced family members, be considerate of their feelings. Never compare the parents to each other.

◆ If your parents are divorced, it's especially important to try to work out potential financial problems before they happen. You might want to open a joint checking account, have each parent contribute equally to the account, and pay all your wedding bills from that account.

◆ If you are faced with signing a prenuptial agreement, make sure you understand exactly what you are signing and why.

◆ If you're feeling overwhelmed by stress, talking to an objective listener can help. Even if you don't seek outside help, you and your partner can keep stress at bay by eating right, getting enough sleep and exercise, and taking an occasional break from the wedding planning.

In This Part

Special Weddings

Every wedding is special. Just ask any bride-to-be, and she'll tell you how special her wedding will be. What I'm referring to in this part are weddings that take on a special flair, unique idea, or specific theme.

Part 5 talks about all these special weddings. I'll share theme wedding ideas, including holiday, outdoor, military, and the latest trend—the personalized themed wedding. I'll talk about what you need to know to pull off a weekend wedding, and finally I'll share information about what a destination wedding is and how to go about planning one.

In This Chapter

- ◆ Considering a theme wedding
- ◆ Ideas for seasonal, outdoor, military, and personalized wedding themes
- ◆ Practical tips to help you plan a theme wedding
- ◆ The weekend wedding

Chapter 17

What's in a Theme?

Weddings with themes are big these days. Brides and grooms want to create a unique atmosphere for their big day and are choosing themes around which they can build this atmosphere. Couples often select a wedding theme based on a particular season or date. One of the biggest trends in weddings today is personalizing the wedding around the couple's likes, careers, or family heritage. That can start the wedding theme idea.

In this chapter, I'll also discuss the weekend wedding concept and share some ideas for making it a delight for all involved.

Seasonal Weddings

A seasonal wedding is one that takes place near a certain holiday or during a certain season of the year. Examples of holidays around which you might choose to hold your wedding include:

- Christmas
- New Year's (both eve and day)
- Valentine's Day
- Fourth of July
- Halloween

In the following sections, I'll give you some ideas for planning a wedding around each of these holidays.

Christmas Weddings

Christmas weddings, in particular, can be wonderfully romantic. I don't know if it's the season, the snow (at least, here in the Midwest), the decorations, or the soft glow of all the candles. The season itself just seems filled with more love, hope, and peace, and those sentiments tend to shine through weddings held during this time. Most facilities and churches decorate for the holiday, which can add a special and lovely touch to your wedding festivities (and actually save you money on decorations).

The white twigs in this centerpiece give it a festive holiday flair. *(Photo by Colter Photography)*

Here are some additional touches to consider for a Christmas wedding:

- Ask musicians to play Christmas carols during the prelude.
- Have a children's choir sing carols among guests at the reception.
- Print Christmas song sheets on parchment paper, tie with red velvet ribbon, and use as a favor.
- Tie the programs with plaid Christmas ribbon.
- Use a small wreath tied with tiny bells and ribbons as a favor.
- Have ornaments printed with your names and hang them on a tree for guests to take as they leave.
- Dress your bridesmaids in the traditional black velvet with Christmas plaid.
- Tuck small silver bells or other holiday ornaments among the flowers in the bouquets.

Having a holiday wedding can save you money on decorations because most facilities are already decorated. Notice the pine cones and holly winding around the candles. *(Photo by Colter Photography)*

Wedding Woes

If you hold your wedding in a Catholic church, be sure to check on exactly when the church will be decorated for the season. Some Catholic churches are decorated late in December. Even if your wedding is on December 20, don't assume that the church will already be decorated. A Catholic church cannot be decorated before the last Sunday in Advent. When in doubt, ask the priest.

◆ Use different sizes of wrapped packages or miniature decorated Christmas trees for the table centerpieces.

◆ Decorate with lots of white lights, icicle lights, and candles.

◆ Carry a white muff instead of a bouquet.

A Christmas tree provides a pretty backdrop for the band. *(Photo by Colter Photography)*

Holiday weddings are special! *(Photo by Colter Photography)*

New Year's Eve or New Year's Day Weddings

You can create a special atmosphere planning a New Year's wedding, whether on New Year's Eve or New Year's Day. For the New Year's Eve wedding, you might wish to have the usual noise-makers and confetti for your guests. Here are some additional ideas for New Year's weddings:

◆ In the center of the dance floor, have a huge sack of balloons tied up, ready to release at the stroke of midnight.

◆ Have guests make New Year's resolutions at their tables, seal them in envelopes, and leave them in a basket by the door. Mail those out later in January to your guests as a reminder of the resolution and of your wedding.

◆ Decorate with lots of confetti, noisemakers, and balloons.

Valentine's Day Weddings

Valentine's Day is already a romantic holiday; add a wedding to the day, and you have the setting for some special happenings. Here are some ideas to consider for a Valentine's Day wedding:

◆ Consider a wedding gown in a pale shade of pink or accented with pink.

◆ Dress your bridesmaids in varying shades of pink or the traditional Valentine's Day red velvet.

◆ Use heart-shape everything at the wedding and reception: candelabrum, unity candles, guest book, napkins, candy favors ... or have two hearts printed on the programs.

Fourth of July Weddings

Talk about fireworks! As the ceremony ends and the officiant pronounces you husband and wife, what's more appropriate than an outdoors fireworks display? Here are some more Fourth of July theme ideas:

◆ It's July, so why not plan for an outdoor reception with red, white, and blue table-cloths?

◆ Lead off the processional with a 1776 traditional drum and fife core. Consider using the "1812 Overture" for the recessional. How majestic!

◆ Have your gown and those of your wedding party made in an eighteenth-century style.

◆ Top off the wedding cake with sparklers, and give children some sparklers to enjoy, too (with adult supervision).

◆ Right before the bride and groom make their exit, gather the entire reception out on the lawn and have a fireworks display to bring your wonderful day to a dramatic end.

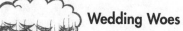

Wedding Woes

Do *not* try setting off your own fireworks. Leave any fireworks displays to the pros!

Make your exit amid sparklers! These extra-long sparklers (two to three feet) are especially made for wedding and parties. *(Photos by Broadway Photography, LLC)*

Halloween Weddings

A Halloween wedding theme might include guests coming in costumes. The waitstaff might be dressed in costume also. Some of the other traditional Halloween elements that you could include are:

- Feature candy apples as favors, wrapped in colorful cellophane and tied with a ribbon.
- Decorate with a black and orange color scheme or other rich fall colors.
- Use corn stalks and pumpkins nestled together around the room for décor. The occasional scarecrow is fun, too.
- An assortment of Halloween masks for guests to use can be waiting for them at their tables or at the place card table (if you are using assigned seating). How fun for guests to don masks in the celebration of your marriage!
- Feature baskets of nuts and berries or an overflowing cornucopia as part of the table centerpieces.
- For favors, leave Halloween treat bags filled with goodies at each place setting for your guests with a note from you and your partner.

Outdoor and Garden Weddings

Outdoor and garden weddings are probably the most difficult to plan and the most risky to carry out. For some reason, people seem to feel that if they opt for an outdoor wedding in Grandma's lovely garden, it somehow will be easier and cheaper than renting a facility and a reception hall. Nothing could be further from the truth.

Teddy's Tips

Choosing an outdoor wedding does not mean it will necessarily be cheaper or less elaborate than an indoor wedding. A great deal depends on your geographic location. If you live in a climate such as California, where the weather is not a major risk factor, planning an outdoor wedding is an easier task. If your wedding will be in the Northeast, however, be prepared for a sudden rainstorm, a chilling cold front, or a sticky heat wave.

You need to be somewhat of a risk-taker to take on and enjoy an outdoor wedding. If you're someone who likes to feel in control of a situation, I suggest that you stick with a more conservative plan and stay indoors. Outdoor weddings can be beautiful, but they certainly are not for the faint of heart. Let's take a look at some of the issues you'll need to consider.

Unpredictable Mother Nature

"It's not nice to fool Mother Nature." Well, trust me, you can't! I know—I've tried. She will do what she will do, and there's nothing you can do about it. If bad weather crashes your outdoor wedding, you need to be ready.

The first thing to consider when scheduling an outdoor wedding is to have a back-up plan for the ceremony and the reception. Ask yourself where the events will take place if the weather doesn't cooperate. Do you have a tent in place or a church reserved in case of bad weather? This is an important agenda item. You just can't depend on Mother Nature to cooperate!

One of my most outstanding wedding memories is a lovely outdoor wedding that was held in a nature preserve. The couple owned property adjoining the preserve, and more than anything, they wanted to be married by the lake. We decided to have tents put up as our back-up plan. The tents arrived on Friday morning. The rain started Friday night. It rained so much that it washed out half the road leading to the property. The wedding was scheduled for 7 on Sunday evening. We had water everywhere—I mean everywhere. I don't think that even Noah himself encountered more water. The tents had bowed at the top from too much water. Two of the uprights came completely out of the ground. We had standing water in some places. You could literally float an air mattress inside the tents. It was a mess!

Bouquet Toss

Superstition says that if it *does* rain on your wedding day, it's a sign of good fortune. That's putting a positive spin on it!

When the wedding day arrived, it sprinkled and the clouds were dark and ominous, but at least it didn't rain. Right before the service, the minister came up to me with a look of panic on his face and asked, "Teddy, what should I do if it starts raining during the ceremony?" I looked him right in the eye and said, "If they're little drops, read fast. If they're big drops, read faster." At that point, there's nothing else you can do.

Dealing with outdoor weddings can be made a little easier if you have the budget. Tents can be floored so the water level won't cause your guests discomfort. Flooring for tents is very expensive. That's one reason why selecting the right site for your tent needs to be left to the professionals. Tents can also be heated (remember in the movie *Father of the Bride*) or cooled.

Both heaters and air-conditioners will heat or cool a tent but not as effectively as being indoors. They, too, are expensive but, as we say in this business, nothing is impossible.

What You'll Need

Another reality of outdoor weddings is that you have to bring everything you'll need outside; you must be completely self-sufficient. For example, your caterer doesn't want to find out that she can't use the water in the well for cooking because it hasn't been tested. Depending on the size of your crowd, you might have to bring in:

- Portable toilets
- Lighting
- Tables and chairs
- Linens
- Décor
- Food and beverages
- Kitchen tent (for preparing the food)

You also want to make sure that you have the bug population under control in the area. It's a pretty awful sight to see a lovely white wedding cake with a trail of black ants marching up the side. Have a professional come to the site several weeks before the event to determine what you need to have controlled. Always let the professionals deal with insecticides.

Let's Get Physical

Okay, so you still want to have an outdoor wedding. Pay close attention to the physical site. Look for uneven places on the ground. Where will the wedding party enter? Wearing high heels on soft ground is not pleasant and might even ruin your shoes.

The physical placement of your ceremony is extremely important. It helps if you can see the site at the time of day you plan for your wedding.

For example, you and your partner do not want to be facing west at 4 on a September afternoon—you will be blinded by the sun. Likewise, you don't want your guests facing into the sun, for the same reason. Therefore, check lighting, sunshine, and sun position so you know what you're up against.

If your wedding is at night, make sure you have sufficient lighting for your guests to safely move around the site. That includes wandering off to the portable toilets (hopefully well away from the main site), to traveling to the parking area and walkways in general. You need to be very careful you provide all reasonable lighting possible. That's your responsibility as the host of this once-in-a-lifetime event. You don't want Aunt Tilly to fall and break a leg. That would put a damper on your day, not to mention hers.

> **Teddy's Tips**
>
> Decide on one focal point for the service so that your guests can focus their attention on one area. Try for something natural: a grouping of trees, a fountain, or the head of a garden. You're outside, so you don't want to compete with Mother Nature—just enhance her.

Park It Here, My Dear

Depending on your property and the size of your guest list, parking can be a major problem. Wherever you schedule the outdoor wedding, make doubly sure that you have adequate parking facilities and attendants. What you don't want or need is someone parking sideways and blocking another car, either the next door neighbor's or a guest's. (You're in big trouble if that person turns out to be your neighbor, who wasn't invited. In fact, if you're planning an outdoor wedding, make sure that the neighbors know what's taking place. You want to keep on good terms with them.)

If the logistics can be worked out, consider having valet parking. This is a great idea, especially if you have a tight area to put lots of cars. Be sure to check with your insurance carrier about the liability of hiring valet parkers. I've hired a church youth choir, a fraternity, and a group of my son Ben's good friends to park vehicles. For the choir and the fraternity, we made a donation to their charity. For Ben's friends, we paid them and then they split the tips.

Another solution is to run a shuttle from a local parking lot (for example, a school or a church) to the site. (Make sure that you check with local authorities in case you need a special permit.) Then hire a company to operate a van or bus.

Tears over Melting Tiers

When choosing your menu for your outdoor wedding, keep in mind that it is going to be outside. You know, among nature—the birds, the bees, the bugs. And the heat. Hire a reputable caterer to recommend a menu that will hold up under the warm-weather sun. Most caterers have cooling units and stove units to keep items hot or cold. But nothing can keep cold items truly cold, for long periods of time, in a summer heat wave. Rely on your caterer's advice. It could mean the difference between a great honeymoon and food poisoning.

Military Weddings

If the bride or groom (or both) are in the armed forces, they may chose to have a military style wedding. The main differences between a military wedding and a civilian wedding are the invitations, the uniformed attendants or the couple in uniform, and the arch of swords (or sabers) at the end of the service. Everything else is the same.

The wording on the invitation needs to be written precisely according to standard etiquette, your branch of service, and your rank. Be sure to check with your bridal consultant or the stationery store expert for the correct military wording on your invitations. There are many different correct forms to use.

For the sword/saber ceremony at the end of the ceremony, all commissioned officers present form two lines opposite each other outside the church or right inside the foyer. As the couple exits, the head usher commands "Draw swords" (Naval officers) or "Draw sabers" (Army, Air Force, and Marine officers). Then, using their right hands, the officers draw out their swords or sabers to form an arch. The couple passes underneath the arch, and the officers return their swords or sabers to their sheaths.

Bouquet Toss

> The tradition of the arch of swords at the end of the wedding started in 1909, when an officer bridegroom and his attendants raised their swords to toast the bride. The idea caught on and has been formalized to be part of military tradition.

Dress can be your dress uniform or full-dress uniform, including medals or merely ribbons. Badges also may be worn. Men or women in uniform do not wear flowers, corsages, or boutonnieres.

If the groom is a member or graduate of one of the academies, you may display its flag in the church along with the American flag.

The groom is dressed in his dress whites for this military-theme wedding. *(Photo by Norma Edelman, The Wedding Casa)*

Getting Personal

Personalizing your wedding is another way to "theme" the wedding. Frank Andonoplas of Frank Event Design in Chicago is a natural at getting ideas from the couples and turning those personal likes and personalities into some wonderfully clever ways to create a unique wedding. Here are some ideas he shares from weddings he's designed:

For two avid golfers:

- Place card table was lined in fresh sod.
- Floral arrangement was created in a golf bag.
- Long-stemmed flowers were mixed in with golf clubs.
- Tables were named for famous golf courses.
- Favors were golf ball and tees with the couple's names and date. They were packaged in clear bags and tied with bear grass.

This couple was married at a train station, then hopped aboard the train for a ride to the reception. They wore his-and-her conductor's caps—hers even has a little veil! *(Photo by Colter Photography)*

Grandpa always did want to be a conductor ....
(Photo by Colter Photography)

A couple who loved poetry:

◆ Invitation had part of "How Do I Love Thee" on top.

◆ Each table was named after a poet with a phrase from a famous work. Those works were then all printed in a booklet placed as the favor.

◆ The groom wrote a poem for his lovely bride and read it in front of the guests (tears flowed).

◆ Guests all received mini poetry books when they left the reception.

Two professional artists:

◆ Invitations were printed on the inside fold so the bride could do an original watercolor on the cover of each invitation.

◆ Tables named for famous artists.

◆ Each table was designed to go with the artist style; for example, Water Lily china for the Monet Table, bright bold colors in china and glasswear for the Picasso table.

◆ Hors d'oeuvres were passed on artist's palettes.

Here are two other ideas for naming tables from Frank:

◆ Favorite Disney characters: Mickey and Minnie, Cinderella and the Prince, Snow White and Prince Charming …

◆ Famous couples: Lucy and Ricky, Romeo and Juliet, Bogie and Bacall, Scarlett and Rhett …

This bride holds a tiny glass slipper given to her by her prince. *(Photo by Colter Photography)*

The Cinderella theme is carried through in details like the castle cake and the table name. *(Photos by Colter Photography)*

And here's the prince putting a real-life glass slipper on his bride (it fits, of course!). *(Photo by Colter Photography)*

You can develop any type of wedding theme as much as you want. You might use only a hint of a theme, or you might go all out and make it a truly thematic wedding, from start to finish. The choice is yours.

Teddy's Tips

Once you've chosen a theme for your wedding, look in the library for books on the subject or search the Internet for information (see Chapter 1).

This couple honors the groom's Scottish heritage by having a bagpiper lead them from the church to the reception. *(Photo by Colter Photography)*

Three men in kilts hoist three merry little maids. *(Photo by Colter Photography)*

The Weekend Wedding

A *weekend wedding* offers your guests additional activities throughout the weekend beyond the normal wedding festivities. Instead of attending only the wedding and the reception, your wedding guests, often coming from all over the country, can choose to participate in several preplanned functions. The wedding and reception are the highlights of the activities, but you can plan other outings to help guests put aside their hectic schedules for a little while and provide them with a mini-vacation. It's a chance to meet new friends, a chance for your two families to do some bonding, and a chance for your friends and family to spend some quality time together—and with you.

> **Nuptial Notes**
>
> A **weekend wedding** offers your guests additional activities throughout the weekend beyond the normal wedding festivities of ceremony and reception.

Many times, the weekend wedding can bring a family back to an area where there is common ground. The University of Notre Dame in South Bend, Indiana, for example, houses a gorgeous cathedral where couples who are alumni can be married. Other colleges and universities have couples return to be married in their facilities. Coming back to a place that holds special memories is not the only reason for a weekend wedding. This kind of wedding also offers the couple the opportunity to include many people in many different activities and to make the wedding a truly memorable event.

Guest Activities

Your guest activities for a weekend wedding can be as unique as the two of you and the location you have chosen. You can arrange those activities around a theme or a time of the year. You should plan for a variety of activities—enough so that guests feel special, but not so many that they become exhausted.

Here's a sample weekend format to give you some ideas:

Thursday, September 4
(for guests arriving early)

6 to 10 A.M.	Continental breakfast in lobby
11 A.M. to 4 P.M.	Shopping in the new mall (bus will transport to and from hotel)
7 P.M.	Notre Dame football practice at the new stadium
8 P.M.	Informal gathering at Coaches Bar
Late night	Hotel hospitality suite—may include snacks, drinks, and board games

Friday, September 5

6 to 10 A.M.	Continental breakfast in lobby
9 A.M.	Golf tournament (see Jim to sign up)
10:30 to 11:45 A.M.	Campus tour—main circle
6 to 7 P.M.	Rehearsal (wedding party) Cathedral of Notre Dame
7 to 7:30 P.M.	Musical ceremony at the Grotto
7:45 to 11 P.M.	Rehearsal dinner at The Commons
Late night	Hotel hospitality suite

Saturday, September 6

7 to 11 A.M.	Continental breakfast in lobby
8:30 to 9:45 A.M.	Campus tour—main circle
11 A.M.–2 P.M.	Notre Dame vs. Michigan football game party in hospitality suite
3–11:30 P.M.	Wedding ceremony at cathedral and dinner and dancing at the Marriott
Late night	Hotel hospitality suite

Sunday, September 7

7 to 11 A.M.	Continental breakfast in lobby
8:45 A.M.	Mass in the Crown Room

This example shows activities for the weekend wedding in which the hotel is the focal point for most guests. This is also an example of bringing the wedding guests to a point of interest other than the hometown location. In this case, the couple chose to bring everyone to the campus of Notre Dame.

This next example involves guests more with family, friends, and hometown activities.

Friday, October 10

10 A.M.	Van picks up guests at airport and delivers them to hotel and guest houses.

4 P.M.	Hospitality time for guests at Aunt Helen's home. Those guests arriving may pick up their welcome packages and get the agenda for the weekend there.
7 to 8 P.M.	Rehearsal at St. Stephen's Church (wedding party).
8:30 to 11 P.M.	Rehearsal dinner at the River House.

Saturday, October 11

10 A.M.	Brunch for all at Brown's Restaurant (hosted by Julia Miller).
1 P.M.	Tour of the art museum or historical society (see John for details).
5 P.M.	Wedding at St. Stephen's Church. Childcare is available at hotel (see John for details).
6:30 P.M.	Wedding reception, dinner, and dancing at St. Mary's.

Sunday, October 12

11 A.M.	Brunch at Uncle Fred and Aunt Margaret's home.

This sample shows more local family members involved. Here are some other ideas you could incorporate into your weekend wedding activities:

- Set up a softball game—maybe a tournament.
- Take a trip to the local zoo.
- Tour a historical district.
- Spend a day at a spa; treat your wedding party to the works: a manicure, pedicure, and body massage.
- Have a picnic or barbecue in a park or backyard.
- Go see a play.
- Have a scavenger hunt through the city with prizes.

Teddy's Tips

Be sure to check with the local chamber of commerce for other events scheduled for the same weekend. If you can stay away from busy times in your chosen city, you'll be better off.

Hear Ye! Hear Ye!

When planning for the weekend wedding (whether you're having it in your home city with family and friends coming in from all over, or whether you've made arrangements for it in another location), there are some do's and don'ts to follow. Always think of your guests' comfort and enjoyment during the weekend. Make sure you take care of their needs. Here are some additional things to help make everyone's visit more pleasurable:

- Get a good travel agent to coordinate the hotel, airlines, shuttle service, and car rentals.

- Get the word out early about the wedding date and location so that guests can begin to think about how they can incorporate your wedding weekend into their plans.

- Send a newsletter closer to the wedding date, including details about parties and other events, weather conditions, hotel information, and maps.

- Update the schedule, and let guests know of major changes.

- Make guests feel welcome when they arrive. Place some kind of welcome package in their hotel rooms. This doesn't have to be fancy or expensive, but it needs to be from you and your partner (or your parents). See Chapter 13 for ideas on creating a welcome basket.

- Leave copies of the wedding weekend agenda at the front desk of the hotel, in the hospitality room, and with both sets of parents. That way, if a guest misplaces an agenda, another one is readily available.

- Provide a list of baby-sitters, or have sitter arrangements made for those guests who are bringing small children for the weekend.

- Have some of the activities geared toward children. Consider hiring a social director to come in and organize a children's party for the kids while the adults are entertained somewhere else, or arrange a visit to a children's museum.

- Try not to overplan. You want to offer activities to your guests so that they can take part, but they should not feel overwhelmed or as if they're at summer camp.

- Remember that the wedding and the reception are the high points of the weekend. Everything else is optional for most of your guests.

Weekend weddings are meant to encompass all the beauty, love, and grace that a one-day wedding holds, plus give your guests more of a feel for celebrating in a variety of ways. Do your homework, stay organized, and plan ahead. You can then relax and enjoy what should be a memorable weekend for everyone involved!

The Least You Need to Know

◆ Build your theme wedding around you and your partner's heritage, hobby, or career. Make it unique to the two of you.

◆ Seasonal weddings are a natural idea if you want to give your wedding a theme. You can have some fun picking a date to plan your wedding around and decorating with seasonal motifs.

◆ Outdoor weddings can be beautiful and fun, but they are risky. Always have a back-up plan in case the weather doesn't cooperate.

◆ Military weddings differ from civilian weddings in the way in which the invitations are worded, the presence of uniformed attendants, and the arch of swords or sabers.

◆ Remember that the wedding and the reception are the highlights of the wedding weekend. No other activity should overshadow these two events.

◆ Don't overplan your weekend wedding. Maintain a balance in your agenda. Consider your guests' interests and needs; give them time to rest and relax.

In This Chapter

- ◆ What's a destination wedding?
- ◆ Planning a destination wedding
- ◆ Activities for your guests
- ◆ What to know before you go
- ◆ Some popular destinations

Chapter 18

Mickey and Minnie, Here We Come: Destination Weddings

I talked about weekend weddings in Chapter 17. A destination wedding is very similar to a weekend wedding in format and principle, but the kind of location you choose for the wedding is the primary difference between the two.

Like a weekend wedding, a destination wedding should offer fun and relaxation for everyone involved. These weddings also require some extra time and organization to pull off successfully. In this chapter, I'll tell you all you need to know!

What Is a Destination Wedding?

A *destination wedding* takes place somewhere where you might take a vacation. That's probably the biggest difference between a destination wedding and a weekend wedding. While a vacation in South Bend, Indiana, or Iowa City, Iowa, might not be at the top of your list, you definitely would consider a vacation to Disney World in Florida or to the Hawaiian islands. Think of it this way: With a destination wedding, the majority of activities you can offer your guests are already in place.

Nuptial Notes

A **destination wedding** sometimes is referred to as a travel wedding (because you travel to the location) or a honeymoon wedding (because the destination also serves as your honeymoon spot).

For example, let's say you're a big country music fan. What better spot could you find than Nashville, Tennessee, and Opryland to enhance your destination wedding dreams? Nashville is a stately southern city filled with beautiful plantations, and the center of the country music industry. Think of all the activities right at your fingertips! For a weekend wedding in South Bend, Indiana, on the other hand, you would have to plan, coordinate, or organize all the activities you offer your guests. Don't get me wrong—destination weddings still require quite a bit of organization and planning to ensure that all systems are go. With a little help from the staff at the site, however, or with other professional help (this is where a good bridal consultant can be a lifesaver), you can be in for a wonderful and memorable event.

A destination wedding can be as elaborate or as simple as you want, depending upon your budget. Many times, families take extended vacations at resort spots and include the wedding festivities.

Keep in mind that with destination weddings, your guests are responsible for their own transportation costs and housing expenses. Very rarely would you house them in family homes at a destination wedding unless there were family members in the vicinity.

How to Plan a Destination Wedding

There are several items to think about when planning a destination wedding. Following are the key considerations.

Do Your Research!

If you have an area in mind or have some interest you want to fulfill, start arranging for your destination wedding by doing research:

- Browse travel magazines.
- Check out websites.
- Talk with other couples who have gone to the same area or resort.
- Contact the tourist boards.
- Contact the local Chamber of Commerce.
- Check on marriage requirements.
- If you are a member of AAA (American Automobile Association) or another travel club, check with them for ideas and details. Most times their advice and information is free to members. They can also send you travel guides and maps of the area or resort.

Mother Nature, Again

Think about the weather conditions where you're hoping to hold your wedding. Maybe a wedding planned for a remote beach in hurricane season isn't such a good idea. A veil blowing gently in the breeze is one thing, but gale-force winds could be overkill. Get some expert advice about the weather at that location at the time of year you're considering.

A Place in Your Heart

When choosing a location, think about a spot that might have some meaning to you. If your favorite fairy tale as a little girl was Cinderella, you might choose a place like Disney World. Or if your family always took skiing vacations, you might consider a place like Aspen, Colorado, for your destination wedding. Consider what's meaningful to the two of you.

The tale of Cinderella comes alive for this bride—complete with beautiful glass coach, six white horses, and two coachmen! *(Photos by The Wedding Specialist)*

Accommodations and Amenities

After you choose a location, you need to select the accommodations you'll use. If you have more specific choices to make, such as choosing a particular Hawaiian or Caribbean island, then you'll want to do more research to find just the right resort for your wedding. Take into consideration the extras the resort offers, such as which amenities are free and which ones guests have to pay extra for (such as golf, tennis, swimming, or sightseeing excursions). You don't want your guests spending big bucks on airfare and hotel accommodations only to find that they have to pay every time they use the pool or ask for a clean towel. Find out those details ahead of time.

> **Wedding Woes**
>
> When selecting the hotel or resort for your destination wedding, be sure read and fully understand the fine print in the contracts. Trust me, there's a reason it's so small!

Is It Legal?

Just because you have every detail in place and have talked at length with the hotel and the airlines, don't make that first deposit until you're *sure* you can be married in your chosen spot. Find out the rules and regulations of marrying at the site you've chosen. Rules vary from state to state and from island to island. Some destinations require a long residency; others require up to a 30-day waiting period after you apply for the license before you can marry there. Take some time now to determine whether your dream location actually can become a reality.

Guest Activities

Unlike the agenda for a weekend wedding, your guest activities are readily available. Because of the locale you've chosen for your destination wedding, planning activities to keep you and your guests busy will not be a chore.

Again, go with the flow. If you're on an island and have great beaches and fishing at your disposal, make that a focal point. Why not have the rehearsal dinner on the beach? Add volleyball and a picnic supper, and your guests can relax, eat, drink, and have fun either enjoying the game or watching the sun set into the ocean.

Let the destination determine what activities you'll have guests involved with; the choices are endless. It's up to you and your groom and just takes a little imagination.

The big moment has arrived. *(Photo by Willis Photography)*

Another popular destination wedding site are the Sandals Resorts throughout the Caribbean. This family headed south for their son's wedding at a Sandals Resort. They've just arrived and are eager to check things out! *(Photo by Willis Photography)*

"Wow—here's where the ceremony will take place. It's a lot different than back home in Iowa!" *(Photo by Willis Photography)*

Can you imagine a more picture-perfect or romantic setting in which to exchange vows? *(Photo by Willis Photography)*

Practical Tips

To make your dreams come true of having your wedding and reception on an island paradise or with a castle as a backdrop, you'll need to make sure you have all your bases covered. Here are some suggestions to help you utilize your resources and still get to the church on time:

◆ Work with the local chamber of commerce or tourist board in the area you've chosen for your wedding.

◆ Hire a bridal consultant from that locale. Many times, the hotels can provide names of local consultants. You can also obtain names of bridal consultants in a particular locale or who specialize in destination weddings by contacting the Association of Bridal Consultants in New Milford, Connecticut, at 860-355-0464 or BridalAssn@aol.com. (Ask for Jerry or Eileen, and tell them Teddy sent you.)

◆ Whether you choose to work with a private company or a staff member at the resort, make sure that you write down all your questions before you make the call to the bridal consultant. E-mail now makes a huge difference. You can actually see the response, not just listen to it. Make good use of both your time and the consultant's time. Include all the items you need to discuss: ceremony site, music, floral arrangements, photography, videography, food, liquor, and the fee for staff. You don't want any surprises 2,000 miles away from home. Get those details in writing now.

◆ Make sure you have the legal requirements for marrying in that locale in writing: waiting periods, residency requirements, and what paperwork you have to bring with you, such as identification, birth certificates, blood test reports, proof of citizenship, passports, and parental consent (in the case of minors). Be sure you know the age requirement for marrying in that particular locale. This fact varies from place to place, so be sure to check. Work out all these kinks ahead of time!

◆ If at all possible, make a trip to the site before the wedding just to be sure that everything is as you want it and that there are no hidden agendas with hotel staff. What you are told and how that statement is interpreted by all parties might not be the same thing. For example, you might be assured that the backdrop for your wedding site is a pure white-sand beach with crystal-clear blue water. The fact that the hotel forgot to mention the oil rigging outfit offshore could be a big interpretation problem. Sometimes a face-to-face conversation can save you misunderstandings later.

◆ If you're marrying during the spring break season, be sure to check to see how popular your resort is with the college crowd. While you're checking, ask about local events that could affect your big day.

Wedding Woes

Don't forget to include in your overall budget the long-distance telephone calls to the resort or facility that will pop up frequently as you plan for this wedding. Although calling is the fastest and most convenient way to communicate with the resort staff carrying out your plans (along with e-mail), it isn't the cheapest. Be sure to build those costs into your budget.

- Be sure to send a newsletter to those guests who have indicated that they would like to share in your destination wedding. In the newsletter, include information on airlines, hotels, costs, choices of accommodations, what's available onsite, dress style for the stay, and anything pertaining specifically to that destination. You can enclose a brochure of the hotel or resort in the newsletter to entice those guests even more.

- Make sure that your arrangements are confirmed and that you have everything in writing. Look over contracts very carefully. Read the fine print—you don't want any surprises.

- If you're bringing your wedding gown with you, it must be boxed carefully with sheets of tissue paper between the folds. Think carefully before you decide to check it through with the luggage: Losing your wedding gown two days before the wedding would be a big headache. You might want to put it in a garment bag and hang it on the plane. Linens and silk taffeta are not good fabric choices for travel; stick with cotton, satin, cotton voile, or a silk crepe for the least amount of upkeep. Check with the hotel or resort about pressing or steaming services.

- If you aren't bringing your gown, think about renting one onsite, or go with the culture of your locale. Instead of our Americanized wedding gown, go with what the locals wear. Have fun!

All this and cake, too! *(Photo by Willis Photography)*

This newly married couple poses amid the natural beauty of the islands. *(Photo by Willis Photography)*

Popular Sites

You can consider any resort area that can accommodate a wedding for your destination wedding. Choose the wedding site as you would choose your honeymoon site. What activities are you interested in? What activities would you like for your guests? Is there a fantasy you would like to fulfill, such as spending time exploring a castle, snorkeling off the coast of St. Thomas, or deep-sea fishing in the waters of Bermuda? Whatever your fantasy is, see if you can find someplace that fulfills it.

This doesn't have to be a big-time resort, either. If there's a state park or nature area that you find particularly inviting and you can envision yourself surrounded by family and friends on top of a mountain, go for it. Make this your special time, and offer your guests the opportunity to participate with you as you celebrate your wedding.

Some popular destination wedding sites include the following:

- Disney World
- Disney Land
- Hawaii
- The Sandals Resorts
- Las Vegas
- Cruise ships

Disney World is probably one of the most fun places to hold your destination wedding. Here we have topiary trees cut out in the shapes of Mickey and Minnie. They will be used at the reception. *(Photo from the author's collection)*

This is to be an outdoor wedding with the reception inside one of the many resorts. This faces the Grand Floridian. The stage is set for the bridal couple.

This wedding guest is getting a personal escort by Mickey and Minnie. *(Photo from the author's collection)*

Teddy's Tips

A fascinating book by Hannelore Hahn, *Places* (see Appendix A), now in its eighth edition, might help you find a unique destination for your wedding. The book's subtitle says it all: "A Directory of Public Places for Private Events and Private Places for Public Functions." Check out this book, and let your imagination run wild.

And speaking of cruise ships, the romantic notion of being married by the cruise ship's captain is false. Unless he is a Notary Public or an ordained minister, the captain cannot perform the service. Most couples have the ceremony at dockside—off the ship—and then go aboard and have the reception, followed by days at sea for the honeymoon. (Don't worry—your guests don't go on the honeymoon with you.)

A destination wedding can be fun, romantic, and intimate for all involved. It can be a wonderful vacation idea for guests and a good opportunity for family and friends to get to know one another. Your options are endless and can be as exotic or out of the ordinary as your budget will allow. Whatever destination you choose, just be sure to do your homework, and enjoy!

Couples can chose from among many themed wedding sites. This one is an island theme complete with gazebo; others might range from King Arthur to a nautical theme. *(Photo by The Wedding Specialist)*

Lake Havasu City, Arizona, is becoming a popular wedding destination. Located south of Lake Mead, it features all kinds of water activities. This is a shot of the famous London Bridge (not the real London Bridge, of course, but a pretty good lookalike). *(Photo by The Wedding Specialist)*

This bride poses with Lake Havasu City's London Bridge behind her. You can see the gazebo through the water fountain. *(Photo by The Wedding Specialist)*

The Least You Need to Know

◆ Destination weddings offer a vacation atmosphere and many of the activities you might want to schedule for your guests.

◆ Make sure that you check about legal requirements for the marriage license in the locale in which you plan to have your wedding.

◆ Wherever you decide to have your destination wedding, work with a bridal consultant either from that area or someone who specializes in destination weddings. The bridal consultant can be invaluable in helping you achieve the type of wedding you desire.

◆ Try to visit the site before the wedding to make sure it's what you have in mind and to make sure you have accurately communicated your desires to the local staff.

◆ Allow enough time for your guests to plan for a destination wedding; send them informative newsletters to help them prepare.

In This Part

Part 6

Surviving the Big Event: Tales from the Altar

Well, this is it! The big day is quickly approaching, and you're ready. You've met with countless vendors, looked at dozens of bridal bouquets, leafed through numerous invitation books, and picked out some wonderful favors for your guests to enjoy. This is where all your hard work and dedication is going to pay off.

In this part, I'll discuss the importance of the wedding rehearsal and tell you how to prepare for your big day so you'll be at your best. I'll walk you through all the activities you might want to include in your reception. You'll learn some valuable tips from the pros, get the scoop on the newest trends, and finally, enjoy a chapter from real-life couples who share their stories with you. Prepare for a day to remember!

In This Chapter

- Practicing at the wedding rehearsal
- Getting yourself ready for the big day
- Reducing your stress level
- Getting down the aisle in time

Chapter 19

Much Ado About Everything: Prenuptial Preparation

I've discussed nearly all the details you need to know to help you prepare for your wedding. Now, you're zeroing in on the big day. Preparation is the name of the game; it has been all along. Now, even more than ever, I want you to prepare just a little bit more as you move right up to the big day!

This chapter will focus on getting yourself ready for the big day, reducing your stress level, and getting down the aisle on time (it's not as easy as it sounds). I'll talk about how important the rehearsal is and what you need to do after all the pre-wedding festivities.

The Dress Rehearsal

The wedding rehearsal is an important event in the wedding planning process. It's your insurance policy that the members of your wedding cast know their lines, places, cues, what to do, and what not to do come wedding day.

The wedding rehearsal usually occurs the day or evening before the wedding is to take place. Sometimes, the rehearsal doesn't take place the eve of the wedding. Many times, the Jewish rehearsal takes place the morning of the wedding. Plan the rehearsal for whatever time your individual circumstances dictate.

The rehearsal is the time to make sure all the details of the ceremony are ironed out. Here the bride and consultant go over some last-minute paperwork with the officant. *(Photo by Colter Photography)*

Practice Makes Perfect

The whole purpose of the wedding rehearsal is to practice what will take place during the ceremony. As in a play rehearsal, the director (officiant or bridal consultant) conducts the rehearsal so that everyone in the cast of characters (wedding party) knows their parts, responsibilities, and duties.

It's best if the musicians are present for the rehearsal. One of the prime functions of the rehearsal is to practice both the processional (when the wedding party enters) and the recessional (when the wedding party exits). If the musicians are not present, it's more difficult for the wedding party to get a feel for rhythm and timing.

I Did Say *Dress* Rehearsal

The rehearsal is a good time to try out any bridal accessories, such as an exceptionally long train or veil, that might require some extra attention or special accommodation during the ceremony. I recommend the bride wear a practice long veil and long train during the rehearsal, if it's

determined that will be a concern. Brides are amazed at how awkward and cumbersome those long veils can be during the wedding; by practicing, it gives them a much better feel for movement and placement.

Bouquet Toss

One bride I worked with chose to wear a full-length veil at the ceremony. It extended four feet behind her on the floor. She did look radiant floating down the aisle on the arm of her father. Dad, naturally, was feeling rather nervous. When they reached the altar area, instead of stepping back away from the veil, he stepped right on it and pulled it completely off the bride's head. He reached down, rolled up the pile of tulle, and tossed it to his wife in the first pew. Words do not begin to describe the look on the mother's face.

Who Should Attend?

Those who should attend the wedding rehearsal include the following:

- All members of the wedding party, including ushers, the flower girl, and the ring bearer
- Readers
- The soloist
- Musicians
- The officiant

If you're including train bearers or pages, they should attend as well. You also will want your parents present, especially if they have a part in the service.

Who's the Boss Here?

The officiant should be in control or in charge of the wedding rehearsal. Some facilities have a wedding director on staff who oversees the rehearsal. If that is the case with your ceremony site, work with that person. Also, if you've hired a bridal consultant, make sure she knows her role at the rehearsal. Unless she or he (we do have male bridal consultants in the Association of Bridal Consultants) has been asked by the officiant to help out, she should assume a back-seat role; she shouldn't run the show.

This couple exits this rehearsal. Notice the bride-to-be is carrying a "bouquet" made from the ribbons that were tied to all her shower gifts. (It's one of those girl things.) *(Photo from the author's collection)*

Over the years, I've found that the best rehearsals are the ones conducted by the person who will perform the wedding service. Whatever circumstances you face, go in with a positive attitude. Try to work out all the ceremony details long before the rehearsal. It does little good for you or the officiant to be deciding on reading selections the eve of your wedding. If at all possible, get those items ironed out beforehand.

If the officiant does not take charge of your rehearsal, you could be in for some rough waters. The more in charge the officiant is at the rehearsal, the smoother the wedding ceremony goes.

Remember to have respect for the person who is going to perform your service. Make him your friend, not your enemy. Above all, remember why you're at the rehearsal in the first place. You're here to practice for your marriage service, the day the two of you vow to spend the rest of your lives together. Don't lose track of what's really important.

A Little Pre-Party Fun

A discussion of the wedding rehearsal brings to mind one other item we should talk about: the bachelor or bachelorette party. Promise me one thing—and don't do this for me (hey, I'm not your mother), do it for yourselves. Do not hold this final fling the night before your wedding. It can be a great time to share with your friends, but the bottom line is that you need to be in good shape for the wedding day. If you've been out too late and partied too much, you might not be in any shape to do anything, much less something as important as getting married. All right, enough from Mother Teddy.

The Bachelor Party

The bachelor party goes back centuries. It began as a way the townsmen could help a prospective young groom get all the philandering out of his system before he took a wife. In our modern times, the bachelor party is an opportunity for the men in the wedding party to get together for a night on the town, a baseball game, or maybe a sailing trip. It has taken on a new meaning as having an evening or even a weekend where the men in the wedding party get together to honor the groom and share in some fun activities. One groom who loved to gamble got his buddies together for a trip to Las Vegas for a weekend. Although this was a more elaborate event than most bachelor parties, they did have a great time, and it gave them a chance to spend some quality time with each other.

If you're a camping nut, why not take your friends to the woods for a camping trip? Fishing and sitting around a campfire telling jokes can be a relaxing—and relatively inexpensive—way to get away from it all for a while and do some male bonding. Some grooms prefer a night in their favorite pub with just a few close friends, or ringside seats at a prize fight. Whatever strikes your fancy, try to incorporate those ideas into your bachelor party.

The Bachelorette Party

While the men are living it up in a local bar or other venue, the women can be doing the same thing with a bachelorette party. One of the neatest bachelorette parties I've ever heard about occurred a few years ago. The maid of honor made up a scavenger hunt for the women in the wedding party. The group divided into several carloads, and each group was given a list of items to find and bring back to the host site within a certain time limit. Of course, there was no alcohol on the road, but a couple bottles of champagne did await the winners. The bride

later shared with me how much she had enjoyed the evening. Many of the items for which they were searching were things her groom-to-be would like, such as a deck of cards or a book on old cars.

Whatever you decide about pre-wedding parties and your friends, just make sure you play it safe, keep it fun, make sure people know the ground rules. And as I've said, be sure to hold the party several nights (or weeks, or even months) before the wedding as well.

Getting Yourself Ready

Okay, time is marching on. You've made it through the rehearsal in one piece, and you have been the honored guests at a lovely rehearsal dinner (see Chapter 6). You say good night and head home for some much-needed rest.

I've tried to emphasize throughout this book how important it is for you to be organized. I don't keep repeating that phrase because I have a limited vocabulary. I say this because of all the ways you can help yourself, staying organized and knowing what to do is the key to a successful, stress-free wedding day.

> **Teddy's Tips**
>
> Use the Planning Check-Off List in Appendix C to help you keep track of all the details in the months leading up to the big event. Keep it handy and refer to it often!

You Are Getting Sleepy

When you come home (or back to the hotel—wherever you're staying the night before your wedding), take a nice, relaxing bath. Now, I'm not a bathtub fan. I much prefer showers, but for this particular event, I think you will find a nice, warm bath very soothing. That's what we're after here. You need to be relaxed so that you can get some much-needed sleep. You've probably been going about 100 miles an hour for the last several months. Now it's time to slow down and savor the day to come.

While you're taking it easy in the tub, try sipping some warm milk (not chocolate, which contains caffeine) or some herbal tea. Warm milk can be very soothing to the body and soul, and research has proven that drinking it releases in the body some chemicals that bring on sleep. As you relax in the tub, imagine a peaceful setting: the green hills of a favorite park, a campfire growing dim, or the brilliance of a sunset. Peace, tranquillity, and a sense of calm (use imagery to stimulate that sense)—that's what you're after. Put on some soft music to help set the mood, or listen to a relaxation tape. Maybe the sounds of water or wind gently blowing can soothe your soul. This is "be good to yourself" time. Indulge yourself. Try to block out every possible negative vision you can. You want to be at peace, inside and out.

When you finish with your bath, follow your normal nighttime routine. Get as much sleep as possible. The wedding day will be exciting but exhausting. You need a lot of sleep now so that you can feel and look great in the morning. A bride or groom with dark circles under their eyes from lack of sleep is not a pretty sight.

You Are What You Eat

Just as important as enough rest is the right kind of food in your body. As I've mentioned in previous chapters, you must keep yourself on track by eating right and getting enough rest. With all the appointments to keep, fittings to schedule, and vendors to call, nourishment is important. Try to avoid fast food and stick with healthier choices.

Even if you're not a breakfast person, try to be one on your wedding day. Even if it's just a bagel and some juice, get a little something in your tummy. Believe me, depending on the time of your service, there might not be time to eat later, or you might be too nervous. And you don't want your stomach growling between silences in the church! If you do enjoy breakfast, then include in your menu some carbohydrates (for energy), some fruit or juice (for vitamin C), and protein (milk, cocoa, eggs, or cheese). If you aren't a heavy breakfast eater, don't change now. Just try putting something light in your tummy. The important thing is to get your body revved up for the day to come.

Teddy's Tips

If your wedding is later in the day, be sure to bring some healthy snacks to the ceremony site for the wedding party to nibble on. Saltines or crackers, nuts, cheese cubes, and fresh fruit are all good choices.

This happy bride arrives at the ceremony site. She looks ready to get this show on the road! *(Photo by Colter Photography)*

Most brides have their hair done and their veils secured by a professional hairdresser before arriving at the ceremony site. *(Photo by Colter Photography)*

Making a List and Checking It Twice

By now you should have a check list of what goes to the church with you, what goes to the reception, and what goes on the honeymoon. Just as I keep emphasizing to keep yourself organized, keeping a list and adding items to it as you think of them will help keep your stress level down and get you to the church on time and with what you need.

What I suggest to my brides is to find a room in their home where they can keep everything that goes to the wedding (church, reception, or on the honeymoon). As you find something or buy that cute bathing suit you've been wanting, put it in that room. That way, when the time comes to divide up all those items, at least you won't have to go all over the house to find things. Make a box or large bag for items that go to the church with you. Make another box for items that go to the reception. Keep your honeymoon luggage open, with a packing list on top, and as you put something in, check it off the list. Lots of things will be happening as your wedding day nears, and the more you can do now to keep organized, the better off you will be.

Something Old, Something New

Whether you choose to dress at home or at the wedding facility, be sure to include in the bag of tricks you're taking with you the items in the verse: "Something old, something new, something borrowed, something blue, and a lucky penny in your shoe."

- "Something old" is used to show a sense of continuity. You can use a family heirloom or carry the family Bible or Prayer Book. I wore my grandmother's onyx-and-diamond ring on my wedding day and carried a handkerchief that belonged to my great-grandmother.

- "Something new" equates to hope for an optimistic future. Most brides consider their wedding gown to fit the bill.

- "Something borrowed" refers to the superstition that happiness wears off on others. So if you borrow something from someone who is happy or from a happily married friend, you'll have a happy future, too.

- For "something blue," brides include a blue item of some kind to bolster the favorite old line, "Those who dress in blue have lovers true." Blue has long been considered the color of fidelity, purity, and love. Brides in Israel wear blue ribbons to denote purity and fidelity. Blue also can be associated with the Virgin Mary. Many brides choose to wear a blue garter.

- In England, "a penny in your shoe" is a sixpence; in Canada, it's a quarter. No matter what the coin, the idea is to ensure a fortuitous married life.

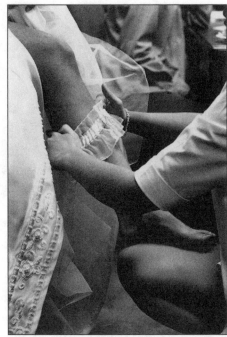

Some brides don't actually wear the garter the entire day. It may be too uncomfortable. Just slip it on right before the garter throw at the reception and no one will know the difference. *(Photo by Colter Photography)*

Bouquet Toss

Other customs around the world suggest what a bride should carry on her wedding day. Brides in Greece, for example, place a lump of sugar in one of their wedding gloves to give them the sweetness of life. Brides in Belgium embroider their name in a bridal handkerchief that is framed after the ceremony and passed on to other brides in the family.

The Emergency Kit

Ah, the emergency kit. If you've hired a bridal consultant to coordinate the weekend activities, you can skip this section; she should take care of having these items available for you.

If you're braving this adventure on your own, well, take heed. Some items you will need at the ceremony site, just for insurance. Of course, you will not need all of these things, but it's a good idea to have them, just in case.

Start with the basics:

◆ Small sewing kit

◆ Small scissors

◆ Safety pins of various sizes

◆ Tissues

◆ Masking tape and a stapler (you might be surprised at the repairs you can make with these two items)

◆ Hand towel

◆ Wash cloth

◆ Soft drinks/juice/bottled water

◆ Saltine crackers (to alleviate nausea)

◆ Static-cling spray

◆ Breath mints or mouthwash

◆ Tampons or sanitary pads (you never know)

"Just a little more fluff here, and you'll be perfect!"
(Photo by Colter Photography)

One last hug before heading down the aisle. *(Photo by Colter Photography)*

There are hundreds of other items you can add, and at every wedding I discover another item that would come in handy. Being prepared, both physically and emotionally, and staying organized are ways to keep you on track for your wedding day. It's time-consuming, but it pays off when you glide down that aisle relatively stress-free and looking wonderful.

Time to Get Dressed!

This is one time in your life where I want you to pamper yourself. This is not the time to be running back and forth setting up the reception décor and then rushing to get ready. This is *your* day and you owe it to yourself to take your time and savor preparing for your marriage.

Most brides today have their hair done professionally at the salon or the hairdresser comes to the ceremony site or home to prepare the bride. This is a great treat for you. Always be sure to have a practice run with your veil and headpiece so there are no surprises. The same goes for with your makeup. Your wedding day makeup should not be dramatically different than what you would mornally wear. If you aren't used to wearing lots of makeup, don't start now. You want to look natural and like you. You will need a little more lipstick color than normal simply because of photos. Having a makeup artist apply the makeup is also a wonderful treat. Again, try out your makeup before the wedding day.

Another nice touch is to have your makeup done professionally. Photographers will tell you they get better pictures when the makeup is done by a professional. And what a treat for all your girls to be able to spend that time together! *(Photo by Colter Photography)*

So you've got your hair done, veil on, makeup looks great, and you're ready to put on the gown. Be careful not to get makeup on the gown. You'll need help here (that's where your trusted bridesmaids come in handy). The final touch is jewelry. The pieces you choose to wear with your wedding gown should accent the gown, not detract from it. You might want to wear gloves if the gown is strapless. When you're all ready, go look in the mirror and see the princess gazing back at you!

"Hold still while I touch up here …" *(Photo by Colter Photography)*

When it comes to getting a bride dressed for her big day, no detail is too small. *(Photos by Colter Photography)*

"Everything's in place ... time for me to go!"

Wedding Woes

Practice walking in your wedding shoes before the ceremony to not only make sure they're comfortable, but to scuff up the soles a bit. Brand-new soles are smooth and can be slippery; a scuffed sole has more traction and can prevent a fall.

Taking That Long Walk

Okay, you're all dressed and ready to go. You've had all your pictures taken before the ceremony (see Chapter 11). You've spent some quiet time with your bridesmaids getting ready, and now comes the moment you've dreamed about for years. Your bridal consultant or the church's wedding coordinator or maybe you get everybody lined up for the processional. If you have a large wedding party, you'll need some help. This is especially true if you have several children in the wedding party (I once had eight flower girls ranging from two to eight years of age!).

The music starts for the grandmothers and they are seated. The moms are next to be seated. Maybe they will light the family candles for the unity candle if you are following that tradition. Next comes the processional for the men and the officiant, followed by your bridesmaids and flower girls and ring bearers. Finally, you hear the swell of the organ, the trumpets sound, you get chills and your tummy is doing flip flops and all of a sudden your dad takes your arm and you are off to meet your groom, the man you will share the rest of your life with.

Here comes the bride! *(Photo by Broadway Photography, LLC)*

The flower girl begins her walk down the aisle. Notice how the pews have been draped with tulleing and flowers. Guests were seated from the sides at this wedding. It really makes a statement, doesn't it? *(Photo by Broadway Photography, LLC)*

This happy bride is being walked down the aisle by both her parents. *(Photo by Colter Photography)*

Don't worry about another thing. Once you reach the altar you will be in the officiant's hands and I'll bet he's never lost a couple at the altar yet. Take his or her direction as you move through the ceremony and try to savor it. It will go by so fast, later on it will seem like a blur.

The priest is standing in front of this couple so their faces are to the congregation. *(Photo by Colter Photography)*

This bridesmaid was also the soloist at the wedding. She's being accompanied by a string quartet. *(Photo by Colter Photography)*

Now this is a good-looking wedding party. Have fun at the reception! *(Photo by Colter Photography)*

Then it's time for the kiss, and you're married. Congratulations! Now go enjoy the biggest party you'll ever have!

The Least You Need to Know

- The rehearsal is a very important part of the wedding activities. Just as an actor wouldn't go on stage without rehearsing his or her lines, don't show up for your wedding day unprepared.

- Make sure everyone who needs to be at the rehearsal is there, including all members of the wedding party and if possible, the musicians.

- The person officiating at the wedding should be the person in charge of the rehearsal. Work with your officiant to make the rehearsal go as smoothly as possible.

- One of the best ways to help get you ready for your big day is to get enough sleep the night before and eat a good breakfast the morning of the wedding.

- Be sure to put together a kit of emergency items to take along to the ceremony site for last-minute crises.

- Allow plenty of time to dress for your wedding so you don't feel rushed. Pamper yourself!

In This Chapter

- ◆ Planning your reception agenda: when to do what
- ◆ Handling wedding gifts at the reception
- ◆ Security considerations
- ◆ Designated drivers and other strategies
- ◆ Special considerations for young guests
- ◆ Making your grand exit

Chapter 20

Let the Party Begin!

You're done with the formalities at the church and/or civil ceremony, and you're feeling somewhat more relaxed. The religious and legal portions of the day are over. Now, prepare to be the guests of honor at one of the greatest parties you've ever attended!

Whether you're having a small, intimate celebration with family and a few close friends, or the party of the century with dinner and dancing until dawn, you and your partner will want to enjoy it. Let others do the worrying for now. This is a time to concentrate on your new spouse and your friends and family who have come from all over to share in this day. The best way to do that is to have certain things decided ahead of time and to make all who need to know aware of the schedule.

Activities to Include

What happens when you arrive at the reception? Should there be some kind of order to the events? Can you just mingle and do things as the spirit moves you? The answers are both yes and no.

Remember that this is *your* reception. The agenda needs to be of your choosing, not what Cousin Sarah says a reception is supposed to include. Discuss your options and what you want to see happen at the reception. For example, do you want your guests to be welcomed with a glass of champagne? When is the best man going to make his toast? Do you want to throw a bouquet and garter? Do you want a rigid dance order that specifies who dances with whom and when? Setting an agenda helps determine how the activities will flow.

Call it whatever you like, but even at an informal, family-only reception, there should be some kind of an agenda. You need an idea of what events are to take place and an approximate time of when each should happen. For your agenda to be carried out, you need someone to help move the events along. This is another place where an experienced bridal consultant can be invaluable.

The new Mr. and Mrs. enjoy a quiet moment alone before the reception. *(Photo by Broadway Photography, LLC)*

Greeting Your Guests

Whether to have a receiving line is a decision based on several factors. If you've taken all your pictures before the wedding, you can easily receive guests after the ceremony and move on to the reception. If you have not taken all the photos, you have to decide if you want to take more time to do the receiving line. A normal receiving line with the couple and both sets of parents receiving 200 guests will take approximately 30 to 45 minutes. Add to that another 30 to 45 minutes for the photographer to finish taking pictures, and you've added 1½ hours to the time after the wedding.

If you have more than 200 guests, consider other options for greeting your guests. Perhaps you and your spouse could move from table to table at the reception greeting guests instead.

Another idea is for the couple to come back into the ceremony site and release the rows as the ushers might do. The bottom line is that your guests expect to be able to say hello to you on your wedding day. They almost feel rejected if time is not built into the schedule for them to wish you the best.

> **Teddy's Tips**
>
> If your guests signed the guest book at the ceremony, there is no need to have it at the reception, although you might want to have it available for latecomers who did not get a chance to sign it.

Mother of the bride   Mother of the groom   Bride   Groom

Positions of participants in a traditional receiving line.

Here's a nice alternative to signing a traditional guest book. *(Photo by Colter Photography)*

Having your guests sign a guest book as they enter the reception provides a record of your special day.
(Photos by Wyant Photography [left] and Colter Photography [right])

A Big Hand for Mr. and Mrs. ...

Many couples want to be introduced as they arrive at the reception. This can be accomplished by working with your band or DJ. Ask them to do the honors if you aren't using a master of ceremonies (MC) for the evening. Most are happy to assist. Consider whether you want your entire wedding party to be announced or just you, the couple. Also, be sure each individual or couple knows where to move after the introduction. Decide whether you want them to walk to the head table or directly to the buffet line. The type of food you're serving for the reception will dictate some of these decisions.

Usually, ushers/groomsmen are introduced first with the bridesmaids they walked with at the ceremony. Then the children attendants are introduced (if they're old enough to participate in this; otherwise, they can be acknowledged at the table where they're seated with their families). The best man and maid of honor are introduced next, followed by the new couple (that's you!).

Welcome the new couple—and don't they look happy! *(Photo by Wyant Photography)*

Raise Your Glasses

When you're finished eating, you might want to schedule in a toast or two. Traditionally, the best man offers the first toast of the evening.

Teddy's Tips

Here is a great opportunity to make a relative or close friend feel very special. Instead of relying on a master of ceremonies, disc jockey, or band leader to make the introductions, why not have someone you know (and who knows the guests and can pronounce their names!) handle this task? Obviously, it should be someone who can stand up in front of a crowd and speak without tripping over his or her tongue!

He stands, gets the guests' attention, and makes a toast to the new couple. The toast should be simple and sincere, and he might choose to share a funny (and tasteful) story. The groom then should thank him and offer a toast to his new bride. After that, it's an open floor (anyone can offer a toast, or it can stop there).

When a toast is proposed, all should rise—except the person or persons who are being toasted. Both the bride and groom would remain seated for the best man's toast. For the groom's toast, only the bride would be seated.

Bouquet Toss

The term *toasting* dates back to the sixteenth century. Those attending a function placed a spice-laden crouton in the bottom of a wine glass. This was either for flavor or nourishment—who knows? Anyway, the last person to drink from the glass and find the toast not only claimed it, but was given good wishes.

These champagne flutes await the guests for the toast. The fresh strawberries add a touch of class. *(Photo by Broadway Photography, LLC)*

If that's not love, then I've never seen it. *(Photo by Colter Photography)*

Cutting the Cake

Following the toast, and depending on what you've decided to do, you can go right into cutting the cake. This is another place you will want formal photographs, so make sure your photographer knows the order of events.

Your photographer will work with you on where you should stand at the cake table. Follow his guidelines and suggestions so he can get the best possible photograph. According to tradition, the groom places his hand over the bride's, and together you cut the first slice. The angle from which the photographer wants to shoot and the way your cake has been constructed usually determine where you make the first slice. Sometimes, the photographer might ask you to pretend to make the first cut from a higher layer so the angle is better for the photograph. After he has snapped the picture, you then can normally cut the first slice from the back of the bottom layer of the cake.

Here's a wonderful example of how important it is to incorporate family traditions into weddings. In this family, the aunts all got together and made the couple a hand-stitched quilt. It provides a special focal point when hung behind the cake table. *(Photo by Morris Fine Arts Photography)*

The cutting of the cake … another Kodak moment! *(Photo by Wyant Photography)*

Have a plate and napkin ready at the table to place the cake on and to wipe sticky fingers. Then take turns feeding each other a small piece of cake. Notice the word *small*. I find it very interesting when a couple gets into a food fight while they are feeding each other the cake. This is supposed to be a tender moment, symbolic of your union and the life you will share. Don't start off that life humiliating your spouse by smushing a piece of cake into his or her face!

> **Bouquet Toss**
>
> As with many of the wedding traditions we observe today, the cake cutting dates back to ancient times. In ancient Rome, the couple would share a hard biscuit, each taking a bite from it. The wedding officiant would then crumble the remaining portion over the couple's heads. This was thought to bring bounty to the couple, good luck, and many children. Guests at these ancient weddings would rush to the site where the biscuit was crumbled to obtain any leftover crumbs for their own good luck. Over the centuries, this cake crumbling has evolved into modern wedding guests having a piece of cake at the reception or taking a piece home with them.

Cutting a wedding cake is an art—don't let anyone tell you otherwise. If the catering staff is willing to cut the cake for you, by all means, let them. If you don't have any expert assistance available, however, this task becomes the responsibility of your cake server, who might never have attempted this task before. The following diagram might help. Be sure to share this information with your server so he or she can be prepared for the big day.

Always remove the layer you want to cut. Never cut a layer while it's on top of another layer. About two inches from the outside of the cake, make a circular cut all the way around the cake. Then, slice off pieces from the outside into the cut. Repeat this process, moving in two inches at a time, all the way to the center of the cake.

Front

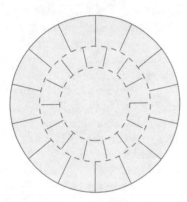

Looking down

Diagram for cutting the cake.

Get Your Dancing Cards Ready

If your reception includes dancing, the dancing can begin following the cake ceremony. The bride and groom are the first to dance at the reception, and some couples choose a favorite song for that first dance. The bride and groom can dance the entire first dance, or the bride's father can cut in and finish that first dance with his daughter. Some brides request the first dance with their groom and the entire second dance with their father. Some popular songs for the dance with dad are "Daddy's Little Girl," "Sunrise, Sunset," and "Butterfly Kisses." (Check with your local music store for sheet music if the band or DJ doesn't have the song you would like played.)

Music can make or break your reception. This 18-piece big band was wonderful! *(Photo by Colter Photography)*

This couple share their first dance as husband and wife as guests blow bubbles around them. *(Photo by Colter Photography)*

Wedding Woes

Don't make the dancing segment of the wedding so complicated that the cast needs cue cards to tell who's dancing with whom and to what song. I normally recommend no more than two or three special dances.

Once you have the first dance or two out of the way, it's time to let loose and get the party moving. This is where the homework you did before you chose your DJ or band should pay off. If your dance floor is filled with dancers most of the night, you get an A for all your advance work.

Looks like they've changed the tempo. "Let's party!" *(Photo by Colter Photography)*

These groomsmen were in a Jewish wedding. They wanted to stomp on a glass, too, so the groom had a glass put in a bag for each of them to stomp on during the reception. *(Photo by Colter Photography)*

I don't know if they're doing the Conga or the Bunny Hop, but whatever it is, they're having fun! *(Photo by Wyant Photography)*

Of all the photos of dancing at receptions, I thought this one was so darling—the bride's grandmother and little friend. This picture is priceless. *(Photo by Colter Photography)*

It's a Toss-Up

Later in the reception, if you choose, you can throw the bouquet and garter. Here again, you will need help to make the announcement. Ask for all single women to join the bride on the dance floor. Work with your photographer, too. Let him determine the best placement. It's customary for the bride to turn her back to the single women and, after a countdown, toss the bouquet. Tradition has it that the woman who catches the bouquet will be the next to marry.

Now it's the groom's turn. Instead of using a chair to sit on while the groom removes your garter, why not ask the best man to kneel on one knee so you can sit on his leg? It makes for a great picture and is certainly warmer than a cold chair. Sometimes, the band or DJ provides a drum roll here and then plays "The Stripper" for the actual garter removal.

When the groom has the garter in hand, he moves off the dance floor and, with his back to his single male friends, tosses the garter. Again, the man who catches the garter will be the next to marry.

Remember, you don't have to incorporate any of these customs into your reception if you don't want to. After all, this is your wedding, and you should plan your agenda around the things you want to include. Many couples today are choosing not to include the garter toss. Some don't include the bouquet toss either or they have the DJ call all the married couples to the dance floor and start listing how long people have been married. The longest-wed "bride" receives the bouquet.

Heads up, girls! *(Photo by Colter Photography)*

Hmmm, how to get the garter off without showing too much leg ... *(Photos by Colter Photography)*

What Else?

There might be more things you want to incorporate into your wedding reception. Perhaps there are some religious customs or prayers you'd like recited (such as the prayers over the wine and bread at a Jewish wedding). Some sororities and fraternities have rituals they perform during the evening. Maybe there's someone you want to honor with a special dance. One father purchased a magnum of champagne at the time of his daughter's birth, with the intention of opening it on her wedding day. He did this, and it was quite a nostalgic moment for the family as he talked about the little girl who had grown into a lovely young woman.

These gals gather around the bride to serenade her—a popular custom among sororities. *(Photo by Colter Photography)*

Handling Gifts at the Reception

According to proper wedding etiquette, all wedding gifts should be sent to the bride's home or her parent's home before the wedding. In our busy society, however, guests often fail to abide by this rule and bring the gifts to the reception. When you talk with the reception site manager, ask to have a table specially set up in the main room for wedding gifts.

Safety First

I hate to have to say this, but your gift table needs to be in a place that is hard to access, such as a distant corner away from any exits. It's much harder to walk clear across the dance floor with gifts than to grab one and go out an exit. Make the table hard to get to, and you'll take home the gifts intended for you.

> **Wedding Woes**
>
> Do not have the gift table set up in an outer lobby. There are too many sticky fingers out there, and you want to make it as difficult as possible for a would-be thief to exit with your wedding gifts.

Assign someone to greet guests and take any gifts they may bring to the reception. This person doesn't need to stand guard over the table all the time—he or she just needs to be there at the beginning of the reception to help guests. If you anticipate receiving cards containing monetary gifts, have either a basket or a box on the table to collect those. If you use a basket, make sure you empty it frequently during the evening. Cards can walk away even more easily than wrapped presents. The best solution here is to have a sealed box that can be opened only by breaking the seal.

It's Not Christmas Morning

You should not open gifts at your wedding reception. The only time when that might be appropriate is at a small, family-only reception where you can do the honors without creating too much hassle. Always have someone record who gave you what so you can send thank you notes. Do assign someone to load up your gifts and secure them for you, especially if you're leaving for your honeymoon.

Security

You might think security is a strange subject to discuss in a wedding planning book, but nothing is further from the truth. Weddings can bring out the good, the bad, and the ugly in your guests. Throw in a little too much to drink, and you can have some fireworks you didn't expect or want.

Most of the larger facilities used for receptions have security guards on the premises who patrol the area just in case they're needed. They're not there to embarrass you or intimidate your guests, but when you need them, you'll be glad they're around.

If you're serving alcohol at your reception and your reception facility doesn't provide security, you might want to look into hiring a security guard for the evening.

"May I Call You a Cab?"

Any discussion of alcohol brings up the topic of watching out for those who have indulged too much. When I first started in this business, I would see people drinking to excess at almost every wedding reception; that usually is no longer the case. It doesn't matter the age of the guests or the age of the couple—fortunately, I haven't been seeing the overindulgence I once saw.

What I do see is a more attentive society with guests taking it upon themselves (and rightly so) to make sure others are sober enough to drive when leaving a reception. I have had couples take car keys from their guests and turn them over only when the driver was someone who had not been drinking. I have had parents book cab companies to come gather guests after a reception and deliver them safely to their homes or hotels. On several occasions, couples have rented buses or trolley cars to transport guests from the reception back to the hotel.

There are all kinds of ways for you to make sure your reception guests do not leave the reception and drive under the influence of alcohol.

The best way to protect yourself from any chance of liability is to make sure that you're working with a licensed liquor agency in your state and that bartenders check the IDs of guests who appear to be underage. It's everyones responsibility to make sure each guest who leaves is capable of driving. You don't need your wedding day memory to be of a terrible auto accident involving one of your wedding guests. Take some time now to develop a plan for seeing that you have a safe and happy reception.

> **Teddy's Tips**
>
> Most reception facilities now require you (the renter) to provide proof of liability insurance that names the facility within the policy. Each facility requires a different amount, depending on the event and circumstances, but most do require the extra insurance. You can obtain this coverage as a rider on your homeowner's policy for a 24-hour period, and the cost is reasonable.

Child Care

"Child care?" you ask. "What does this have to do with my wedding?" Well, for openers, if I live to be 100, I will never understand why parents cart their toddlers and babies to weddings and receptions, especially evening weddings. Parents don't enjoy the time spent at the wedding or reception when the baby is along. There's nothing enjoyable about trying to keep a crying baby still during the wedding vows or trying to keep Junior from playing leapfrog on the dance floor with the other two dozen children.

The only people invited to the wedding and reception are those whose names appear on the inner envelope. So if the outer envelope says "Mr. and Mrs. John Smith" and the inner one says "The Smith Family," technically the Smiths can bring the entire family. If the inner envelope says "John and Mary" or "Mr. and Mrs. Smith," they are the only ones invited. Some clients ask me if they can put "Adult Reception" on the reception card. The etiquette answer is no, but as long as Emily Post isn't on your guest list ... well, you get the point.

Some couples want children at the wedding and reception. Others do not. My advice is to spread the word about whether the children are welcome at the reception.

If your guests insist on bringing their children, try to provide some activities kids will enjoy. Children like to be kept busy; children are basically very busy little people. And I love kids; truly, I do.

You can apply the following ideas to both the ceremony and reception:

◆ Hire someone to supervise the children. When I hire college girls (many are elementary education majors) to supervise a children's room for a wedding, I give them specifics. I hire one girl for every five kids so I've got enough hands.

◆ If the church or reception facility has a separate room, ask to use that room as the entertainment lounge. Give it a fancy title so the kids think they're getting a great deal.

◆ Rent some cartoons and bring in a VCR and a TV for "movie night." Provide some kid snacks and nonsugared drinks (apple or orange juice).

◆ Have coloring books, crayons, easy-to-read books for the older children, puzzles, trucks or cars, and maybe some blocks.

◆ Check with a local university (early childhood department) or a high school home economics class (family development) to see if you can hire students to come in and work with the children. Notice I said "work with," not "watch"—there is a vast difference between the two.

Teddy's Tips

It helps to know in advance the ages of any children who might be attending the wedding and reception so you can plan appropriate supervision and activities. Consider including an additional enclosure card with the invitations you send to those with small children. This card can have blanks for the names and ages of the children, and guests can return them in the same envelope as the reception response card.

For one wedding reception, the couple decided that because several children would potentially be at the reception, they would plan something specifically for them. At the beginning of the dancing segment, one of the groomsmen brought out a heart-shape piñata and had all the kids line up and take turns trying to break it. When it finally broke apart, the kids scrambled for the candy and trinkets inside. They were occupied for several hours playing with the trinkets and sampling candy (try to keep the sugar count down). The adult guests enjoyed watching the kids have their own special fun.

House-Sitters

During the final consultation with my clients, I suggest that if they don't have a good security system on their property, they consider hiring a house-sitter to stay at their home during the ceremony and reception. At the very least, you need to make sure the neighbors know what's happening on the wedding weekend, and ask them to watch out for anything or anyone unusual in the area.

Burglars know when weddings are happening—they watch for them. These potential party poopers scan the newspapers for wedding and engagement announcements and marriage license announcements. They know there will be a lot of movement and a lot of gifts arriving at the home, and they know they can count on the family being gone for hours the day of the wedding. Don't give them the opportunity to steal you blind. With a little preparation now, you won't be sorry later.

It's also a good idea to add a rider for your wedding gifts to your insurance policy. This is a short-term policy you can usually add through your homeowner's or renter's insurance policy. It doesn't cost much, and it can save you thousands of dollars if you happen to be unlucky enough to be robbed. This is different from the liability rider I talked about earlier. Check with your insurance company for details.

Making Your Getaway

The time has come, my dears, to make your grand exit. You and your groom need to decide when you want to leave your wedding reception. Most of the couples I work with want to stay for the whole reception. After all, it's a party for you, given in your honor. Most of these couples don't want to miss anything: the fun, the music, the dancing, and talking with friends and family members they've not seen for months. So if that's what you'd like to do, go for it.

But let's say you do want to leave earlier than most of your guests. Maybe you have a plane to catch or you just want to find some time for yourselves. If you're changing clothes at the reception, you need to do that before you leave. It will be easier not to travel in a long gown complete with train. Besides, you can leave your gown with your mom or a good friend to be taken to the cleaners. (Check with a reputable dry cleaner before your wedding to see about having your gown cleaned and then preserved in an airtight box.)

After you've both changed clothes and gathered the items you need to take with you (hopefully your luggage for the honeymoon will already be in the car), it's time to say good-bye to your folks. Now, most times, moms and dads at this stage of the game are glad things have gone well. They're happy, they're sad, they're tired, and they love you. Give your parents a hug; thank them for this wonderful day and for all their support. Do the same with your new parents-in-law. Then, make your exit. If you have petals or birdseed you want guests to toss as you make your mad dash to the waiting car, have one of your bridesmaids gather guests by the exit and pass out the petals or birdseed. The showering simply means good luck and, according to legend, also promotes fertility.

Guests gather to blow bubbles at the couple as they make their exit. *(Photo by Colter Photography)*

Wedding Woes

One bride lost a $100 deposit when a guest, not knowing the rules, passed out birdseed to the guests to toss. The church claimed the deposit as a cleanup fee. So check with facility beforehand!

The photographer will want to capture this moment on film. Give her time to get set up and then run—do not walk—to the car and wave good-bye. Now, you're off. You're alone for the first time since earlier that day, or maybe even the previous day. It's now your time to enjoy each other, relax, and have a great honeymoon!

Off in a blaze of glory! *(Photo by Broadway Photography, LLC)*

The Least You Need to Know

◆ Plan a reception agenda so the reception has a continual flow and so the photographer can be ready for each activity—but don't feel you have to incorporate any or all customs into your reception.

◆ Have the reception manager place a table for gifts in the main room of the reception, and ask a friend to direct guests bearing presents to this table.

◆ Check with the reception manager about having security available during the festivities. It's good to have some expert assistance if guests become rowdy or out of control.

◆ Make sure you have a plan for getting home any guests who might have a little too much of the bubbly.

◆ If you anticipate children at the reception, provide some appropriate activities for them or hire someone to watch them.

◆ Check into hiring a house-sitter during the wedding weekend when you will be gone for an extended time. Also check into purchasing a short-term rider to your homeowner's or renter's insurance policy to protect the value of your wedding gifts in case you're burglarized.

In This Chapter

- ◆ Valuable free advice from experienced bridal consultants and vendors

- ◆ Hot wedding trends around the country

- ◆ Trends that seem to be losing popularity

- ◆ Tips and advice from the professionals

Chapter 21

Tips from the Pros: What's Hot, What's Not

One of the benefits of belonging to the Association of Bridal Consultants, an international trade association, is the opportunity to meet people from all over the world who share a common desire: to provide the best possible services and products for wedding clients. Over the years, I've had the pleasure of hearing other professionals speak and the opportunity to share ideas about our profession. I've learned so much from them, and I want to share some of this valuable information with you.

This chapter includes tips, trends, and free advice from professionals to you, the prospective bride and groom. These wonderful consultants and vendors have included trends they are witnessing in their particular areas of the country. Enjoy this free advice as you read on.

East Coast Trends

The East Coast offers everything for your wedding from bright city lights to small villages that dot the mountains in Vermont. The weddings and customs here are sometimes a bit more formal than in other parts of the country.

Colin Cowie

Colin Cowie, owner of Colin Cowie Lifestyle, has been designing and producing weddings for 18 years. His business is a full-service event, design, and production company with offices both in New York and Los Angeles. He is the author of numerous books, including *Colin Cowie for the Bride: A Guide to Style and Gracious Living*, *Colin Cowie for the Groom: A Blueprint for a Gentleman's Lifestyle*, and *For the Bride* (see Appendix A).

These wonderful books hit on subjects that other authors either leave out or don't know how to write about. Not only is Colin a brilliant producer of some of the most famous weddings in the world, but he is also a humble, kind gentleman and has a wonderful sense of humor. He is a member of the Association of Bridal Consultants, appears on *Oprah*, and is a contributing editor to *InStyle* magazine. Colin sees the following general trends in the wedding industry:

> There are a few big trends I've noticed and some great ideas that we've have been embracing in the weddings I'm designing for my clients. Lately I've been seating guests at long banquet tables instead of using round tables. We've been serving food "family style" on large platters placed directly on the table for guests to help themselves … it makes for a warm and welcoming environment … it also helps to break the ice. If guests are being seated at round tables, it's best to use a table no larger than a 60 inches round for 10 guests. Any bigger and the distance between your guests can make it difficult for conversation.
>
> And don't be afraid to use color … brides are using color more than ever. Try to identify a color you want to use throughout your wedding and start by setting the stage with your invitations. Infuse the color in your table, your flowers, your printed menus and certainly the attire of your wedding party. Even the ink for your thank you notes can be a color of your choice.

> Most important, the best advice I can give you is to make sure you have fun whatever you decide and enjoy the whole process. It's an important day, and as long as you're relaxed and enjoy yourself your guests will enjoy themselves as well.

Shelby Tuck-Horton

Shelby Tuck-Horton, owner of Exquisite Expressions and Events, Inc., in Mitchellville, Maryland, has been in business for 18 years. She is a Master Bridal Consultant through the Association of Bridal Consultants and also a member of the International Special Events Society. Shelby sees these trends:

- Instead of corsages, mothers are carrying small nosegays.
- Hand-tied bouquets are very popular.
- Brides and grooms are honoring their heritage by incorporating ethnic customs into their ceremony.
- More couples are writing their own vows.
- To create an atmosphere of romance, candles—in various sizes, heights, and shapes—are very popular for centerpieces.
- The stacked, often simple yet artistic, wedding cake is one of the most popular.
- Groom's cakes are increasing in popularity and are being served at the rehearsal dinner.
- An exciting alternative to the buffet is the action station, which offers guests multiple tasting stations; for example, carving, stir-fry, and pasta stations. Mashed potato bars are a big item in many locations!
- Couples are choosing specialty drinks to be served at the bar. The theme drink is usually a favorite of the bride and groom.

◆ The use of uplighting on the walls and ceiling is becoming much more popular at the reception.

◆ Couples are sending "save-the-date" cards so guests know of the wedding date months in advance.

◆ Couples are finding creative alternatives to the guest book, such as having guests sign a photo mat of their engagement picture or putting well-wishes on quilt patches.

◆ Coffee bars are featured at the reception, usually with cake or dessert.

◆ Photojournalistic-style photography for wedding albums is becoming popular. Other albums are a combination of color and black-and-white photography.

◆ Classic cars are very popular, as is the use of luxury SUV limos.

◆ Weddings are lasting the entire weekend, beginning with the rehearsal dinner, golf outings, spas, ceremony, reception, and after-wedding brunches.

◆ Couples are giving their guests practical or edible favors.

Trends that have lost popularity include the following:

◆ Long head tables.

◆ The garter toss.

◆ Receiving lines (instead, couples visit their guests at each table during the reception).

◆ Disposable cameras on every table.

Beverly Ann Bonner

Beverly is president of The Wedding Beautiful, Inc., in Norwood, Massachusetts. She has been in the business of helping brides for 20 years and is a Master Bridal Consultant and State Coordinator for Massachusetts with the Association of Bridal Consultants. She notices that many couples are planning weekend celebrations that incorporate touches of New England, and even couples who don't live in New England are planning long-distance weddings because they love the area. Touches of New England flair might include the following:

◆ Cuisine—from clambakes to Parker House rolls.

◆ Choosing educational institutions for the ceremony or reception site, such as Boston University Chapel or the Harvard Fogg Art Museum.

◆ Taking in a sporting event such as the Red Sox or the Bruins.

◆ Historic venues such as Plymouth Plantation and Newport mansions.

◆ Couples are choosing to have their wedding in the snowy winter months or in the fall to celebrate the colorful fall foliage.

◆ Couples want their guests treated like family.

◆ Guests receive information in advance via "save-the-date" cards and/or websites.

◆ Information is included on how to dress for certain events and entrée choices for the reception.

◆ Welcome bags delivered to the hotels are filled with New England treats such as Yankee candles, Cape Cod potato chips, Toll House cookies, Boston Harbor tea, a tourist map of area, Bruins or Celtics playing cards, a *Cheers* mug, or salt water taffy.

◆ Transportation is arranged so guests are picked up at their hotels in a trolley car or bus and taken to the ceremony and then on to the reception.

◆ Two or three entrée choices are offered for the reception.

◆ Couples are registering for larger items or a honeymoon fund. Because many couples are older, they are registering for fewer toasters and more coffee tables or books. A group of friends might share the cost of buying a larger gift.

◆ Couples cherish items used during the wedding as keepsakes in their home. More brides are drying their bouquets and transforming them into topiaries to grace their homes.

◆ Couples are keeping the less fortunate in mind by requesting that leftover food be given to a food bank and floral pieces delivered to nursing homes.

Lois Pearce

Lois Pearce is president of Beautiful Occasions in Hamden, Connecticut. She has been helping brides plan wonderful weddings since 1986. She is a Master Bridal Consultant and the Director of Ethnic Diversity of the Association of Bridal Consultants and is the 2002 recipient of the association's highest honor, the Miss Dorothy Heart Award. Here's Lois's take on the latest trends in her area:

◆ Wedding budgets are remaining fairly the same, but the guest list is shrinking. Average wedding is $20,000 to $25,000, with a guest list of 100 to 135 persons. This wedding budget now includes the wedding and a post-wedding celebration such as a brunch.

◆ Brides are thinking about every detail of the wedding. Wedding programs are more widely used and include more information. In some cases they are a memento of all the wedding day activities. Aside from the actual wedding information, if there are mixed cultures or religions, there are descriptions of each ritual. Directions to the reception from the church are included, as are notes honoring any deceased family member, a personal thank you note from the bridal couple, and perhaps their new at-home address.

◆ Pampering is big. Brides are including their bridal attendants in a spa activity, which might include the basics of a manicure and pedicure to facials and massages including lunch.

◆ Newsletters and/or "save-the-date" cards are being utilized to encourage guests to attend and help them get right into the spirit of the wedding by knowing some background information about the members of the wedding party, information about the sites, and hotel information.

◆ Hospitality bags for the guests as they check into their hotels might be as simple as a box of chocolates with a thank you note for coming, up to a small fruit basket with a description of things to do (or where-to-find-it information—local drug store, etc. vs. a mall) during the weekend.

◆ Ethnic music for either the ceremony or the reception is big. Particularly at the reception, ethnic music from Scottish jigs to salsa dancing gets the crowd up and moving.

◆ Comfort foods for the reception and/or cocktail hour, such as mashed potato martinis during the cocktail hour and one-bite hors d'oeuvres (so as not to mess up the guests).

◆ Signature drinks that the couple can decide on before the reception.

◆ Oversize invitations with organza ribbon ties.

◆ More delayed honeymoons. Couples may marry over the weekend, take a few days off, then return to work. Later (sometimes a month or two), they will take an extravagant vacation. This may reflect the lifestyle of the newlyweds who may be cohabitating before the nuptials and "sneaking off" is not as important to them as a wonderfully planned vacation taken after the hoopla dies down.

◆ More brides and mothers of brides are working with wedding consultants. The consultant reviews the wedding day plan to make recommendations that the day go smoothly and/or is included during the final months up to the wedding day.

◆ Mini-buses (stocked with bar supplies, TV, and VCR) are used instead of limousines to shuttle guests, family members, and the bridal couple. The bride and groom, parents, and bridal party all enjoy the company of each other as they move from ceremony to photo site to reception.

◆ CDs are given as favors. They might include either a song written specifically for the bride and groom or a thank you message to the guests from the bridal couple.

◆ Photo review on the internet. Guests can purchase pictures from a website, and those guests who were unable to attend are able to share in the pictures.

◆ DVD of the wedding and reception rather than a videocassette tape.

JoAnn Gregoli

JoAnn owns Elegant Occasions, Inc., in New York City. And elegant events she does! JoAnn has been in business for 15 years and is a Master Bridal Consultant and the New York metro State Coordinator for the Association of Bridal Consultants. Here are some of trends that JoAnn sees in the Big Apple:

◆ Smaller weddings, including simpler wedding parties and fewer guests.

◆ Strings played during dinner with swing bands for entertainment.

◆ Seating at long banquet tables.

◆ Specialty drinks and food stations, such as a martini bar, caviar bar, or sushi bar (complete with sushi chef).

◆ Fine wines and wonderful champagnes to accompany the meal.

◆ Printed menu cards and pairing of wines with each course.

◆ Offering a cheese course during the meal.

◆ Simple wedding gowns.

Trends that are on the way out include the following:

◆ Lavish cocktail hour.

◆ Tall table centerpieces.

◆ DJs at the reception.

◆ Viennese table.

◆ Gothic-looking wedding gowns.

Bouquet Toss

Here's one idea JoAnn had that sounds like a really nice way to end the reception: "We give away pretzels at the end of the evening or Krispy Kreme donuts with hot apple cider during the cold winter months. During the summer, we give out little bags of fresh cherries and blueberries along with fresh fruit punch."

Midwest Trends

The Midwest is considered the "heart" of the country. We are more laid back here. The pace is slower. New ideas take a while to make it to our doors. But we still have some spectacular weddings as well as wonderful consultants and vendors, who offer these trends.

Mary Jane Miles

Mary Jane Miles owns The Perfect Wedding in Evansville, Indiana. And indeed, her weddings are almost flawless. She has been treating brides to her creative talents since 1989 and is an active member of the Association of Bridal Consultants. She shares some of these tips and trends:

- Favors are back!
- Tented receptions.
- Food stations with no assigned seating.
- Fewer couples live together before the wedding.
- Fresh flowers in the hair for both bride and bridesmaids.
- Bands.
- Specialty linens (for example, two layers of linen, an overskirt of organza on top of a tablecloth, for a beautiful finished look).
- Rose petals—everywhere.
- Goody gift bags for hotel guests.
- Classic cars instead of limos for the couple's exit.

What's out in trends include the following:

- DJs at the reception.
- The garter and bouquet tosses.
- Wedding party dance.

- Fewer unity candles.
- Black and white as the colors for weddings.

Mary Jane suggests one way to personalize the wedding reception: "Have the bride and groom introduced at the reception and then have them introduce their wedding party members. Guests are much more attentive when the bride and groom do the introducing."

Frank Andonoplas

Frank Andonoplas, owner of Frank Event Design in Chicago, Illinois, is another Master Bridal Consultant with the Association of Bridal Consultants and winner of the Miss Dorothy Heart Award. I have watched Frank's business grow as he has developed and found his style with couples. He's an excellent consultant who celebrates his tenth year in business this year. He is also on the Advisory board of *Special Events Magazine* and is The Knot.Com Chicagoland Wedding Expert. Frank has noticed these trends in the Windy City:

- Sit-down dinners are the most popular.
- Buffet/action stations for cocktail hour.
- Centerpieces that are different yet coordinated in style.
- Table names, not numbers.
- Choice of entrées for mixed grill.
- Black limousines.
- The couple's parents serving as the best man and matron of honor.
- Showering the couple with flower petals as they leave the church.
- Detailed tabletops, featuring napkins treatment, personalized menus, and individual salt and pepper shakers.

The "outs" are:

◆ Double linen treatments (two different linens on the same table).

◆ The bride and groom not seeing each other until the ceremony (get those photos done!).

◆ Showering the couple with birdseed.

◆ The bouquet and garter tosses.

Be sure to check the color section of this book for a gorgeous garden wedding Frank created in a ballroom, complete with a meandering garden path aisle runner.

Kay Krober

Kay Krober, from Carmel, Indiana, owns Kay Krober Bridal Consultants. She has consulted on many very large-scale weddings and earned a great following in the Indianapolis area over the past 11 years. She is an active member of the Association of Bridal Consultants and the International Special Events Society. Here are some trends Kay sees in the heartland:

◆ Variety in reception entertainment. Brides are wanting more than strings or jazz for cocktails and dinner and a band for dancing, such as a gospel choir, a barbershop quartet and a mime artist to entertain guests during cocktails and/or dinner.

◆ Receptions with a "club" atmosphere for dancing. When the facility has space, move to a different room for the dancing with décor, lighting, seating, and special bars, like a nightclub.

◆ Brides are wearing more lace, beads, and pearls instead of simpler-style gowns.

◆ Tables in all shapes and sizes. Use square, oval, and long banquet in addition to round tables. The centerpieces are different for the various shapes and sizes of tables. The room is much more interesting than having all round tables with identical centerpieces.

◆ Specialty linens are a must, including chair covers.

◆ Bridesmaids dressed in champagne or ivory.

◆ Monograms on everything. It's a great symbol of the couple coming together with a symbol that is unique to them.

◆ Videographers are producing more journalistic coverage of the wedding weekend.

◆ Black-and-white photography.

Some trends she's seeing disappear are:

◆ All round tables.

◆ Chairs without chair covers.

◆ Bridesmaids wearing black or red.

◆ Long videos of the couple's "growing up" years.

> **Bouquet Toss**
>
> Kay offers this wonderful idea for the right bride: "I had a bride who loved ballet. She had studied for many years. As a surprise to her, we arranged for 10 little ballerinas, aged 8 to 10, in white flowing costumes, to dance from the front of the church, down the aisle, and open the doors for the processional of the bride and her attendants. It was spectacular!"

Southern Trends

Ah, the South. Thoughts of plantations, long, winding tree-lined driveways, and lazy summer afternoons sipping mint juleps come to mind. Weddings in the South are steeped in tradition and usually by-the-book etiquette decisions.

Carol Marino

Carol hails from Fairfax, Virginia, and owns A Perfect Wedding, Inc. She has been in business for 10 years now and is a Master Bridal Consultant with the Association of Bridal Consultants, a Certified Wedding Specialist with Weddings Beautiful, and a member of International Special Events Society. The trends she see in the Fairfax area include:

- Bold colors and lots of texture on guests' tables.
- Vignettes of flowers and candles instead of single centerpieces.
- Brass ensembles for ceremony and cocktail music.
- Invitations or "save-the-date" cards that feature photos of the bride and groom.
- Handheld flowers or *tussie mussies* for the mothers.
- Serving lots of comfort foods such as beef and mashed potatoes—real Americana.

Nuptial Notes

A **tussie mussie** is a silver cone-shape flower holder used in the Victorian times. Today many brides have the mother's flowers put into these charming keepsakes. A wedding I just coordinated used these, and each had a silver charm engraved with the mother's first initial. What a delightful keepsake!

- Wedding newsletters that showcase the personalities of the bride and groom.

Carol's biggest pieces of advice: "Set your budget *first*, before selecting any wedding vendor, even the site. And personalize everything!"

Mackenzie Spalding

Mackenzie Spalding is a special young woman to me. She owns and operates One Fine Day Wedding Consultation in Bardstowon, Kentucky. She's been in business six years and is a member of the Association of Bridal Consultants. I met Mackenzie while she was still in college studying to be a nurse. She wanted to see what this business was all about and came to an association state meeting to gather all the information she could. She not only went on to graduate but also decided to take the plunge and start her own business. She was married two years ago and had not one but seven bridal consultants help her with her wedding. And what a wedding it was! As a newer member of this business, here are some trends she is seeing in the South:

- All photos taken before the ceremony.
- Weddings with a regional flair. In this area, couples are sharing a taste of Kentucky with their guests, such as horse farm weddings and receptions, mint julep cocktails, and an equestrian theme commemorating the Kentucky Derby.
- April, May, and October are popular months for weekend weddings.
- Couples are spending more on the welcome baskets with local favorite items rather than typical wedding favors at the reception.
- Rehearsal dinners are more of a casual event.

Southwestern Trends

The Southwest is an exciting place, with brilliant sunsets and mariachi bands. Southwestern weddings have a greater ethnic flare than other parts of the country simply because of the Spanish and Mexican influence.

Salli Goldstein

Salli Goldstein operates Salli G in Dallas, Texas. She's been in business 17 years and is an active member of the Association of Bridal Consultants. Here's what Salli is finding out about trends in the Lone Star state:

◆ More sit-down dinners.

◆ Big bands playing during the reception.

◆ More ethnic foods served.

◆ Fewer dessert choices—more wedding cake served as dessert.

◆ More showy linens and table covers.

◆ Chair covers.

◆ Smaller but more detailed weddings.

And here's a tip or two from Salli:

◆ Have a wedding you can afford. Do not go into debt!

◆ Spend the money, no matter who is paying for what, as if it were your money, and spend it where it is needed.

Christine McFall

Christine McFall owns Celebrations! Bridal Consulting and Special Event Planning in Albuquerque, New Mexico. She's been in business there eight years and certainly has a beautiful area of the country to work with. She is a member of the Association of Bridal Consultants. Trends in her area include:

◆ Brides are going to salons to have their hair and makeup done by professionals.

◆ Bridal gowns are sleeveles or strapless or have spaghetti straps. The style is classic and elegant. Bridesmaids' gowns are flattering to individual figures, and all are made of the same or coordinating fabric.

◆ Semi-formal to informal weddings. Couples in New Mexico enjoy garden, backyard, and outdoor weddings because of the great weather and lovely scenery.

◆ Floral arrangements and bouquets that feature lots of color.

◆ Half of table linens are white or ivory. Accent linens are colored to coordinate or contrast with the color scheme.

◆ Biscochitos and Mexican wedding cookies are a favorite favor here. Christine's favorite favor is a candy and short message wrapped in a tamale husk and tied with a ribbon.

◆ DJs are popular.

◆ Ethnic music—mariachi bands, classical guitar.

◆ Formal pictures with addition of photojournalism to the albums.

Bouquet Toss

Christine says, "Many destination weddings occur in Albuquerque and Santa Fe, and I strongly recommend using a wedding coordinator. It's a beautiful area, plus the cost of getting married here is about the same as most locations with the exception of New York, Chicago, and Beverly Hills."

Mimi Doke

Mimi Doke is "The Wedding Specialist." That is the name of her business, which she's owned for the past 26 years. She hails from Lake Havasu City, Arizona. She's a member of the

International Special Events Society, is a Master Bridal Consultant with the Association of Bridal Consultants, and is a member of the American Rental Association. She's also a wonderful photographer! Mimi offers two trends you might not have heard before:

◆ More weddings are taking place during the week (Monday through Thursday). Couples may choose a weekday wedding to commemorate the date they met or were engaged, to coincide with the date of the full moon, because it's a "good luck" day for them, or to cut costs because fewer guests would be able to attend.

◆ Many weddings have small guest lists (20 to 50).

Evelyn Spiker

Black Tie Optional Custom Events, in Santa Fe, New Mexico, is owned by Evelyn Spiker. Evelyn is a new member of the Association of Bridal Consultants and is also certified by Weddings Beautiful and a member of the International Special Events Society. She's been in business just three years but has some good ideas and sees these trends in the Land of Enchantment:

◆ Creative lighting—paper lanterns, soft colored gels between the layers of draped fabrics, different styles of votive and candle holders, and spotlights on the cake.

◆ Wedding planners—brides and their families are beginning to understand the value of coordinators.

◆ Using more fabric in décor and fewer florals.

◆ Photojournalism in wedding photos.

◆ Welcome parties—these larger and less-formal gatherings are replacing the rehearsal dinner to include all or a very large portion of wedding guests. This acts as an ice-breaker to kick off the weekend festivities.

◆ Using candles and linens to supplement the décor.

What's not so hot in the Southwest:

◆ The bride and groom shoving cake in each other's faces (thank goodness!).

◆ Drunken sprawling pre-wedding night parties.

◆ Decorated limos.

◆ Dollar dances.

West Coast Trends

The West Coast has a laid-back, go-with-the-flow atmosphere. Because of the wonderful weather in this part of the country, many wedding ceremonies and receptions are held outdoors.

Merry Beth Turpin

Merry Beth, owner of Aisle of View, Inc., in Kirkland, Washington, has been contributing to the wedding industry for the past 14 years. She's a very creative gal who has done all kinds of weddings, and she's an active member of the Association of Bridal Consultants. Here are some trends she sees in the Northwest:

◆ Fireworks at the reception.

◆ Organic juice bars (fruit smoothies, wheat grass) or espresso bars at the reception.

◆ Casino at reception for entertainment. Have custom poker chips made to play with that can double as favors.

◆ Flower petals used for more than just tossing as the couple exits.

Jean Picard

Jean has been coordinating weddings in California for the past 10 years. Her business, Jean Picard Wedding Consulting, is in Ventura, California. She is a Master Bridal Consultant and the California State Coordinator with the Association of Bridal Consultants. She has an eye for presentation and for detail. Trends that she is seeing include the following:

◆ Smaller weddings (70 to 150 guests).

◆ Whatever the style, weddings are very elegant.

◆ Themes that reflect the couple's personal interests.

◆ Chair covers and specialty linens.

◆ Different shapes and sizes of tables.

◆ Menu cards.

◆ Good use of lighting: spotlighting the dance floor or the head table area, or using color gels in the lights to give off a soft glow.

◆ *Personalization* is the watchword!

◆ Creative food presentation.

◆ Good food, period. Couples are more interested in what is served and *how* it is served.

Jean says one-sided head tables are not so popular now (here's hoping they're gone for good!).

Norma Edelman

Norma Edelman, owner of Wedding Casa, has been planning and producing hundreds of weddings for the past 22 years. She is a member of the Association of Bridal Consultants and winner of the Miss Dorothy Heart Award. Norma has seen it all, and here are some trends she sees on the West Coast:

◆ Being near the water—on a cliff, on a beach—anything to get a view of the bay or water.

◆ Bright, warm colors; citrus colors like orange and lemon.

◆ Bountiful buffets.

◆ Stations of cooking foods.

What's out in trends:

◆ Receiving lines.

◆ Fluff and frou-frou.

◆ Full bar.

Some trends that are unique to the Wedding Casa are:

◆ The family reunion portrait—taken immediately after the wedding before everyone scatters.

◆ A bright red aisle cloth (see the color section for a picture).

◆ Bells are rung to announce the beginning of the wedding.

◆ Music such as a bagpiper or mariachi band lead the bride and groom with all their guests to the reception.

◆ Using a unique vehicle to take the couple away: sailboat, pedacab, antique car, old Jeep, truck, gondola, etc.

Vendors

As you move through your planning stages, you will obviously meet with many vendors. Vendors also see styles and trends come and go. The vendors here offer what they have seen lately in their particular fields of expertise.

Invitation Specialist: Gloria Boyden

Gloria knows invitations inside and out. Based in Indianapolis, Indiana, she is a member of the Association of Bridal Consultants, the Invitation Dealers of America, and the International Special Events Society. She's also very creative and has designed some outstanding invitations.

Gloria says, "Today's bride is looking for something different. I am selling more ensembles that are custom designed. Very often we are able to take a very simple invitation and embellish it to make it truly unique to the bride and groom. It has increased in value because it is no longer a 'book' invitation but rather one of a kind."

Here is some advice from Gloria about buying your invitations:

- Be sure to proofread them carefully. Have three people look at the copy and be sure one of them is not closely involved with the wedding. Their objectivity could be priceless.

- Order enough. Invitation companies price per 25 invitations. To do the typesetting and begin the process for your order, the beginning price for 25 invitations might be $100. To order 100 invitations, the price might only go up by $30 to $40. However, to do a re-order (you didn't count right and you need more, or maybe the dog ate some), you will start all over again with the higher pricing. Don't be penny-wise and pound foolish.

- When the order comes in, your invitation specialist should count each piece and inspect the entire order, thus saving you time. If you use some other sources you will have to do this yourself. You can resolve problems with incorrect copy or insufficient numbers if you do it quickly. Be sure to have your invoice number and source for the problem.

BBJ Linen: Lanie Hartman

BBJ Linen is based in Skokie, Illinois, but services clients all over the country and beyond. Lanie is a member of the Association of Bridal Consultants, the National Association of Catering Executives, the Meeting Planners International, and International Special Events Society. And can she create some gorgeous tables! (See the color section for some of her creations.) Here's what Lanie is seeing across the country in linen trends:

- Color, color, color! People are slowly getting away from the traditional white or ivory weddings. Brides are getting much more daring and using colors like fuchsia, orange, or rich terracotta and burgundy in the fall.

- Chair covers are in—what a difference they make!

Lanie also offers this sage advice: "Hire a wedding planner, even if just for the day. My daughter recently got married, and being in the business, I decided that I could do this by myself. *Never again*. You need help that day, and just for your own peace of mind, hire someone. You'll enjoy your day!"

IT Travel: Virginia Pfrommer

Virginia is a hardworking travel consultant in Terre Haute, Indiana, and works with IT Travel (International Tours). Trends in honeymoon spots are the same as they were several years ago, with the number-one choice Sandals Resort; number two, a Caribbean cruise; and number three, Hawaii.

The biggest change is in the amount of money couples are spending on their honeymoons. Most have larger budgets than in years past. The average is about $5,000. Many couples register for honeymoon travel funds through the agency and instead of getting a toaster or a set of glasses, so money goes toward the honeymoon. Virginia says their bridal registry is very popular.

The Least You Need to Know

- ◆ Bold, vibrant color is in.
- ◆ Specialty linens and chair covers are very popular.
- ◆ Another hot trend is mixing and matching tables in various sizes and shapes to give your reception site a more interesting look.
- ◆ Photojournalistic wedding photography is big.
- ◆ Comfort foods and specialty drinks are two popular trends at the reception.
- ◆ Personalize: Make this wedding about the two of you!

In This Chapter

- ◆ Brides and grooms share their wedding stories
- ◆ What worked for them
- ◆ What they would do differently
- ◆ How they incorporated their uniqueness into their weddings

Chapter 22

True Confessions: Couples Tell How They Survived

A long time ago, I learned to listen and take advice from those who had experienced a similar situation I was about to enter. After all, they got through it and lived to tell about it, so why couldn't I?

In this chapter, five couples share their wedding stories with you. You should find this chapter especially fun to read. These gracious couples offer ideas they used and things they would either keep the same or change. They tell you what they learned in the process of planning their weddings and give advice on how to avoid some of the pitfalls they experienced.

These couples were asked to be part of this book because of the ways in which they handled their wedding planning process and the type of wedding they had. We have everything from the mom helping plan to the couple doing it all themselves. There are some very emotional stories and a lot of creativity. Their stories are sure to inspire you, so read on!

Amy Diersen Koeneman and David William Hopper

Date: June 30, 2001

Hometown: Santa Monica, California

Guests: 200

Colors: Navy, light blue, and pastel flowers

Attendants: Five maids, five groomsmen, four ushers

Reception: Tented reception with hors d'oeuvres and buffet

Music: Band

Amy and David are both graduates of DePauw University and decided to come back to DePauw to be married (a weekend wedding). When I first met with Amy, she knew exactly what she wanted in the way of the ceremony and the reception. She and David wanted to bring their families together and have a relaxed, fun time. They incorporated family members to help, so that gave more meaning to the wedding planning.

A very close family friend performed the ceremony. Amy's uncle is an organist. Her new mother-in-law is an interior decorator. Amy asked these people to be a part of the planning process, and the end result was very lovely.

They were married in one of the classroom buildings on campus. It actually reminded me of a church setting. It had beautiful wooden pews, a large area for the ceremony, and an organ, and its simplicity fit with Amy's no-frills style.

The reception was tented. The caterer took care of the food and beverage, and the rental company supplied everything else: linens, table, and chairs.

And finally, the weather cooperated! As I've mentioned earlier, you need a backup plan for outdoor events. We had one but didn't need to use it. Whew!

Here's what advice Amy has to offer:

On June 30, 2001, I married my best friend after dating 10 years and a year and a half engagement. We met in college; live in Santa Monica, California; and are from the Chicago area. After debating whether to get married in California or Illinois, it came to us that we should get married where we met each other and most of our friends. DePauw University, in the middle of Indiana, is where we tied the knot! Our friends from LA were interested in a visit to "the middle," our friends from college were up for a reunion, and friends and relatives from Chicago were delighted to attend a summer, country wedding.

My mother-in-law is an interior decorator, so I asked her to help me with the decorations. My mom and dad are terrific entertainers, so I used them to plan the menu, bar, and seating. Our family friend is a Lutheran minister who would conduct the ceremony, and my uncle is an organist who played all the music. But the most important appointment I made was to hire a wedding planner. Living in southern California and planning a wedding in Indiana was a chore. Our wedding planner, Teddy Lenderman, helped us with everything—the florist, caterer, photographer, cake, band, tent, alternative venue (in case of rain), party favors, etc. She and her staff allowed us to enjoy the wedding without having to worry about the details you can't imagine as a new bride (paying the vendors, guarding the presents, cueing the speeches and special dances). We arranged all the meetings over two weekends. I brought clippings and photos of what I wanted (even photos of how I would like our photographs to look). The clippings helped all the vendors have an idea of the theme, feel, and look of the wedding I imagined.

Being the first to be married in both of our families, everyone was interested in helping and being a part of this event. However, as the saying goes, "too many cooks …." What I learned from this experience is to focus on what is most important to us. The photos, invitations, programs, and ceremony were the things I deemed most important. On those subjects I would not budge. However, I also learned to delegate. With that knowledge I also had to pick my battles. At a point in your planning you realize that regardless of the insignificant details, at the end of your wedding day you are marrying the man of your dreams and that is all that matters. Spend more of your time planning your marriage rather than your wedding.

Some of the best ideas happened by chance. If you overplan, the magical accidents that make your wedding special don't occur. For example, I was very nonchalant about the bridesmaids' dresses (all I said was "wear blue"). When shopping for shoes, I noticed dresses on sale. I thought I should take a look. What a stroke of luck! On the sale rack were five navy blue Ralph Lauren tank dresses in my bridesmaids' sizes at half price! I bought the lot and made the dresses a part of my gift to them. The other gift was a last-minute purchase of raw silk wraps in various spring colors. Another stroke of luck—the wraps matched the colors in the flowers, and the girls decided to wear the wraps during the ceremony. This new accessory was just the right touch of color to brighten the ceremony. Last, our wedding was close to Independence Day, and many of our friends from LA were shocked to learn you could buy fireworks in Indiana. So our silly but brilliant friends bought boxes of fireworks and lit them after the reception as guests were leaving. What a marvelous spectacle to see my friends and family dancing around in the grass with sparklers under the light of fireworks.

In a nutshell, the most important things to remember while planning and enjoying your wedding day are:

1. *Delegate!*

2. *Allow for "magical accidents."*

3. *Spend more time planning for your marriage than your wedding.*

4. *Wear comfortable shoes.*

5. *Take a moment with your new husband to observe your wedding reception. Soak in all the details. Realize how blessed you are.*

6. *Take note of who is there to share this wonderful day with you.*

Susan Michelle Dinkel and James Knolle Jensen

Date: October 13, 2001

Hometown: Terre Haute, Indiana

Guests: 300

Colors: Steel gray and bright multicolored fall flowers

Attendants: 11 maids, 11 groomsmen, 2 flower girls, 1 ring bearer

Reception: Food stations with heavy hors d'oeuvres

Music: DJ

I met Susie at another wedding I coordinated, and I was very flattered when she called and asked me to help with hers. She was one organized bride! And she was a planner to the nth degree. That's not a bad thing, but I have seen brides who are so much into the planning that they can't let go of it come wedding day and they miss their own wedding. But Susie knew her limits, and I knew when it came time to let me do my job, she would.

I want you to read Susie and Jim's story carefully. She offers some really fun and unique ideas. And I want you to think about family and how important family members are to us. Life is not fair sometimes, so it's important to make the most of what we have now.

Enjoy!

From the early stages of our planning process, we knew we were going to have a large wedding but we also knew we wanted to unite our two families with some special touches. I encourage all newly engaged couples to sit down and research their names and heritage. It's lots of fun, and you might find something you can incorporate into your wedding to make it "you."

All girls dream of their wedding day, and I was no different. And just seconds after I got engaged, I was already planning. Planning and organization are two keys into carrying out a perfect wedding.

I'm a perfectionist and a micro-manager, and I have a hard time delegating tasks to others. It's not that I don't trust my friend and family, I just always have to have my hands in everything. My wedding was no different.

Here's how I tackled my wedding mission:

Number one, hire a wedding coordinator! I hired Teddy. She kept me focused, level-headed, and on track! Her job was to keep me guided in the right direction and to tie everything together in the end. And she most definitely did. I had an amazing ceremony and reception to prove it.

I consider myself the Head Contractor of my big day. First, I made two blueprints: one for the ceremony and one for the reception. Then I separated everything into categories, from flowers to favors.

I bought all the wedding magazines I could find. They gave me some great ideas to help develop my perfect wedding. I also surfed the Internet for wedding websites. They, too, provided me with a lot of great ideas. I tore out magazine pictures and articles and filed them into designated folders. I took this file case with me as I searched for the vendors that would make my ideas become reality.

When it comes to vendors, don't just hire the first vendor you talk with. Investigate, ask questions, and look into their track record. You should also talk with other brides who have used their services. And remember, sometimes cheaper doesn't mean better. Shop around, get estimates, and get proof of their performance.

You can spend thousands of dollars on your big day. So before you start making decisions, make a budget and prioritize what means the most to you. My still photography was my number-one choice.

And to this day, I do not regret spending a significant amount of money on my pictures. They are moments in time I can go back and remember just like it was yesterday. I would recommend a photographer who understands the importance of capturing special moments. My abstract photos have really impacted me. They truly take me back to my special day and recreate the jitters, the joy, and the tears from that day.

From there, build your team of wedding helpers. Choose individuals you can trust to get their jobs done for you.

Make a timeline. Set daily, weekly, and monthly goals.

I can't express to you just how important it is that you delegate your many chores and tasks. This is "your" special day, and it's extremely important that you don't lose focus of you. Exercise and get massages, manicures, pedicures. Do things that make you feel good. Do non-wedding-related things, too. Otherwise you'll suffer from wedding burnout.

If I had it to do over again, I wouldn't change a thing. Well, maybe one thing. The weather! Boy, did it rain. It poured all morning, afternoon, and all night long. Just realize there are things you cannot control, and the weather is one of them. Life is full of twists and turns.

Here are some special things I incorporated into my wedding to make it unique.

My maiden name is Dinkel, which is German for "wheat." I had my florist include wheat in all our floral arrangements. It was harvest time, so the wheat fit right in. Instead of using traditional bouquets and pew pieces, we used cornucopias. They were festive, fun, and different. Again, we carried out the fall theme.

A German good luck charm is the ladybug. So to have a little fun with my bridesmaids, I planned the "Little Ladybug Luncheon" to thank each of them for being part of my special day. This was the highlight of the pre-wedding festivities. I want to encourage brides to bring this tradition back. I reserved a tearoom and created an unbelievable ladybug wonderland. From the cake, placemats, napkins, table centerpieces—everything was ladybugs. It was a perfect thank you to my special friends. I even gave them ladybug-theme Swatch watches as their gift. We had so much fun with them. And it kept everyone on time to all the wedding events.

I carried the theme into the big day. My reception favors were individually wrapped cookies. The cookies were made by a local professional, and yes, they were in the shapes of ladybugs and flowers. All were decorated with funky bright icing, placed in a clear bag, and tied with bright raffia ribbon. We placed them in a big clear pickle jar so the color showed through. Then we put a sign that read, "Sweet dreams. Thanks for coming. Susie and Jim." Guests helped themselves as they left the reception.

We created a signature drink with our caterer: a Cosmopolitan with lemon twist garnish. It was red and worked beautifully with our décor.

Music was very important to us. We created a music wonderland at the ceremony. We had a brass quartet, a choir, and an organist. The music added beauty to the ceremony. It added emotion and feeling and really tied everything together. Music is powerful. Pick the instruments you like, and create your ceremonial mood.

Another thing I did that was a big help was creating a fake bouquet out of silk flowers in the colors I thought I would like for my real bouquet. I showed it to the florist and took it with me when picking out the bridesmaids gowns to see how it worked with the color I had chosen. I also took it to the linen company and the baker. It really helped explain my color scheme to those vendors.

Use a different form of a guest book. My aunt created a piece of artwork for me. She drew a picture of my wedding bouquet with my hands holding it.

I had it mounted on a wide mat board. At the ceremony and again at the reception, we placed this art piece on an easel and guests signed it. Some wrote messages, others just their names. It now hangs in our new home as a treasured keepsake.

My matron of honor loaned me her silver cake stand, which had been used at her wedding. We started a new tradition and every couple who borrows the cake stands has their names engraved on the underneath side of the stand. Try to think of things like this. Start your own traditions. Who knows, maybe my daughter will use that cake stand.

When I got engaged, my mom started a silver charm bracelet for me. Each month of my engagement I received another charm. When I finally reached my wedding month, I had a full charm bracelet loaded with charms pertaining to my wedding—everything from wedding bells to a marriage license. It's a great keepsake and something I can pull out and wear on our anniversaries.

I have only been married a short time, but don't lose sight of the fact that your life could change instantly. I am daddy's little girl. He's my heart and soul. He had as much fun, if not more, than me at the wedding. A little more than two months after our wedding, he was diagnosed with cancer. He died in November 2002, 13 months after our wedding. I thank God for allowing my daddy and me that special day, and I look back at my priceless photographs for our happy time together. I dedicate my wedding story to his memory.

Bouquet Toss

When the photographer who did Susie's wedding heard of the death of her father, he gathered all the photos he had of her dad, the ones the couple hadn't purchased, and sent them to her. That is going above and beyond the call of duty.

Michelle Lynn Roseff and Michael Alan Beachkofsky

Date: June 8, 2002

Hometown: Philadelphia, Pennsylvania

Guests: 250

Colors: Red and white

Attendants: Six bridesmaids, six groomsmen, two ushers

Reception: Hors d'oeuvres and luncheon

Music: Band

Michelle and Michael had an interesting wedding weekend. They were actually married at the rehearsal on Friday. In the Jewish tradition, couples cannot be married from Friday sundown to Saturday sundown. So unknown to most of the guests, a rabbi performed their service the night of the rehearsal. We *signed the Ketuba* then also. Knowing that this was going to all take place, Michelle hired her photographer for Friday and Saturday so he could capture those wonderful moments from the rehearsal, too.

> **Nuptial Notes**
>
> **Signing the Ketuba** is a Jewish custom handed down from generations. It is a contract that outlines the groom's responsibility to his bride. It is signed before the service by the bride, groom, rabbi, and two witnesses. Some couples use this signing time as part of the actual ceremony; others make it more private. Today's Ketubas are often beautiful pieces of artwork that are framed and hang in the couple's home.

The ceremony on Saturday was the legal part of this union. A judge friend of the family performed the ceremony incorporating some of the Jewish traditions.

They had a tented ceremony and the reception at a country club. We used golf carts to move around the place, which worked quiet well. And the weather could not have been more beautiful!

Here's what advice Michelle has to offer:

We were married at 11:30 A.M. in a tent on the grounds of the local country club. The ceremony was followed by a luncheon reception, which lasted until late afternoon. My wedding coordinator was a lifesaver. There are just so many details the day of the wedding, especially with ours, that made having a wedding coordinator invaluable.

Here are some things I loved about my wedding. The wedding coordinator helped with absolutely everything. In days prior to the wedding, she met the tent company and finalized plans with the photographer, caterer, florist, and the cake baker. The day of the wedding, she ensured that I was not a disaster nor was anything else about the day. Honestly, if something went wrong, I didn't know about it. She fixed the problem before I heard about it.

After the wedding ceremony, we had to go about a half-mile to the clubhouse. We decided to use golf carts—one for us and two more for the wedding party. This was a great idea and tons of fun. Plus the pictures from that were wonderful. We also rented a big van to transport the wedding party from the clubhouse to the tent and then take the guests from the tent to the clubhouse.

Recycle your flowers. We used all our ceremony flowers at the reception and my throw bouquet as the cake topper. We used the food station concept at the reception. The guests enjoyed the various foods, there was less waiting in line, and it was visually appealing. My dad was very nice to provide an open bar. With an afternoon wedding, not as many people were drinking like they might at an evening reception.

I had a hard time deciding whether to have reserved seating or open seating for the reception. In the end we went with open seating. This way no one felt snubbed because they were seated in the back. If we had served a meal, I would have done assigned seating.

My photographer, Michael Colter, is the best. Although it took a little while to get my prints, the quality of the photos was unbelievable. Also, he is extremely flexible and open to anything you want to do. Working with Michael was so much fun, and he was always so relaxed. I've heard other brides complain about photographers who stress out when the bride is late (as most brides are), but Michael was wonderful. He took my husband and me first to do our pictures and didn't let anyone else come along. It was nice to be by ourselves for these pictures. We decided to take all our pictures before the wedding. It was so nice to have all of that out of the way so we could arrive at the reception the same time as our guests. Taking pictures beforehand just made the day run so much smoother.

My florist, Miller Floral, was also incredible. Their prices were reasonable, and their flexibility allowed for unique ideas that we created together.

We tried to plan our wedding according to the type of guests who were attending. We had many out-of-town guests so we planned an early-in-the-day wedding. This way people could get up early on Sunday morning and head back to their homes without having been out really late the night before. Also, people who lived only an hour or so away could travel back to their homes on Saturday night. For those who did stay in a hotel, we provided Welcome Packs complete with snacks, maps, local information, and sightseeing suggestions. It was a little extra cost but made the out-of-town folks feel welcome and provided a personal touch.

Band versus DJ—the ultimate dilemma. We decided on a band and were very happy with that decision. They were more lively, flexible, and very willing to do whatever we asked. We also decided to combine the bride and father and groom and mother dances into one. It saved some time and was still very meaningful to us.

There are some things I wish I would have done or done better, such as going table to table to really see all my guests and thanking them for sharing in my special day. It's a good way to meet all those people you don't know—the distant cousins and your husband's long-lost grade-school friend. We had a receiving line outside as guests entered the reception. It was too hot and the line got very long. Plus, hugging sweaty people in my heavy dress was not fun at all. Honestly I think it's a waste of time for guests to stand in that long line just to say a quick hi. I wish I had done some of my food stations outside the clubhouse. That might have been fun and spread out my crowd. Our reception ended about 5 P.M. Both sides of the family had casual gatherings after the reception for out-of-towners and family. There was too much for us to do after the wedding, and it was very difficult to balance our time. I would have liked to have skipped both post-wedding events and spent the evening with my new husband, but you have to remember that these people have traveled far and spent money to see you, so you should try to spend some time with them.

After getting up at 5 A.M., being at the hairdresser's at 6 A.M., and finally going to bed around 2 A.M. the next morning (once we drove to the airport for our early morning flight), it was a long day. But it was a wonderful day filled with great memories. The biggest compliment you can hear after your wedding is for potential brides and grooms to say, "We want a wedding just like yours."

Michelle had some really good points in her words of wisdom.

Audra Janell Schwinghammer and Jay Ryan Hamlin

Date: September 28, 2002

Hometown: Lakewood, Colorado

Guests: 250

Colors: Bright fall colors

Attendants: Six bridesmaids, six groomsmen

Reception: Tented reception at the bride's home with food stations

Music: DJ

Audra is the second daughter in this family I've helped with weddings. I was very excited when her dad called and booked me. Our biggest challenge with her wedding was to try to make it different from her sister's wedding two years before. Both had church weddings followed by tented reception at their home. Our first step was to try to find something that made Audra and Jay's wedding unique. In talking with the couple, I found out that they were both very much into nature and the outdoors. Then Audra showed me the wedding cake she wanted, and once I saw that, I knew what our theme or unique part of the wedding would be.

Audra's mother had passed away a year before her wedding, so the planning sessions were difficult, even for me. She and Jay did a beautiful job putting things together, and I know her mother smiled down on the wedding day.

Here's Audra's advice:

The first thing to do is be sure to hire an experienced wedding coordinator. (Hire Teddy if you can!) If you have budget constraints, don't let this be the part you eliminate or cut back on. An experienced coordinator will be your best investment. For me, the wedding planning was extremely emotional for several reasons. I was getting married a little over a year after my mother passed away. Therefore, it was extremely important for me to have someone kind and trustworthy to guide me in my planning. With her experience and kindness, Teddy was the perfect match. No one believed I would be able to step back and release control of our wedding day, but with Teddy and her staff, I knew and trusted that everything was under control. Let the coordinator and her staff handle the details. If something doesn't go as planned, chances are you'll never even know it because they know what to do. It's their job, and it's yours is to be married and enjoy the once-in-a-lifetime blessing of your wedding day.

Jay and I planned together as much as possible. From our first meeting with Teddy, she told us it was our wedding and we should do it our way. So decide what is important to both of you, not everyone else, and work from there.

- *Set aside at least 15 minutes sometime before the ceremony for you and your groom to "meet" each other alone. The day is so fast-paced and hectic, you tend to lose sight of the real meaning. Use this as your chance to focus on each other. It will also help relieve some of the nervous feelings.*

- *Take as many pictures before the ceremony as possible. That way you can arrive at the reception and not keep your guests waiting for hours.*

- *Be flexible—things will not be perfect. Roll with it!*

- *The most important thing to remember is not to get caught up in the details. As long as you are married at the end of the day, that's all that matters. The important thing is that in the end, you and the most important person in your life will become one for life before God.*

And from Jay, the groom:

As the groom, I would definitely suggest taking your own travel route to the ceremony. The day has plenty of commotion and people who want to help. But those few minutes before the ceremony alone are a great chance to just collect yourself before it all begins. I also would suggest you use a fast convertible to drive yourself to the ceremony. It's a nice way to clear your mind.

I know it's not the first thing on the groom's mind, but being an integral part of the planning process helped make the day a better, more fulfilling one for me. Planning together helped set the tone for the marriage and the decisions we make together today.

(I've had more than one couple say this!)

Penny Leigh Hehman and Daniel Paul Heater

Date: April 12, 2003

Hometown: Atlanta, Georgia

Guests: 170

Colors: Tiffany blue, lilac, with touches of silver

Attendants: Six bridesmaids, three junior bridesmaids, five groomsmen, three flower girls, two ring bearers

Reception: Buffet

Music: DJ

Penny had been a bridesmaid in two of my weddings. She knew my style and the way I worked. When she called to see if I was available, it was like "old home week." These gals had been together for each other all through school and in each other's weddings. It was fun to see the former brides. Penny and I met only once. This was a weekend wedding with most guests coming in from all over.

We met at the reception facility and at the same time met with each of the vendors. Then for the rest of the time, we e-mailed and faxed each other with the various lists and who does what. Penny was *very* organized and had a lot of detail in her plans. She made a point of telling me that for her wedding day she wanted to be the princess. And Princess Penny she was! She and Dan were delightful to work with, and they did have a great wedding.

Here's what Penny has to say:

Things I would do again:

I would highly recommend using a wedding coordinator. I was able to sit back on my wedding day and simply enjoy my time with my family and friends and let the wedding coordinator do all the worrying and running around with the last-minute details. It also forced me to organize my thoughts and how I wanted the day to flow.

I also recommend spending time with your photographer and bringing pictures from magazines that you like. By doing this, Dan and I were able to get the exact type of pictures that matched our styles and personalities.

My family played a huge role in adding meaning to my wedding. All my aunts pitched in to create an amazing quilt that will become a family heirloom. One of my aunts created wedding charms for both the wedding and my bridal shower. These were given as favors to our guests.

I had food catered to the church so the attendants and those who came early for pictures could snack. This was a big hit, as most had a three- to four-hour wait before dinner that night and it seemed to keep the moods up.

Things I would do differently:

I would rely more on vendors and less on trying to do things myself—I tried to do unique things with candles and so on, but the job of gathering them and bringing them to the reception and wedding site and then packing them back up to take home was one thing I wish I had to left to someone else.

I would host a brunch the morning after the wedding for our out-of-town guests. We had an impromptu brunch that was so much fun I wish now I had planned a full brunch to have one more chance to see my family and friends from out of town.

I wish I had spent more time with the contracts and had everything in writing. My flowers ended up being late, and I am still battling with the florist regarding the time discrepancy. The DJ took it upon himself to do some things that I would have preferred not happened, like having me sit on my brother-in-law's lap for the garter toss. I felt this was a bit tacky, but it would have been awkward to not go ahead with it.

The best advice I received:

- *Be sure to never get separated from your groom—we made it a point to stay with each other the entire night!*
- *Take a moment to look around and soak it all in. It goes by so fast!*
- *Only have people in your wedding party who have meaning to you, even if your wedding party numbers don't match.*

Well stated, Penny!

Some Final Thoughts

Over the past 18 years, I've learned so much about people, about commitment, and about what is *really* important to a wedding, the celebration that follows, and life in general. I've worked with some absolutely delightful couples in my experiences. The trust and respect they have given to me makes me very humble. No amount of money could ever give me the satisfaction I've received from knowing these fine young men and women and being honored by them to help with one of the most important days in their lives.

The weddings you just read about are all different and unique to the particular couple—and they should be. This is *your* wedding—make it part of the two of you. It still amazes me how very different we all are and how we can take that uniqueness and use it to make the magical essence of our own weddings.

Enjoy this planning time. Spend it wisely, and enjoy this time with each other. And I do sincerely hope that no matter where you are, all your dreams come true and you live happily ever after. With blessings and my very best wishes!

The Least You Need to Know

◆ Use your imagination and uniqueness to make this *your* wedding.

◆ If at all possible, take all the photos before the ceremony.

◆ Make sure you read your contracts carefully.

◆ Don't sweat the small stuff.

◆ Most of all, be sure to have fun at your wedding!

Further Reading

There are literally hundreds of books on the market involving weddings, from decorating the cake to making the favors to sewing your own gown—yes, there is a book on that subject. Listed in this appendix are some of my favorite book which cover a variety of topics. Enjoy!

Books

Aertker, Paul, and Katherine Aertker. *Write After the Wedding*. Paint Press, LLC, 1994.

Baldridge, Letitia. *Legendary Weddings*. HarperCollins/Madison Press, 2000.

Batts, Sidney. F. *The Protestant Wedding Sourcebook*. Westminster/John Knox Press, 1993.

Bigel-Casher, Rita, Ph.D. *Bride's Guide to Emotional Survival*. Prima Publishing, 1996.

Cleary, Noelle, et al. *The Art and Power of Being a Lady*. Grove/Atlantic, Inc., 2002.

Cowie, Colin. *For the Bride: A Guide to Style and Gracious Living*. Bantam Doubleday Dell Publishing, 1999.

———. *For the Groom: A Blueprint for a Gentleman's Lifestyle*. Bantam Doubleday Dell Publishing, 1999.

Diamant, Anita. *The New Jewish Wedding*. Simon & Schuster, 2001.

Effenger, Tracy, and Suzanne Rowe. *Wedding Workout: Look and Feel Fabulous on Your Special Day*. Contemporary Books, 2002.

Editors of *Don't Sweat the Small Stuff. The Don't Sweat Guide for Weddings*. Hyperion, 2002.

Eklof, Barbara. *With These Words ... I Thee Wed*. Adams Media Corporation, 1989.

Exley, Helen. *The Bride*. Exley Gift Books, 1998.

Feinberg, Steven L., ed. *Crane's Blue Book of Stationery*. Doubleday, 1989.

Goldman, Larry. *Dressing the Bride.* Crown Publishers, 1993.

Gulh, Tracy. *For Your Wedding Accessories.* Friedman/Fairfax Publishers, 2000.

Hahn, Hannelore. *Places: A Directory of Public Places for Private Events and Private Places for Public Functions.* Tenth House Enterprises, 1989.

Hawkins, Kathleen. *The Bride's Guide to Wedding Photography.* Amherst Media, 2003.

Heckman, Marsha, et al. *Bouquets: A Year of Flowers for the Bride.* Stewart, Tabori and Chang, 2000.

Jones, Leslie. *Happy Is the Bride the Sun Shines On.* Contemporary Press, 1995.

Joos, Ellie. *Glorious Weddings.* Friedman/Fairfax Publishers, 2001.

Kingma, Daphne Rose. *Weddings from the Heart: Contemporary and Traditional Ceremonies for an Unforgettable Wedding.* Red Wheel/Weiser, 1995.

Klausner, Abraham J. *Weddings: A Complete Guide to All Religious and Interfaith Marriage Services.* Alpha Publishing, 1986.

Lluch, Alex, et al. *Your Rehearsal Day.* Wedding Solutions Publishing, 1999.

Lluch, Alex, and Elizabeth Lluch. *The Ultimate Guide to Wedding Music.* Wedding Solutions Publishing, 2002.

Matlins, Stuart, ed. *The Perfect Strangers Guide to Wedding Ceremonies.* Skylight Paths Publishing, 2000.

Metrick, Sydney Barbara. *I Do: A Guide to Creating Your Own Unique Wedding Ceremony.* Celestial Arts, 1992.

Moore, Cindy, and Tricia Windom. *Planning a Wedding with Divorced Parents.* Crown Publishing, 1992.

Munro, Eleanor C., ed. *Wedding Readings.* Penguin Group, 1989.

Naylor, Sharon. *1,000 Ways to Have a Dazzling Second Wedding.* New Page Books, 2001.

Packham, Jo. *Wedding Toasts and Speeches: Finding the Perfect Words.* Sterling Publishing, 1998.

Passere, Kathy. *Centerpieces and Table Accents.* Friedman/Fairfax, 2002.

Smith, Lauren. *Colors for Brides.* Acropolis Books Ltd., 1989.

Smith, Susan Lee. *Wedding Vows: Beyond Love, Honor, and Cherish.* Warner Books, 2001.

Tincher-Durik, Amy, coordinator. *Weddings for All Seasons: 90+ Ways to Personalize Your Wedding.* Krause Publications, 2001.

Werner, Marilyn. *The Bride's Thank You Note Handbook.* Simon & Schuster, 1985.

Winner, Sue. *The Complete Idiot's Guide to Budgeting for Your Wedding.* Alpha Books, 2000.

Woodhman, Martha. *Wedding Etiquette for Divorced Families.* McGraw-Hill Trade, 2002.

Magazines

These are some of the more popular bridal magazines. All are available at your local bookstore or by subscription. Subscription information is always available in the front of these magazines or on the magazine's website, if they have one. These are general wedding magazines. There are specific ones for cakes, décor, flowers, gowns … just look and you will find.

Bridal Guide

Brides (www.Brides.com)

Elegant Bride (www.ElegantBride.com)

InStyle Magazine (wedding edition)

The Knot Wedding Magazine (www.theknot.com)

Modern Bride (www.Modernbride.com)

Southern Bride

Town and Country Weddings

Victoria

Wedding Dresses Magazine

Wedding Worksheets

I talk about keeping yourself organized all through the process leading up to the big day. The worksheets found in this appendix will help with that organization. Each worksheet refers to the chapter where that specific material is discussed. For example, catering is discussed in Chapter 8, so if you have questions as you are filling in the catering worksheet, you can turn back to Chapter 8 for help. And although it's not technically a worksheet, I've also included a handy list that tells who pays for what.

These worksheets are meant to be used. They're not here to add pages or just to look pretty. Using them will help you so much in the long run as you choose and work with different vendors. Good luck!

Catering Worksheet (Chapter 8)

Name of caterer: _____

Address: _____

Telephone: _____ E-mail: _____ Fax number: _____

Menu format:

     Buffet _____ Hors d'oeuvres _____ Served dinner _____

     Other: _____

Menu ideas: _____

_____

_____

_____

Cost per person: _____

Deposit made: _____

Balance due: _____

Guarantee of numbers due: _____

Next appointment with chef: _____

Notes: _____

_____

_____

_____

_____

_____

_____

_____

_____

Ceremony Site Worksheet (Chapter 3)

Name of facility: _____

Address: _____

Telephone: _____ E-mail: _____ Fax number: _____

Contact: _____

Meeting(s) with contact: _____

Date available: _____

Fee: _____

Includes:

     Organist _____   Officiant _____   Janitor _____   Other: _____

     Kneeler _____   Aisle cloths _____   Candelabra _____   _____

Number of guests facility can accommodate: _____

Musical equipment provided: _____

Dressing room facilities: _____

Parking areas: _____

Wedding policy booklets: _____

Facility restrictions: _____

_____

Added fees for rental items (candelabra, kneeler, aisle cloth, etc.): _____

_____

Special accommodations for people with disabilities (parking, access, restrooms, etc.): _____

_____

_____

Notes: _____

_____

_____

Choosing the Caterer Worksheet (Chapter 4)

Name of caterer: _____

Address: _____

Telephone: _____ E-mail: _____ Fax number: _____

Referred by: _____

_____

Pricing system (per person or per item): _____

_____

Labor charges: _____

Linen charges: _____

Delivery charges: _____

Menu format (buffet, hors d'oeuvres, seated dinner): _____

_____

Will incorporate family recipes? _____

Notes: _____

_____

_____

_____

_____

_____

_____

_____

_____

_____

_____

Choosing the Reception Site Worksheet (Chapter 4)

Facility: _____

Contact: _____

Telephone: _____ E-mail: _____ Fax number: _____

Rental price: _____

Includes:

      Linens _____   Tables _____   Security _____

      Skirting _____   Chairs _____   Plants, decorative items _____

Ample parking? _____

Distance from ceremony: _____

Catering requirements: _____

      In-house: _____

      Outside: _____

Number of restrooms: _____

Accessible to people with disabilities? _____

Date available: _____

Notes: _____

_____

_____

_____

_____

_____

_____

_____

_____

_____

Cost Comparison Worksheet (Chapter 2)

Item	Vendor Name and Contact	Cost Estimate
Jewelry store		
Engagement ring	_____	_____
Wedding rings	_____	_____
Bridal consultant	_____	_____
	_____	_____
Ceremony site rental	_____	_____
	_____	_____
Reception site	_____	_____
	_____	_____
Caterer	_____	_____
	_____	_____
	_____	_____
Bridal shop		
Gown	_____	_____
Veil	_____	_____
Attendants' dresses	_____	_____
Wedding stationery		
Invitations	_____	_____
Announcements	_____	_____
Enclosures	_____	_____
Other paper	_____	_____
Photographer	_____	_____
	_____	_____
	_____	_____

Item	Vendor Name and Contact	Cost Estimate
Videographer	_____	_____
	_____	_____
	_____	_____
Florist	_____	_____
	_____	_____
	_____	_____
Musicians—ceremony	_____	_____
	_____	_____
	_____	_____
Musicians—reception	_____	_____
	_____	_____
	_____	_____
Wedding cake	_____	_____
	_____	_____
	_____	_____
Groom's cake	_____	_____
	_____	_____
	_____	_____
Attendants' gifts	_____	_____
	_____	_____
	_____	_____
Men's formal wear	_____	_____
	_____	_____
	_____	_____
Party rental equipment	_____	_____
	_____	_____

Item	Vendor Name and Contact	Cost Estimate
Limousine	_____	_____
	_____	_____
	_____	_____
Favors	_____	_____
	_____	_____
	_____	_____
Programs	_____	_____
	_____	_____
	_____	_____
Honeymoon		
Hotel	_____	_____
Travel	_____	_____
Tours	_____	_____
Wardrobe	_____	_____
Gifts	_____	_____
	_____	_____
	_____	_____
	_____	_____
	_____	_____

Favors Worksheet (Chapter 13)

Ideas: _____

_____

_____

_____

_____

_____

_____

_____

_____

Cost per person: _____

Contact: _____

Telephone: _____ E-mail: _____ Fax number: _____

Hotel contact who will make sure favors are delivered to guest: _____

Hotel phone number: _____

Notes: _____

_____

_____

_____

_____

_____

_____

_____

_____

_____

Floral Worksheet (Chapter 9)

Company: _____

Address: _____

_____

Telephone: _____ E-mail: _____ Fax number: _____

Type of flowers desired: _____

_____

_____

Wedding colors: _____

Ceremony site flowers: _____

_____

_____

Aisle cloth wanted? _____

Floor plan for ceremony: _____

_____

Floor plan for reception: _____

_____

Ideas for reception flowers: _____

_____

_____

Centerpieces: _____

_____

Notes: _____

_____

_____

_____

Honeymoon Worksheet (Chapter 7)

Activities to include: _____

_____

_____

_____

_____

Travel agent: _____

Telephone: _____ E-mail: _____ Fax number: _____

Budgeted amount: _____

Destination: _____

Hotel: _____

Mode of travel: _____

Meals included? _____

Extra expenses: _____

_____

Documents required (passports, IDs): _____

Luggage needed: _____

What to pack: _____

_____

_____

_____

Notes: _____

_____

_____

_____

_____

_____

Invitations Worksheet (Chapter 12)

Company: _____

Address: _____

_____

Telephone: _____ E-mail: _____ Fax number: _____

Contact: _____

Discount available: _____   Paper number: _____

Quantity needed: _____   Ink color: _____

Style or theme: _____

Enclosures

    Reception cards: _____

    Response cards and envelopes: _____

    Maps: _____

    Within-the-ribbon cards: _____

Accessories

    Napkins: _____

    Informal notes: _____

    Toast glasses: _____

    Place cards: _____

    Programs: _____

    Matches: _____

    Cake knife: _____

    Scrolls: _____

    Favor ribbons: _____

    Thank you notes: _____

    Cake boxes or bags: _____

Notes: _____

_____

Liquor Worksheet (Chapter 8)

Dealer: _____

Telephone: _____

Address: _____

Contact: _____

Requested:

      Open bar _____   Limited bar _____   Cash bar _____

Method of accountability: _____

Liquor requested: _____

_____

Number of bartenders needed: _____

Time for setup: _____

Notes: _____

_____

_____

_____

_____

_____

_____

_____

_____

_____

_____

_____

_____

_____

_____

_____

Musicians Worksheet (Chapter 9)

Company: _____

Address: _____

_____

Telephone: _____

Contact: _____

Contact phone number for the musicians: _____

Referred by: _____

Type of music (band, DJ, single instrument): _____

_____

_____

Do they provide song list to choose from? _____

What is attire for reception? _____

How long will they play? _____

How many breaks will they take? _____

What are overtime charges? _____

Will they help with introductions and garter and bouquet toss? _____

Next appointment: _____

Notes: _____

_____

_____

_____

_____

_____

_____

Photography Worksheet (Chapter 11)

Photographer: _____

Address: _____

_____

Telephone: _____ E-mail: _____ Fax number: _____

Website: _____

Referred by: _____

Type of photography (portraiture, candid, photojournalistic, soft focus, natural light): _____

_____

_____

_____

_____

Deposit paid (date): _____

Package plan (including time limit, overtime charges, charge for proofs, number of pictures, albums, etc.): _____

_____

_____

_____

_____

Next appointment: _____

Balance due: _____

Notes: _____

_____

_____

_____

_____

Programs Worksheet (Chapter 12)

Type of program desired: _____

Method of producing:

     Self _____   Printer _____   Invitation company _____

Contact: _____

Telephone: _____ Fax number: _____

Deadline for production (date): _____

Deposit paid (date): _____

Suggested wording: _____

_____

_____

_____

_____

_____

Notes: _____

_____

_____

_____

_____

_____

_____

_____

_____

_____

_____

_____

Reception Site Worksheet (Chapter 4)

Reception facility: _____

Address: _____

_____

Contact: _____

Telephone: _____ E-mail: _____ Fax number: _____

Time for reception to begin: _____

Time for reception to end: _____

What the facility will provide (linens, skirting, mike hookups): _____

_____

_____

_____

Fee for site: _____

Deposit paid (date): _____

Floor plan layout (sketch here):

Appointments with manager: _____

Balance due: _____

Notes: _____

_____

_____

Rehearsal Dinner Worksheet (Chapter 6)

Place: _____

Address: _____

_____

Telephone: _____

Contact: _____

Time to begin: _____

Time to end: _____

Menu ideas: _____

_____

_____

_____

_____

Meal price: _____

Bar charge: _____

Agenda ideas ("roast the couple," slide show, etc.): _____

_____

_____

_____

_____

_____

Equipment needed: _____

_____

_____

_____

Invitations ordered: _____

Responses received:

Guest's Name	Address	# Attending
_____	_____	_____
_____	_____	_____
_____	_____	_____
_____	_____	_____
_____	_____	_____
_____	_____	_____
_____	_____	_____
_____	_____	_____
_____	_____	_____
_____	_____	_____
_____	_____	_____
_____	_____	_____
_____	_____	_____
_____	_____	_____
_____	_____	_____
_____	_____	_____
_____	_____	_____
_____	_____	_____

Notes: _____

_____

Special Transportation Worksheet (Chapter 10)

Mode of transportation desired: _____

Contact: _____

Telephone: _____ Cell phone _____

Referred by: _____

Contract used: _____

Contract/deposit returned (date): _____

Hours needed (time of day): _____

Special instructions/directions sent: _____

_____

_____

_____

_____

Notes: _____

_____

_____

_____

_____

_____

_____

_____

_____

_____

_____

_____

A beautiful moment is frozen in time as
doves circle overhead. Amazing!

The wind catches this bride's veil, but I don't think she's worried.

What a natural setting for this couple. This gazebo lends itself to this bride and groom.

What a beautiful site for a wedding—Jamaica—can't you just feel that salt water mist on your face?
And by the looks of things, I'd say this couple is having a great time!

Our golfing couple looks like they're headed off to wander those blue hills.

The couple prepares for their marriage service in a ritual of "Ganesh Poojan." Prayers are offered to Lord Ganesh, the deity of peace and remover of all obstacles, for peace and tranquility to prevail throughout their marriage.

(opposite page) This handsome couple poses for their wedding service. Henna has been applied to the bride's hands and feet, as is the custom. It signifies the beauty of the unity of marriage and embodies all well-wishing.

An absolutely breathtaking arch of flowers shelters this couple as they say their vows.
Notice how the columns have been wrapped with fabric and tied with greenery.

A shower of rose petals greets this couple as they make their exit. This photo is done in black and white with the color added.

Here's a handsome couple posing before their wedding ceremony.

The bride walks to meet her parents, who will escort her to the chuppah. The white rose petals scattered on either side of the aisle set off the red carpet.

Instead of standing at the actual altar for the picture, move forward so the background of the church can be seen. This one is lovely.

It looks like this groom is proposing all over again in this lush garden scene.

These little ladies seem to be telling the bride a secret. Children can steal the show sometimes!

These lovely ladies gather for a quick picture right before the walk down the aisle. Notice how the bride has coordinated several fabrics into the dresses and pulls everything together with the bouquets.

(Photo by Morris Fine Art Photography)

I'm not sure how this photographer got the trees to drop their leaves and turn colors on cue, but it's an amazing photo.

(Photo by Wyant Photography)

What a great-looking wedding party. These gals are all ready to go. Notice how the lavender in the bride's bouquet is just enough color to help pull everything together.

Make your wedding unique! This bride is dressed in a yellow gown amid downtown Chicago traffic. The wedding party was dressed in blue.

Incorporate your ethnic heritage into your wedding day.

Pretty maids all dressed in black show off their tans as well as their gorgeous pink rose bouquets.

These lovely ladies pose for the camera. Notice the beautiful embroidered bodice of the bride's gown. The flowers pull everything together.

Weddings are for sharing your happiness.

These two grandmothers have just arrived at the church only to find that they purchased the same dress for the wedding! And the photographer captured this priceless moment.

(Photos courtesy of the Association of Wedding Gown Specialists)

Take a look at what a good restoration company can do to make your antique wedding gown look like new (top) or to update an older wedding gown (bottom).

Can't you almost smell the aroma of that bouquet? Just like it was picked from my grandmother's garden.

(Photos by Colter Photography)

The colors in these bouquets coordinate beautifully with the gowns or provide a splash of vibrant color to enhance a white gown.

(Photo by Janet Klinger Photography)

Here's a beautiful idea for using flowers instead of a chair cover. It can be used for the bridal couple's chairs as well as the wedding party's chairs. The flowers are wired together and then gently tied to the back of the chair.

A red aisle cloth (a trademark of Norma Edelman and the Wedding Casa) makes a statement, especially with these beautiful pew pieces.

(Photo by Monique Feil)

This ceremony site among the trees is quite unusual. Notice the background for the focal point. Tree branches, grapevines, bear grass—very fall.

Pretty fall flowers with wheat stalks nestled in them carry out the fall theme of the wedding.

(Photo by Garbo Productions)

This meandering garden path was created in a ballroom in Chicago! It looks like a garden (except for the columns and chandeliers). Notice the ivy linking the two urns of flowers at its entrance. That usually means guests are seated from the sides so the only people to walk down the aisle will be the wedding party. Fabulous!

San Diego is the setting for this beautiful wedding. Notice the red aisle cloth. It's a nice change from all white.

(Photo by Monique Feil)

This setting for the reception is formally set with silver as the predominant color choice. Very striking!

A place setting with lots of candles gives it a warm glow. Did you know that everyone looks so much better in candlelight?

This is a posed picture for BBJ Linen Company to show the various ways to use the same linen with different florals. Notice how the red linen table has three centerpieces that could all go with the linen color and yet give three different styles for centerpieces.

(Photo by Garbo Productions)

This very dramatic table setting features a yellow flower in the napkin's fold at each place. Notice the large candles at the base of the centerpiece. Very elegant.

In this fall table design, one color is used for the table-cloth and another contrasting color for the napkins. The result is a very warm and friendly table.

A simple setting for a luncheon reception. Notice the pear wrapped in paper and tied with a message about "The Perfect Pair." Don't be afraid to use color with your linens. It really makes a difference.

Bridal Party

This round, stacked cake features rolled fondant icing with light blue icing detail. Pink roses on top and around the base make this cake a lovely addition to the reception.

Talk about dramatic! The vases behind this magnificent cake hold the bridesmaids' bouquets. See how that adds to the overall look of the cake table.

The African American tradition of "Jumping the Broom" is featured in this unusual cake topper.

Mmmm, cheesecake, carrot cake ... This sweet table also holds the wedding cake (yes, the leaning tower of color in the center of the table). Notice, too, all the color of the linens on the table.

(Photo by Colter Photography)

This groom's cake features chocolate-covered strawberries designed like tuxedos. Very nice—and very good!

This groom's cake is certainly cute. It's a love stamp cake because the groom works for the U.S. Postal Service.

(Photo by Colter Photography)

Check out this sweet table and the heart-shape cookies with the couple's names on them. This can be an added part of the reception menu.

This beautifully presented sweet table is adorned with two ice sculptures, which appear to be a horse pulling a carriage—maybe Cinderella's carriage. Don't go here if you're counting calories!

Fireworks provide a spectacular ending to an unforgettable day!

Tuxedo Worksheet (Chapter 10)

Name of store: _____

Address: _____

_____

Telephone: _____ E-mail: _____ Fax number: _____

Salesperson: _____

Price: _____

Style number: _____

Color: _____

Tie/cummerbund/vest/shirt color: _____

Accessories

     Shoes: _____

     Gloves: _____

     Hats: _____

     Other: _____

Deposit made: _____

Name	Phone Number	Paid
_____	_____	_____
_____	_____	_____
_____	_____	_____
_____	_____	_____
_____	_____	_____

Notes: _____

_____

_____

Videography Worksheet

Company: _____

Address: _____

_____

Telephone: _____ E-mail: _____ Fax number: _____

Website: _____

Contact: _____

Referred by: _____

Type of video requested (edited or unedited): _____

_____

_____

Attends rehearsal? _____

Number of cameras needed: _____

Music selection: _____

_____

_____

Provides cordless microphone for groom: _____

Special effects used (baby pictures? credits? animation? fade in or out?, etc): _____

_____

_____

_____

Notes: _____

_____

_____

_____

_____

Wedding Budget Worksheet (Chapter 2)

Item	Estimate	Actual
Rings		
Engagement ring	$_____	$_____
Bride's wedding ring	$_____	$_____
Groom's wedding ring	$_____	$_____
Other	$_____	$_____
Bridal consultant (name)		
_____	$_____	$_____
Other	$_____	$_____
Ceremony		
Site rental fee	$_____	$_____
Officiant's fee	$_____	$_____
Ceremony assistants' fee	$_____	$_____
Other	$_____	$_____
Reception		
Site rental fee	$_____	$_____
Food	$_____	$_____
Beverages	$_____	$_____
Service personnel	$_____	$_____
Party rentals (chairs, tables, linens, etc.)	$_____	$_____
Other	$_____	$_____
Wedding cake		
Charge for cake	$_____	$_____
Delivery fee	$_____	$_____
Groom's cake	$_____	$_____
Other	$_____	$_____
Reception		
Napkins	$_____	$_____
Personalized matches	$_____	$_____

Item	Estimate	Actual
Favors	$_____	$_____
Toasting goblets	$_____	$_____
Cake knife	$_____	$_____
Scrolls	$_____	$_____
Other	$_____	$_____
Bride's clothing		
Gown	$_____	$_____
Headpiece and veil	$_____	$_____
Alterations	$_____	$_____
Shoes	$_____	$_____
Gloves	$_____	$_____
Hose	$_____	$_____
Jewelry	$_____	$_____
Garter	$_____	$_____
Lingerie	$_____	$_____
Other	$_____	$_____
Photography		
Engagement announcement photo	$_____	$_____
Wedding portrait	$_____	$_____
Wedding photographs	$_____	$_____
Wedding albums	$_____	$_____
Other	$_____	$_____
Videography		
One camera	$_____	$_____
Two cameras	$_____	$_____
Three or more cameras	$_____	$_____
Fee for extra tape	$_____	$_____
Editing charge	$_____	$_____
Other	$_____	$_____
Flowers		
Ceremony flowers	$_____	$_____

Item	Estimate	Actual
Reception flowers	$_____	$_____
Personal flowers	$_____	$_____
Other	$_____	$_____
Wedding stationery		
Invitations	$_____	$_____
Announcements	$_____	$_____
Reception cards	$_____	$_____
Response cards	$_____	$_____
Thank you notes	$_____	$_____
Informals	$_____	$_____
Maps	$_____	$_____
Newsletters	$_____	$_____
Other	$_____	$_____
Music		
Ceremony		
Soloist	$_____	$_____
Organist/pianist	$_____	$_____
Reception	$_____	$_____
Other	$_____	$_____
Groom's clothing		
Tuxedo or suit	$_____	$_____
Shirt	$_____	$_____
Tie	$_____	$_____
Vest or cummerbund	$_____	$_____
Shoes	$_____	$_____
Accessories	$_____	$_____
Other	$_____	$_____
Gifts		
Attendants	$_____	$_____
Gifts to each other	$_____	$_____

Item	Estimate	Actual
Parents' thank you gifts	$_____	$_____
Other	$_____	$_____
Transportation		
Limousine	$_____	$_____
Parking	$_____	$_____
Other	$_____	$_____
Rehearsal dinner (included, even though traditionally paid for by groom's family)		
Food	$_____	$_____
Beverages	$_____	$_____
Service personnel	$_____	$_____
Room rental charge	$_____	$_____
Flowers/decorations	$_____	$_____
Other	$_____	$_____
Honeymoon		
Hotel accommodations	$_____	$_____
Transportation	$_____	$_____
Tours	$_____	$_____
Meals	$_____	$_____
Passports	$_____	$_____
Traveler's checks	$_____	$_____
Other	$_____	$_____
Additional expenses		
Marriage license	$_____	$_____
Postage for invitations	$_____	$_____
Gratuities	$_____	$_____
Blood tests/physicals	$_____	$_____
Hair stylist	$_____	$_____
Makeup artist	$_____	$_____
Bubbles or petals	$_____	$_____
Other	$_____	$_____

Wedding Cake Worksheet (Chapter 8)

Baker: _____

Address: _____

_____

Telephone: _____ E-mail: _____ Fax number: _____

Price: _____

Delivery fee: _____

Deposit on cake pieces: _____

How to get items back to baker: _____

Number of servings: _____

Description of wedding cake: _____

_____

_____

_____

_____

Description of groom's cake: _____

_____

_____

_____

Number of servings: _____

Notes: _____

_____

_____

_____

_____

_____

Wedding Gown and Bridesmaids' Dresses Worksheet (Chapter 10)

Shops to visit: _____

_____

Referred by: _____

Date of appointments: _____

_____

Contact at shop: _____

Telephone: _____

Style of gown: _____

_____

Color selection: _____

Budgeted amount for gown and veil: _____

Budgeted amount for accessories:

      Bra: _____

      Slip: _____

      Shoes: _____

      Jewelry: _____

Deposit paid (date): _____

Payments to be made (dates): _____

_____

Bridesmaids' dresses

      Number of attendants: _____

      Color choices: _____

      Style of dresses: _____

      Cost of dresses: _____

      Cost of alterations: _____

Attendants' names, phone numbers, and addresses:

1. _____

   _____

   _____

2. _____

   _____

   _____

3. _____

   _____

   _____

4. _____

   _____

   _____

5. _____

   _____

   _____

6. _____

   _____

   _____

(Add more paper if needed.)

Next appointment: _____

Notes: _____

_____

_____

_____

_____

What's Important to Us Worksheet (Chapter 2)

Number of guests: _____

Number of attendants: _____

Time of day: _____

Time of year: _____

Other (limousine, photography, videography, special items [hot air balloon, vintage cars], decorations, flowers [silk vs. fresh], and attire):

_____

_____

_____

_____

Reception:

- ❏ Cake and punch
- ❏ Hors d'oeuvres
- ❏ Buffet
- ❏ Sit-down dinner

- ❏ Open bar
- ❏ Limited bar
- ❏ Cash bar
- ❏ Champagne toast

- ❏ Music
- ❏ Dancing
- ❏ Favors

Other ideas: _____

_____

_____

_____

_____

_____

_____

_____

_____

Who Pays for What Worksheet (Chapter 2)

The Bride and Her Family:

- ◆ Wedding dress, headpiece, and accessories
- ◆ Ceremony site rental
- ◆ Bridal consultant
- ◆ Reception site rental
- ◆ Reception food and drink
- ◆ Flowers for the ceremony

- ◆ Flowers for the reception
- ◆ Groom's wedding ring
- ◆ Invitations, announcements, and enclosures
- ◆ Gift for the groom
- ◆ Gifts for the bridesmaids

The Groom and His Family:

- ◆ Bride's engagement and wedding rings
- ◆ Gift for the bride
- ◆ Rental of formal wear
- ◆ Marriage license
- ◆ Officiant's fee
- ◆ Boutonnieres for the men in the wedding party

- ◆ Bride's bouquet
- ◆ Corsages for the mothers and grandmothers
- ◆ Gifts for the men in the wedding party
- ◆ Honeymoon
- ◆ Rehearsal dinner

The Wedding Party:

- ◆ Their wedding attire
- ◆ Accessories to go with the attire (shoes, headpieces)

- ◆ Gift for the bride and groom
- ◆ Transportation to the city (if out of town)

Notes: _____

_____

_____

_____

_____

_____

_____

Appendix C

Countdown to Your Wedding Day

This handy check-off list can help you stay on track in the months and weeks leading up to your wedding day. I suggest you read through the list completely (just disregard any items that don't apply to your wedding). Get a handle on what you need to do when, and then as each item is dealt with, you can check it off as done!

Planning Check-Off List

Six to Twelve Months Before the Wedding

- ❏ Announce your engagement.
- ❏ Plan the engagement party or make the announcement to the rest of your family and friends.
- ❏ Attend bridal shows.
- ❏ Talk with a bridal consultant/wedding coordinator. Make an appointment for a consultation.
- ❏ Together with both sets of parents, discuss wedding plans, including formality.
- ❏ Determine a budget.
- ❏ If you are sharing expenses, decide who will pay for what.
- ❏ Select a date and time for the wedding.
- ❏ Call the church or synagogue for an appointment with the officiant.
- ❏ If it will be a civil ceremony, call the officiant.

- ❏ Meet with the officiant.
- ❏ Ask friends and family to serve as wedding attendants.
- ❏ Start comparison shopping for services, such as florist, caterer, photographer, and videographer.
- ❏ Select wedding rings and make arrangements for engraving.
- ❏ Begin writing your guest lists.
- ❏ Gather ideas for reception: menu, beverages, entertainment, favors, and so on.
- ❏ Reserve your reception site.
- ❏ Reserve your vendors: caterer, photographer, videographer, florist, musicians, limo, and so on.
- ❏ Shop for your wedding gown and headpiece. Also look for attendants' dresses.
- ❏ Begin to plan the wedding ceremony and reception music.
- ❏ Register with department stores for bridal gift registry.
- ❏ Order your gown, veil and/or headpiece, and the attendant's dresses.

Five Months Before the Wedding

- ❏ Select and order your gown, headpiece, and attendants' dresses.
- ❏ Discuss honeymoon plans with your fiancé, and speak with a travel agent.
- ❏ Check samples of wedding invitations, announcements, and enclosure cards.
- ❏ Begin shopping for your wedding invitations, enclosure cards, thank you notes, and informal notes.
- ❏ Begin shopping for your wedding cake.
- ❏ Reserve blocks of rooms at hotels for out-of-town guests (include this information with invitations).

Four Months Before the Wedding

- ❏ Select and order your wedding stationery: invitations, announcements, enclosures, informals, scrolls, napkins, and thank you notes.
- ❏ Get necessary travel documents (passport, birth certificate).
- ❏ Draw maps with directions to the ceremony and reception site for out-of-town guests.
- ❏ Make an appointment with the caterer or banquet manager to discuss your reception menu.
- ❏ Make an appointment with your bridal consultant to "touch base" and get your questions answered.

Three Months Before the Wedding

- ❏ Decide on honeymoon destination, and call for reservations.
- ❏ Begin making a list of clothing and other items you will need for the honeymoon. Start shopping for those.
- ❏ Finalize your guest list, check for duplicates, and correct spelling and addresses.
- ❏ Review musical selections with your musicians.
- ❏ Arrange for an engagement picture for the newspaper.
- ❏ Make an appointment with the florist to discuss floral budget and floral decorations.
- ❏ Check with local authorities about requirements for marriage license and blood test.
- ❏ Make an appointment with your doctor for a physical.
- ❏ Begin addressing the inner and outer invitation envelopes.
- ❏ Complete honeymoon plans. Buy air or cruise tickets.

Two Months Before the Wedding

❑ Order the wedding cake and groom's cake.

❑ Have a physical examination, blood tests, and any required inoculations for foreign travel.

❑ Accompany groom to the formal wear shop and choose formal attire for the male attendants.

Seven Weeks Before the Wedding

❑ Meet with the caterer or banquet manager and firm up reception details. Ask for a banquet room floor plan.

❑ Consult a party rental store if equipment is needed at the reception.

❑ Schedule an appointment with the bridal consultant.

❑ Talk with musicians, and review your selections.

❑ Make an appointment with your photographer for your formal bridal portrait.

Six Weeks Before the Wedding

❑ Call the church or synagogue, and confirm rehearsal date and time.

❑ Discuss music with the church organist and soloist.

❑ Plan the rehearsal dinner with the caterer.

❑ Visit the church and reception site, and do a floor plan (if not done earlier).

❑ Have the males in the wedding party, including the fathers, rent their formal wear at the same store.

❑ If there are out-of-town male attendants, have the local store send them the tux information and a postcard to return with their measurements so they can order the tuxes.

❑ Order wedding programs.

❑ Order favors (if using).

Five Weeks Before the Wedding

❑ Mail all the invitations.

❑ Select and buy gifts for all attendants.

❑ Get swatches of attendants' dress fabric and have shoes dyed in one lot.

❑ If attendants live out of town, arrange for their dresses to be sent to them for fittings and alterations.

❑ Meet the florist and order your flowers. Take samples of fabric and pictures of your gown and attendants' gowns.

❑ Purchase or borrow bridal garter, guest book, pen, cake knife, and toasting glasses.

Four Weeks Before the Wedding

❑ Prepare the wedding announcement for the local newspaper.

❑ All invitations should be in the mail.

❑ Make an appointment with your hair stylist and a makeup artist to try out makeup and hairstyles for your wedding day.

❑ Finalize arrangements for the rehearsal dinner.

❑ Finalize arrangements for the reception.

❑ Check with attendants regarding their accessories.

❑ Wrap attendants' gifts and have them ready to present.

❑ Make an appointment for the final fitting of your gown.

❑ Begin recording invitation acceptances and regrets.

❑ Begin addressing announcement envelopes.

❑ Select wedding gifts for each other.

❑ Arrange for transportation of the wedding party to the wedding and reception.

❑ Discuss the ceremony with the officiant.

❑ Make a seating plan for the rehearsal dinner and reception.

❑ Write place cards for the reception (if using).

❑ Decide whether you will use a receiving line.

❑ If you are moving to another town after the wedding, call the movers and make arrangements.

Three Weeks Before the Wedding

❑ Have your final fitting.

❑ Notify all participants of rehearsal date, time, and place.

❑ Have your formal portrait taken.

❑ Check on honeymoon tickets and reservations.

❑ Set up a table to display your wedding gifts.

❑ Record gifts and continue to send thank you notes.

❑ Get marriage license.

❑ Confirm transportation to ceremony and reception.

❑ Attend showers given in your honor.

❑ Arrange for bridesmaids' luncheon.

❑ Ask a friend to handle the wedding gifts at the reception.

❑ Make arrangements for gifts to be taken from the reception to your home or to storage.

❑ Hire a house-sitter for the rehearsal and wedding day for your home, your parents' home, and your fiancé's home.

❑ Ask someone to be the guest book attendant.

❑ Check with cleaners about preserving your gown.

❑ Assign someone to take your gown to the cleaners.

❑ Pick up tickets and confirm reservations for honeymoon.

Two Weeks Before the Wedding

❑ Finalize hotel arrangements for out-of-town guests.

❑ Plan a "welcome" package for out-of-town guests to be in their hotel rooms when they arrive.

❑ Send your photograph and wedding announcement to the newspaper.

❑ Check on accessories for the groom and male attendants.

❑ Make an appointment with your hair stylist, makeup artist, and manicurist.

❑ Give addressed and stamped announcements to someone who will mail them the day after the wedding.

❑ Follow up on guests who have not returned their response card. You must have an accurate count for the caterer.

❑ Meet with your bridal consultant to go over all the final details.

One Week Before the Wedding

- ❏ Eat right and get plenty of rest this week!
- ❏ Give the caterer a guaranteed count for the reception.
- ❏ Double-check all service providers: florist, photographer, caterer, church, and so on.
- ❏ Pay balances due on services required before the wedding.
- ❏ Have money or checks in envelopes for your consultant to hand to organist, soloist, musicians, minister, and anyone who needs to be paid the day of the wedding.
- ❏ Attend the bridesmaids' luncheon.
- ❏ Remind everyone of the time and place of the rehearsal.
- ❏ Pack for the honeymoon.
- ❏ Give gifts to attendants (if not planned for rehearsal dinner).
- ❏ Spend some quiet time with your family.
- ❏ Have "something old, new, borrowed, and blue" ready.
- ❏ Explain any special seating to your bridal consultant.
- ❏ Attend the bachelorette party (*not* the night before the wedding).

Two Days Before the Wedding

- ❏ Check the weather conditions for the wedding day, and make adjustments if needed.
- ❏ Lay out everything you will need to dress for the wedding in one place at home.
- ❏ Your bridal consultant should provide a care package: safety pins, thread, bobby pins, hairspray, soft drinks, juice, crackers, and more for your use.
- ❏ Make sure the cars involved have gas.

One Day Before the Wedding

- ❏ Attend the rehearsal.
- ❏ Make sure you and your groom are comfortable with the rehearsal and have no questions.
- ❏ If you are leaving for your honeymoon directly from the reception, place your luggage in the car you will be driving and lock it.
- ❏ *Relax.* Take a hot bath. Have a glass of warm milk or hot tea, and get a good night's rest.

The Big Day!

- ❏ Have your bridal consultant get your gown, veil, and/or bridesmaids' gowns from the bridal shop and take them directly to the ceremony site (if the shop doesn't deliver).
- ❏ Eat a good breakfast—something that will last. You want to include protein items and some bread items (for energy). You might be too nervous to eat closer to the wedding time.
- ❏ Give yourself plenty of time to get ready. Don't rush! Enjoy this time. You may even indulge and have a makeup artist and hair stylist come to the ceremony site to apply your makeup and do your hair.
- ❏ Your consultant should make sure that anything belonging to you that needs to go from the church to the reception will be taken there or assign this task to a reliable friend.
- ❏ *Enjoy this day!* You've planned well and now you can relax.

Best wishes for a lifetime of happiness!

Index

G

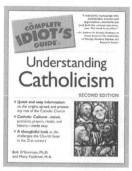
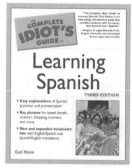
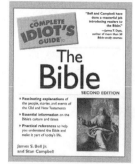